Free Market Conservatism

A Critique of Theory and Practice

edited by
Edward Nell

London
GEORGE ALLEN & UNWIN
Boston   Sydney

© Editorial selection, Edward J. Nell, 1984 ✗
© Individual chapters: Robert Heilbroner; Rosemary Rinder; Edward Nell and Alex Azarchs; Jan Kregel; Bob Cherry, Pat Clawson and James Dean; Jagdish Handa; Edward Nell; Teresa Amott; Geoff Hodgson; Antonio Schneider; Edward Nell; 1984.

George Allen & Unwin (Publishers) Ltd,
40 Museum Street, London WC1A 1LU, UK

George Allen & Unwin (Publishers) Ltd,
Park Lane, Hemel Hempstead, Herts HP2 4TE, UK

Allen & Unwin Inc.,
9 Winchester Terrace, Winchester, Mass 01890, USA

George Allen & Unwin Australia Pty Ltd,
8 Napier Street, North Sydney, NSW 2060, Australia

First published in 1984

British Library Cataloguing in Publication Data

Free market conservatism.
1. Economics   2. Conservatism
I. Nell, Edward J.
330.12′2   HB171
ISBN 0-04-330339-0
ISBN 0-04-330340-4 Pbk

Library of Congress Cataloging in Publication Data applied for

Set in 10 on 11 point Times by Phoenix Photosetting, Chatham
and printed in Great Britain by Billing and Sons Ltd,
London and Worcester

Contents

List of Contributors

TERESA AMOTT
Wellesley College, Wellesley, Massachusetts and University of Massachusetts, Amherst, Mass.

ALEX AZARCHS
St John's University, Queens, New York

ROBERT CHERRY
Brooklyn College, City University of New York, Brooklyn, New York

PATRICK CLAWSON
World Bank, Washington, D.C.

JAMES DEAN
Simon Fraser University, Burnaby, British Columbia, Canada

JAGDISH HANDA
McGill University, Montreal, Quebec, Canada

ROBERT L. HEILBRONER
Graduate Faculty, New School for Social Research, New York

GEOFF HODGSON
Newcastle upon Tyne Polytechnic, Newcastle upon Tyne

JAN KREGEL
Rijksuniversiteit, Groningen

EDWARD NELL
Graduate Faculty, New School for Social Research, New York

ROSEMARY RINDER
Citibank, and New School for Social Research, New York

ANTONIO SCHNEIDER
Terra Inc., and New School for Social Research, New York

Q: How many Conservative economists does it take to change a light bulb?

A: None. Conservative economists just sit in the dark and wait for the Invisible Hand to do it.

Acknowledgements

When I first began work on these essays I asked Zoltan Acs to collaborate with me. Our subsequent discussions contributed greatly to shaping this volume. He later had to drop out of this project to concentrate on his own work, but his efforts are remembered.

In addition to their written contributions, Alex Azarchs, Rosemary Rinder and Antonio Schneider helped plan the book. Nicholas Brealey, editor, and Liz Paton, copyeditor, not only were a great pleasure to work with, but suggested many improvements both in style and in substance.

But my greatest thanks go to Margaret Dunbar, my wife, who insisted from the beginning that a critique of conservative economics had to deal with both theory and practice. She helped in editing several of the papers, and she did research for, and wrote preliminary drafts of sections of the concluding chapter. The final shape of this work reflects her influence more than anyone else's.

1 Introduction – Capitalism as *Gestalt*: A Contrast of Visions

A question seems to elude the grasp of modern economists, or rather to escape their interest: *what is economics*? In an impatient way, of course, we all know the conventional answers. Economics is 'the study of mankind in the ordinary business of life', as Marshall put it; or it is 'maximizing subject to constraints', as the mainstream of methodology from John Stuart Mill through Lord Robbins would have it; or perhaps it is the 'practice' of praxiology, as von Mises would insist. But if the question is pressed harder, these conventional answers lose their self-evident authority. What is the 'ordinary' business of life? Maximizing what, how? Are commissars praxiologists? Pressing the question home this way leads to the uneasy suspicion that we do not know exactly what economics is.

One aspect of this ignorance is our embarrassed inability to explain clearly why economists disagree. I do not mean why economists disagree about next month's GNP, which is no more puzzling than why meteorologists disagree about next week's weather. The question, rather, is why economists disagree about the main thrust of the system, its central tendencies, its inertial properties, its inherent vitality or morbidity. An easy answer to this problem would be that economists begin from identical premises – a set of institutions X, of behavioral vectors Y, of institutional channels Z – but thereafter proceed to apply different analytical methods, or to force the same analytical procedures to yield the results that they want of them. But I do not think that most economists would be happy with that explanation. The pride of the profession lies in its science-like clarity, in the existence of chains of causal and logical sequence that force economists of the most different 'persuasions' to arrive at the same conclusions, given the same initial conditions, drives, frictions and the like. Is it not the fact that Smith and Marx both agree that an increase in demand will result in a higher price of labor despite differences as to its effect on growth? Do not Malthus and Ricardo see eye to eye on the effects of population change on rent, although they disagree about the social usefulness of rentiers? Are not the supply-sider and the Keynesian of one mind that the multiplier will be determined by the size of the leakage fraction, although one wants high savings propensities and the other wants low ones?

In other words, economics per se does not seem to be the reason why economists disagree. What, then, is the reason? I have already given away the answer when I mentioned those 'persuasions' that seem to lodge in economists' heads before they begin their analytical work. Economists disagree because they are political animals, and because the practice of economics, like any social analysis, is shot through with the political suppositions and assumptions of its protagonists.

I do not intend to pursue here the manner in which these political premises enter into, and help determine, the complex work of scenario-building that is the task of economics. This is a matter I have looked into elsewhere (Heilbroner, 1973; 1983). Instead I would like to make a preliminary reconnaissance of the very important, but insufficiently explored terrain of those preconceptions themselves. What is the 'mind set', the 'ideology', or simply the beliefs that we recognize in others (not so often in ourselves) as radical and conservative? There exists no official canon of conservative or radical tenets, so I shall have to formulate my own.

I shall begin with five theses that to my mind capture the essence of the modern conservative position. This is a nutshell description of 'capitalism', the socioeconomic order that prevails in all advanced industrial nations, save only the USSR and its satellites (which also contain capitalist-like elements).

1   Capitalism is a 'natural' economic system, in that it accords in some deep way with human nature. It is the manner of organizing production and distribution to which mankind will spontaneously drift, once impediments of various kinds (including ignorance) are taken away.
2   Capitalism is an evolutionary system. Its evolutionary tendencies are described by the term *growth*, which means an increase in real per capita income. This increase, accruing first to entrepreneurs and innovators, then trickling down to the rest of the population, is perceived as bringing useful social and political consequences: higher individual morale, less political dissatisfaction.
3   Growth arises naturally within capitalism from the interplay of its two elemental constituents. One of these is the profit motive (embodied in both individual and institutional agencies) acting as a force for innovative and expansionary economic activity. The other is the restraining mechanism of competition. These two forces together comprise the thrust and feedback of the market system.

4 The capitalist economy contains two sectors, one public, one private. The private sector is mainly responsible for growth. The public sector's main responsibility is the provision of defense, law and order, and necessary public goods. Beyond these functions, whose boundaries are admittedly not always clear-cut, government is deemed to weigh on, and to diminish the vigor of, the private sector.

5 Capitalism is an international system, in that its constituent nation-states are bound together by market forces. There is therefore a world economy that exerts a restraining, and ultimately commanding, influence over the movements of its national capitalist members.

This is certainly not a complete listing of the identifying elements of capitalism as seen from the conservative side, but I think the vision that emerges is true to its conservative intentions. At any rate, it will serve as a contrast to the radical vision that I outline below. I make no attempt at a point-by-point refutation or comparison of these two visions. The two conceptions are so fundamentally different as to be almost impossible to compare in detail. Nor is the choice between them a simple empirical matter, for they are at too high a level of abstraction to be simply 'set against the facts'. The following seven radical theses can be seen only as a rough counterpart to the conservative view:

1 Capitalism is quintessentially a means of organizing labor to produce a social surplus. By a surplus, I mean the production of wealth over and above that needed to replenish and restore the system. The line between surplus and replenishment is always blurred, as are most social distinctions, but in the large there is no difficulty in distinguishing the form and extent of surplus in all surplus-producing systems.

2 Capitalism is not the first surplus-producing system. Indeed, all social orders above the most primitive produce surpluses. This is true of ancient Egypt, European feudalism and the contemporary USSR. What is distinctive about capitalism is the form that its surplus takes. Other social orders use surpluses for war, for public adornment, for religious observances and for the maintenance of privileged classes. Capitalism also uses its surplus in part for these purposes, and indeed distributes increments in consumption more widely than any prior system. But its primary use is something else: *surplus is employed to create the means to gather additional surplus*. That is, 'wealth' under capitalism takes the form of machines, equipment, plant, factories. Such a form of surplus

exists in no prior society. Its persistence in the USSR and in other industrial 'socialist' societies testifies to their incomplete separation from capitalism.

3   Another distinguishing characteristic of capitalism is the manner in which surplus is gathered. Unlike other systems, it is not extracted by naked force, or by tradition backed by latent force. Surplus under capitalism accumulates as a consequence of the existence of wage labor as the mode by which production is carried on. Wage labor has the historically unique attribute of legally denying the worker the ownership of his labor-product, which belongs instead to the owner of the physical equipment with which he works.

In this regard it is always enlightening to reflect on who owns the cars that roll off General Motors' assembly line. The workers? No. The technicians? No. The management? No. The stockholders? No. (Try going in and claiming a car, waving a stock certificate as justification.) Who, then? The company – the fictional person who owns the assembly line itself and the products that emerge from it. This is the unique capitalist wage-labor relation to which John Locke referred when he wrote, 'The grass that my horse has bit, *the turfs my servant has cut*, and the ore I have digged in any place . . . become my property without the assignation of consent of anybody'. What a host of assumptions and mystifications lie in that italicized phrase, which goes to the core of the surplus-gathering process!

4   The separation of work from the right to claim the product of work establishes the rationale for the organization of the work process that is typical of capitalism. This is an organization in which the volume of output per hour takes precedence over most other considerations, such as fatigue, interest, creativity, etc. The hallmark of this mode of organization is the 'division' of labor, not just by occupational variety but by the fragmentation of physical and mental tasks into their simplest components. This division of labor is not a 'natural' tendency of mankind, and is not found in other societies to anything like the degree we find it in capitalism. The division of labor endows capitalism with its immense superiority with respect to productivity, but also saddles it with the need to maintain the strictest supervision over, and discipline within, the labor process.

5   The productive activities of capitalism are coordinated by market exchange among individuals and firms. This is the vaunted market mechanism, the source of capitalism's remarkable adaptability and its self-regulating properties. There are, however, two vital areas into which the buying and selling mechanism does not enter.

The first is the allocation of work *within* the office or factory. Production itself is carried on by socially constrained fiat, not by exchange. Second, the market does not make crucial macro allocations. Government often determines the direction in which the economy will go, as well as braking or accelerating it. For example, government builds the road network without which the auto industry could not function. So, too, government provides the research and development on which the agricultural sector depends, the schools from which its trained workforce emerges. In these ways government provides an indispensable, although usually overlooked, foundation for the accumulation process.

6 The wage-labor system effectively creates an 'economy' distinct from a 'society'. This separation of an economic sphere from its social matrix creates two pathologies for capitalism. The first is the generation of problems that arise because we systematically exclude consideration of the social consequences of economic behavior. Thus, agricultural enclosures, undertaken for economic reasons, bring unanticipated social distress; the creation of the factory brings the undesired mill town; the free workings of competition plunge regions into social decline or thrust them into the disorders of sudden affluence; the extension of the wage-labor system destroys the extended family; the development of advertising, indeed of marketing in general, corrodes moral virtue. It is characteristic of capitalism that it perceives no connection between these 'problems' and its underlying mode of production.

The second, more familiar pathology is the continuing difficulty in successfully accumulating surplus. Potential disruptions and mismatches lurk at every stage of the process, from engaging a labor force, through assuring its disciplined performance, to selling its output. These difficulties are recognized by conventional economists. A radical view stresses the self-generated nature of these problems, largely rooted in the wage-labor relation, and emphasizes the 'curative' role that crises can play in restoring the conditions for further accumulation.

7 Capitalism is a world system, but not merely because it is linked by market forces. The core of the world system of capitalism is the extension of the wage-labor system from the developed center to the 'underdeveloped' periphery, for the purpose of gathering surplus on a global scale. On the whole, this international surplus is gathered as effortlessly as is the case within national capitalisms, although resort may be had to military intervention from time to time, as is also the case within national capitalisms when troops are used to put down strikes.

The existence of a world system does not preclude tensions,

even wars, among 'center' countries, just as national systems often suffer severe conflicts among factions of the nation, all of whom benefit from the surplus. The systematic unity of the system, on a national or a global scale, is not perceived within, but only from without. This mystifying aspect of capitalism was first noticed by Adam Smith, who used the term the Invisible Hand to describe the coordination of individuals, unbeknownst to themselves. The equivalent of the Invisible Hand imposes a system of accumulation on a world scale over the appearance of international capitalist rivalry and discord.

This is assuredly not a complete enumeration of all the crucial elements of capitalism. The purpose of this sketch is only to project a vision that can be contrasted with and used to criticize that of modern conservative economics.[1] Yet, in spite of some overlaps, it must be plain that they are simply two different *gestalts*. To my mind, the essential difference between them is the absence of a historic dimension in the conservative view, to which it will no doubt be returned that they see history, but not *my* history. Perhaps we must fight over *gestalts* as well as values. But it does not follow that we cannot say anything at all. Indeed, the only way we can decide between them is to explore their logic and implications.

Two very important conclusions follow from these alternative visions. Even if we cannot finally establish which vision is true and which a mere wraith, it will help us form a judgement to make these conclusions explicit.

First, the role of government is entirely different in the two visions. I have already indicated that government is regarded from the conservative side as an encroaching force, an intruder into the private sphere, a weight on the system. Its necessity is not denied, but its virtues are held to be minimal. In the radical view this demarcation becomes blurred and ambiguous. The designations 'private' and 'public' refer to functions that are directly, or only indirectly, connected with the generation of surplus. Both public and private roles and functions are seen as actively supporting the process itself.

From this viewpoint, the fact that there is often conflict, even bitter conflict, between those who directly work with the surplus-generating process and those who work at a remove from it is not surprising: the Roman imperium fought bitterly against senatorial privileges to maintain the empire; monarchs warred against barons to preserve an aristocratic social order; Parliament acted against the immediate interest of English factory owners to secure the future of the capitalist order; Roosevelt curbed the prerogatives of bankers and industrialists to ward off a feared social revolution. Governing elements within all social systems must often curb the activities of privileged groups within the system.

Second, conservative economics sees the capitalist order as tending 'naturally' – that is, in the absence of the artificial impediments and distortions introduced by government – toward equilibrium and harmony. By equilibrium I mean that there are no perceived obstacles that stand in the way of more or less steady growth, well-limited departures from full employment, reasonably smooth micro adjustments. Or rather, if there are such impediments, they stem from government intervention into the flux of the market process. By harmony I mean that the successful achievement of economic growth will bring social morale and political stability. In a word, there are no economic or social contradictions in the system, in the sense of dysfunctions brought about by the *success* – not the failure – of capitalist processes.

The radical view sees an almost opposite picture. The system tends naturally toward economic disequilibrium and toward social and political tension. The economic strains (crises) are the consequence of matters I have already mentioned, namely the difficulties of pursuing the accumulation process without constantly overreaching it. This is a matter that cannot be argued here. It rests on the long history of the theory of instability whose roots are to be found in Marx. The radical view also sees the process of change militating against harmony. In politics there is an intrinsic conflict between the 'horizontal' tendencies of a democratic (egalitarian) view and the 'vertical' tendencies of a hierarchical (inegalitarian) structure. In social life there are the strains that result from the continuous restructuring of 'life' as the side-effect of economic 'growth'. Indeed, in place of the conventional assumption of a tendency toward stability and harmony, the radical view asks how it is possible to maintain social continuity in the face of continuous economic fluctuation, social insecurity and political strain. The answer is essentially by the use of government as a sustaining and restraining force.

This has been rather heavy going, so let me relax the pace by taking up two less momentous matters. The first of these concerns the question of government waste – the squandering of resources by the public sector to which supply-side economics devotes so much attention. I would be the last to deny the presence of waste: the MX missile system, the space shuttle, the tax subsidies to various upper-income groups, not to mention the petty cadging and occasional grand larceny among welfare groups. No doubt one could argue about all these instances. However, I want to call attention first to a curious aspect of the question of waste. *It is that there is no waste in the private sector!* This is the case because all 'wasteful' operations are eliminated by the market. Contrariwise, whatever survives the test of the market is not waste. The five giant buildings being erected between 53rd and 57th Streets along Madison Avenue in New York are not waste, unless they cannot be rented. The Cadillac Seville is not waste, assuming that it sells. There is no waste in the production of *anything* that sells, because the very act of purchase provides the justification for whatever resources have been used.

Is this not interesting? Clearly it establishes that there are entirely different criteria for waste in the public and private domains. Suppose that the scrutiny ordinarily directed at government were brought to bear on private output, and that each act of production had to justify itself by some *non-market* criterion. Would we not find a great deal of waste in the private sphere? And suppose that the government produced only those things it could sell – pocket-sized armaments and vendible services of all kinds. Would not all waste now disappear from the public sphere? This leads one to think about the unnoticed distortions introduced from the vantage point of conventional economics.

I turn to a second related matter, namely the ideological element that colors our social perceptions, such as waste. To be sure, all social orders have ideologies, and none could exist without them. Therefore societies never think of their prevailing views as being 'ideological', but rather as expressing self-evident or natural truths. As Immanuel Wallerstein (1974, p. 351) has acutely remarked, during most periods of history there is effectively only one class that is conscious of itself, and this dominant class sincerely expresses its own views as representing those of the entire society. Thus the senators of Rome, the lords of the manor, the monarchs of France and England and the members of the Soviet elite all speak with unself-conscious assurance in the name of their societies. None feels itself to be a 'privileged' class or thinks its views to be other than universal.

The upper class in capitalism also speaks with a universal voice – as witness the degree to which it speaks for the working man. Nonetheless, the view of the upper class under capitalism is more clouded than under other dispensations. This is the consequence of the rise of democratic, egalitarian and even revolutionary ideas at the same time as, and indeed as part of, the bourgeois struggle for ascendancy. These ideas remain to haunt the bourgeois serenity of spirit: as Schumpeter wrote, '. . . capitalism creates a critical frame of mind which, after having destroyed the moral authority of so many other institutions, in the end turns against its own' (1942, p. 143). As a result, bourgeois ideology at its most refined strikes a defensive posture unlike that of any other social order. It recognizes the violent historic origins of capitalism, the vulnerability of its property rights, the shortcomings of its philosophy. Against these deficiencies it ranges the very great achievements of its economic system and the unparalleled political and intellectual accomplishments of bourgeois culture. Here we find the defense of capitalism offered by Schumpeter, by Weber, in a manner of speaking even by Marx himself.

There is, however, another vein of ideology – one that marshalls arguments that cannot withstand the examination of history, philosophy or social science in general. Here, for example, we find the most vulgar materialist reductionism, in which capitalism is presented as embodying a primordial and unchanging 'economic man'. Jude Wanniski (1978), for instance, writes, 'In mother and father . . . the child has a diversified portfolio', a point of view that pervades his book. Such a view, which puts to shame the most blatant 'economism' of the Left, would be treated with the scorn it deserves if it were adduced as a defense of, say, the Marxian view of history. Yet it is treated with respect, even by so Burkean a critic as Irving Kristol. Or George Gilder (1981) tells us that love and altruism are the true essence of capitalism (they used to be trotted out as the soul of monarchy), and this equally grotesque statement is also treated as a 'serious' pronouncement. I console myself that Gilder will take his place alongside Bruce Barton, who wrote in the 1920s that Jesus was the most successful businessman who ever lived.

The question to be pondered is why modern conservatism has attracted the worst ideology, and why it has dulled the sensibilities of the best ideologists. I am ashamed to state the reason that occurs to me. It is that 'neoconservative' policies, such as supply-side tax cuts, have as their immediate objective the improvement of the conditions of the rich. What bonanzas will result from the lowering of the high marginal rate on property income and on the reduction of the capital gains tax! I, too, rub my hands at the prospect. To be sure, like all policies, the *ultimate* objective of supply-side economics is said to be the improvement of the condition of everyone. Just the same, I do not think neoconservative economic policies would adduce quite the same fervor, or quite the same dulling of critical sensibilities, if their *immediate* aim were the improvement of the poor and their *ultimate* aim the bettering of the rich. Self-interest has extraordinary powers of persuasion.

I have tried to remain at a distance from my subject, which is the exploration of the *gestalts* that precede economic analysis proper. But it must be apparent that my own *gestalt* lies much closer to the radical than to the conservative view. I should perhaps add that there are elements in the older conservative tradition, exemplified in Smith's *Theory of Moral Sentiments*, that seem to me to fill large lacunae in the radical analysis – elements that deal with the nature of authority and hierarchy, for example – but that is a matter for another paper.

If my purpose in this chapter is primarily expositional, however, I would not wish to conceal its complementary critical intent. The policies and programs of modern conservative economics have, to my mind, brought great and unnecessary suffering to the Western world, and my basic intent is to plumb the conceptions on which these policies and programs ultimately rest. I cannot claim that my interpretation of the conservative view of the social universe is the correct one, but I can at least challenge my critics to bring forth an exposition of its fundamental premises that is more cogent and persuasive than my own.

NOTES

1   The word 'modern' should be stressed. Conservative persuasions can certainly be traced back to the classical founders of our discipline, but their constitutive elements would depart in significant ways from that of the modern school, whether in its bland neoclassical version or its extreme supply-side incarnation. Adam Smith's conception, for example, embraces some aspects of the radical view in its perception of capitalism as a surplus-acquiring system and of social problems as integrally associated with the surplus-producing mechanism — namely the degradation of the workforce as a consequence of the division of labor. Conservative *gestalts* can thus embody different premises. In the synopsis I have given, I have tried to capture the main elements of modern conservatism, without overemphasizing its more extreme supply-side variants. I have also tried to embrace a synoptic radical view that avoids the various special emphases that distinguish schools within that general orientation.

REFERENCES

Gilder, G. (1981) *Wealth and Poverty*, New York: Basic Books.

Heilbroner, R. L. (1973), 'Economics as a value free science', *Social Research*, Spring.

Heilbroner, R. L. (1983), 'Economics and political economy: Marx, Keynes and Schumpeter', paper prepared for the Centennial Symposium on Marx, Keynes, and Schumpeter, University of Colorado at Denver, 20 April, 1983, forthcoming.

Schumpeter, J. (1942) *Capitalism, Socialism and Democracy*, London: Allen & Unwin.

Wallerstein, I. (1974) *The Modern World System*, Vol. I, New York: Academic Press.

Wanniski, J. (1978) *The Way the World Works*, New York: Basic Books.

PART I: Theory

Conservative economic theory divides into three distinct and not always mutually supportive camps. Supply-siders believe in Say's Law and the gold standard, support tax cuts and deregulation, abhor government interference with markets but do not mind deficits, and believe that the money supply adapts to market pressures, like any other supply. Monetarists likewise believe in free markets, but have reservations about Say's Law and abhor deficits, while holding that control of the money supply is a central responsibility of the government, failure to control it being the chief cause of inflation and unemployment. Rational expectations theorists began as a sub-species of monetarists, intent on demonstrating the impotence of government macro policies, but have by now developed a substantial new approach to certain parts of economic theory.

What unites these different schools is a common belief in the efficiency and optimality of free markets and, as a corollary, a determined opposition to Keynesian policies of demand management. None of them is conservative in the traditional sense – which involves a reverence for the past and a loyalty to the established values and social order. Traditional conservatism certainly placed a high value on private property, but it also stressed the values of the community and asserted the reciprocity of rights and duties: property and privilege entail obligations to the community.

No such ideas can be found in any of the three versions of free market conservatism. Reverence for the past and for established institutions is out of the question. The welfare state, the graduated income tax and the minimum wage are all established institutions, with a long history and widespread community support, but to free marketeers they are anathema and Thatcher, Reagan and Pinochet have all cut them back. What we have here is not so much conservatism as programs and apologetics for radical plutocracy. For all three approaches firmly support the maximum free scope for the activities of capital. Regulation should be abolished wherever possible, taxation should be curbed, welfare cut, labor disciplined by threats of unemployment, and potential profit should guide all business decisions. The interests of the community, its traditions, customs, values, the reciprocal relations of rights and duties, the ceremonial trappings of the established order, all these matters dear to the hearts of old-fashioned conservatives not only play no role whatsoever in the political discourse of free marketeers, they are also quite likely to be utterly obliterated by the forces of the market. No matter how famous its product, how central to the culture, if a business cannot pay its way it will go under. As for the traditional values of family life, nothing undermines them like unemployment, yet that is what is prescribed to cure inflation (although supply-siders are expansionist, and regard the unemployment their programs bring as merely 'transitional').

Let us consider each school in turn. Supply-side economics has recently made off with most of the headlines, but it is in fact the least respectable intellectually. It amounts to little more than a few flourishes added to a very literal-minded interpretation of neoclassical theory. When competition is vigorous, markets will clear, say the textbooks. Moreover, markets achieve equilibrium positions that are supposedly optimal, according to certain criteria. Hence, in equilibrium, all unemployment will be voluntary, reduction of taxes will increase supply by enhancing price incentives, and government policy will not be needed to move the economy toward equilibrium – indeed, it would be likely to move it away. In view of the great discrepancies between idealized and actual conditions, mainstream economists substantially qualify the textbook propositions on which these conclusions rest. Even more important, these propositions all stem from *partial* equilibrium theory; in a *general* equilibrium approach such claims could not be sustained. Markets do not necessarily clear; an equilibrium may not exist or there may be many, even infinitely many; some or none may be stable. Frank Hahn (1981, p.126) puts the point clearly and forcefully: 'A bad nomenclature . . . together with much carelessness in textbooks, often misleads people into thinking that there is some theorem which claims that a competitive equilibrium is socially optimal. There is no such claim.' There is such a claim, of course, and the supply-siders make it all the time. But it is not valid.

Monetarists likewise begin from an uncritical acceptance of partial equilibrium market analysis, though a number of important recent works have tried to establish its characteristic propositions in simple general equilibrium models. This is extremely difficult because general equilibrium models, being based on complete futures markets with complete information and an assumed absence of uncertainty, cannot easily accommodate even a rudimentary monetary system (Arrow and Hahn, 1971). Hence very little work has been done with general equilibrium theory, and the traditional marginalist models of supply and demand remain the starting point.

The concept of the 'natural rate of unemployment' illustrates this very well. This rate of unemployment is the result of voluntary quitting and job search – the normal turnover – when real wages are such that labor supply equals labor demand; it is the rate of unemployment associated with labor market equilibrium. In the long run this cannot be changed (unless the parameters of the labor market change) but, in the short run, a rise in demand due, say, to government demand management may push up prices, thereby lowering the real wage and leading employers to offer more employment. Thus unemployment will fall as a consequence of (unanticipated) inflation – just the sort of relationship embodied in the Keynesian Phillips curve (the empirically observed inverse relation between price inflation and unemployment). But, according to the monetarist doctrine known as the 'natural rate hypothesis' (NRH), this relation can hold only in the *short run*. In the long run, when employers and employees find out that the real wage has fallen below its equilibrium value, employment will return to the natural rate. In the short run, government policy can fool people; in the long run, the equilibrium will reassert itself. The only difference will be that money prices will be permanently higher. Thus the government, trying to reduce unemployment, will have caused inflation.

But how can prices be higher? Aggregate output is the same and monetary institutions are unchanged, which means that velocity must be the same, so the only possibility is that the money supply must have been increased in the course of the government's attempts to manipulate demand. Indeed, monetarists argue that fiscal policy without monetary expansion will be ineffective. So demand management boils down to controlling the money supply. The argument shows that a monetary expansion may have a temporary effect on employment and output, but in the long run it affects only the price level. Money is 'neutral, in the long run: it affects only nominal values.

Rational expectations theory developed largely out of the debates around the NRH. The central point can be made very simply: if employers and workers understand 'the way the world works' – that is, understand the correct theory – then they will short-cut the adjustment process and move directly to the equilibrium. So government policies will have *no* impact on employment and output, and can affect only prices, even in the short run.

The three approaches have large overlaps but also substantial differences. Perhaps the least significant are the differences between the rational expectations writers and the monetarists, for these seem to be chiefly matters of emphasis. Rational expectations is concerned largely with theory in relation to policy – chiefly with proving that the government is powerless to affect the economy's equilibrium position. This is also crucial to monetarism, although it is only one of its several and interrelated core propositions. To date, the chief application of rational expectations methods has been to models involving the natural rate hypothesis, which, we shall argue, have serious defects, but rational expectations can also be applied to quite different models, when it will no longer yield the typically monetarist conclusions.

By contrast, a serious gulf divides supply-siders, on the one hand, from both monetarists and rational expectations theorists, on the other. Monetarists and rational expectations theorists have argued that government taxing and spending simply 'crowds out' private activity, so that the net effect is zero. Government regulation of business and family life generates compensating or offsetting private behavior: requiring public education simply reduces private instruction provided by the family; subsidies like school lunches and family allowances simply reduce private expenditure on children and private effort in the labor market, respectively. But if the government is powerless to affect the economy's equilibrium position, then there cannot be any net gain from a supply-side tax cut, or from deregulation, or from any of the other much-touted conservative programs. They will simply substitute private for public activity. Conservatives regard this as desirable in itself, of course, but, as Heilbroner points out in the Introduction, they provide no reasoned case for such a judgement.

Supply-siders, on the other hand, believe that the government *can* influence the economy. Its impact reduces private initiative by more than it increases public activity; hence cutting taxes and eliminating regulations and controls will provide net stimulus. Even more heretical is their belief that not only do deficits not do harm, they also provide a stimulus – of a Keynesian sort. Finally, supply-siders argue that the banking system acts like any other business, increasing its supply in response to increased demand and introducing product innovations if necessary. The money supply tends to adapt to the demand for money, either directly or by way of new forms of payment, like credit cards or electronic funds transfers. It is useless and footling to call for rigid rules controlling the growth of the money supply, since such control is not within the power of central banks. If an automatic money supply is wanted – and supply-siders agree that it is required to control inflation – it will be necessary to return to the strict gold standard. Some monetarists might accept the conclusion, but they cannot accept the argument.

Clearly there are serious differences within the general framework of conservative economic theory. We shall now look at each approach in turn, both to see what each says and to assess it critically. We shall conclude with an examination of a somewhat surprising extension of conservative thought to family policy.

REFERENCES

Arrow, K. J. and Hahn, F. (1971) *General Competitive Analysis*, San Francisco: Holden-Day.

Hahn, F. (1981) 'General equilibrium theory', in Bell and Kristol, eds, *The Crisis in Economic Theory*, New York: Basic Books.

2 Supply-Side Economics: Incentives and Disasters

Rinder provides a critical survey of the main doctrines of the supply-siders, covering their advocacy of Say's Law (the doctrine that there can be no involuntary unemployment due to shortage of demand), their theory of incentives, especially as it applies to taxation and the labor market, their treatment of government spending, particularly as regards welfare and regulation, concluding with their advocacy of a return to the gold standard. When she first wrote the article, she ended with a forecast of what we could expect from supply-side policies in practice: a disastrous recession, rising unemployment, an increase in poverty and crime, together with a worsening of pollution and more frequent environmental disasters. The first two years of the Reagan administration have borne her out very well.

SUPPLY-SIDE ECONOMICS

Introduction

This paper examines the theoretical underpinnings, such as they are, and the policy recommendations of supply-side economics. Many economists have, in recent years, shifted focus from the sufficiency of effective demand to the productive capacity of the economy and the willingness of firms to use it and to expand it. While these economists are concerned with supply, they are not necessarily part of that camp called 'supply-siders'. This study will explore supply-side economics as expounded by George Gilder, Arthur Laffer and Jude Wanniski, and as embraced in 1980 by the Reagan administration.

Supply-siders consider capitalism a natural and progressive economic form: it expresses the individualism inherent in human nature and offers economic growth balanced by the harmonious equilibrating mechanisms of the free market. Entrepreneurs seek opportunities through innovation, which provides the creative power of capitalism. The masses maximize utility by responding to monetary incentives. Their instinctive knowledge of economic principles guides them in their responses and reactions to political and economic leadership.

These reactions provide the masses with considerable control over leadership in the long run.

There are no *proofs* to confirm or refute the supply-side vision, unfortunately. Supply-siders hold their opinions fervently, and evidence can be used to support almost any proposition, for something can always be argued to be less (more) than it would otherwise have been, had different policies prevailed. 'It is inconceivable, for example, that Friedman would consider . . . the recent riots in Britain or high US stagflation as suggesting the slightest blemish on his monetarist views', though Thatcher and Reagan pursued monetarist policies (Gardner, 1981, p. 30). Economic theories, then, must be judged on the plausibility of their world-views, and against a common-sensible examination of history. But my common sense is lunacy to the supply-siders, and I largely return the compliment. Readers must judge our relative merits for themselves.

Here, it will be argued that capitalism is wasteful and destructive as well as creative; that entrepreneurs, while they sometimes innovate, mostly react to their sales and inventory levels; that individuals are encrusted in family and neighborhood ties, in habits and customs, and that their responses – not always consistent – to monetary incentives are variable.

Supply-side theorists invoke Say's Law, espouse essentially neoclassical theories of the supply of and the demand for labor, postulate that government operations are largely harmful or useless, and suggest that inflation be ended by reinstatement of the gold standard. These various points will be examined in turn.

Say's Law

The supply-siders first resurrect Say's Law ('supply creates its own demand') to justify their exclusive focus on the incentives to supply. Say held that since consumption is the goal of production, all production (supply) constitutes at the same time a demand for goods of equal value. 'Apparent' gluts of goods (and there were plenty in the eighteenth and nineteenth centuries) were only partial, balanced by insufficient production in other parts of the economy. If products piled up everywhere, it was the result of artificial hindrances to their exchange – tariffs and the like. In the modern parlance of supply-sider Gilder: 'There can be no such thing as a general glut of goods. There can be a glut of 'bads', but in the world of necessary scarcity in which the very science of economics finds its meaning, an apparent glut of all goods merely signifies a dearth of creative production, a lack of new supplies and fresh demands' (Gilder, 1981 p. 39).

Say's Law holds for a barter economy, where an act of supplying a dozen eggs to market is at the same time an act of demanding an equal value of goods in return. In that type of primitive economy there can be no general glut of goods. But Say's Law does not hold for a money economy, where hoarding in hopes of better opportunities later is possible. Keynes' general theory explained how unemployed workers and unemployed factories could coexist in a rational economy supposedly driven by scarcity (Keynes, 1936). Gilder, however, shrugs off Keynes' insight: 'Private savings, moreover, in the current inflationary environment, are invested', he says (Gilder, 1981, p. 39). That they maybe invested in gold, jewels, art or other non-productive forms is not suggested.

Incentives

Having eliminated the problems of the match between aggregate production and aggregate demand by assuming Say's Law, the supply-siders move to microeconomics. Here they employ their particular concept of human nature: humankind responds principally to monetary incentives. For higher pay and lower tax rates, workers will work longer hours with greater application. Moreover, as tax rates decline, they will work more in the public market, rather than bartering their services with neighbors. (Wanniski, 1978, considers the barter market to be very large.) Individuals will also save a higher proportion of their incomes when after-tax returns to saving rise. In Wanniski's writings, all individuals are calculating utility-maximizers, *à la* Gary Becker, having learned marginal principles in their cradles. Infants maximize parental attentiveness by carefully calculated marginal doses of crying. Affection, habit and custom, those crucial determinants of human behavior, are disguised manifestations of the desire to maximize utility – usually income.

Entrepreneurs will similarly respond to monetary incentives. They will save and invest when prospects of after-tax profits rise, and they will hire workers and buy material inputs more when wages and input costs decline. The rich will also save more and eschew tax shelters when tax rates are low, allocating funds to more efficient investments. This appears logical, but it ignores the critical role of sales. Entrepreneurs increase investment and hire more workers when sales are rising – which does not usually happen when wages are falling. For supply-siders, increased savings present no problem in the form of declining sales of consumer goods, for Say's Law prevents recession.

Even leaving aside the problem of the sufficiency of aggregate demand, there is the question of its composition. Shifting spending from consumption to investment, as the supply-siders urge, would hurt producers of consumer goods, bringing layoffs in that sector and thus further declines in consumer spending. Producers of capital equipment would step up production, assuming they and their suppliers had excess capacity. The probability of costs and prices rising in this sector is high. Moreover, if consumer goods production is more labor-intensive than capital goods production, the shift from consumption to investment would increase unemployment, even if aggregate demand did not fall. The point is, shifting resources from consumption to investment would create severe adjustment problems and, unless carefully planned, could easily result in recession in the consumer goods sector and inflation in the investment goods sector (Nell, 1978).

The Labor Market

The supply-siders' view of the function of monetary incentives embraces the neoclassical theories of supply and demand for labor. These theories were developed at the end of the last century during the 'marginalist revolution' in economics.

The determination of the supply of labor to the public, taxable market is as follows: Individuals, in order to maximize utility, will weigh the inherent disutility of work (the utility of leisure) against the utility of money and decide whether and for how long to offer their labor services. For them, the wage must exactly offset the value of forgone leisure – otherwise they would gain more utility by staying home than by going to work. As employment rises for an individual (longer hours), the marginal utility of leisure also rises, and a higher wage is necessary to bring forth additional work. Aggregating from the individual to the economy as a whole:

$$W = MU_{\text{L}}.$$

The wage in equilibrium must equal the marginal utility of leisure. The marginal utility of leisure rises as employment rises. If the wage falls, workers will withdraw from the markets; if it rises, additional workers will seek work. This relationship constitutes *the supply of labor*.

The supply of labor to the private, barter economy works in essentially the same way. But the allocation of workers between taxable and barter markets depends on the tax rate (an incentive to barter) and the desire to expand business (an incentive to move to the taxable market), for barter markets are necessarily limited.

The demand for labor is determined by firms in a way analogous to labor supply. But while labor responds to rewards (wages), firms respond to input costs, and assume that the rewards in the form of sales and profits will be forthcoming. In order to maximize profits, firms will hire workers (subject to diminishing returns) to operate a fixed capital stock up to the point where the additional worker adds to the value of output an amount equal to the wage received. Aggregating from the firm to the economy as a whole:

$$W = MP_{\mathrm{L}}.$$

The wage in equilibrium must equal the marginal product of labor. The marginal product of labor, with fixed capital, declines as employment rises. If the wage falls, additional workers will be demanded; if the wage rises, fewer. Thus, this relationship constitutes *the demand for labor*.

Together, the response of workers to wage incentives and the response of firms to cost incentives determine the level of employment and the real wage (see Figure 2.1). Following the standard format, the wage is on the vertical axis. From bottom to top, the vertical axis thus represents progressively higher wages. From left to right, the horizontal axis represents rising numbers of workers. The upward slope of the supply of workers shows that, as the wage rises, additional people seek work. The downward slope of the demand for workers shows that, as the wage falls, firms will seek to expand hiring.

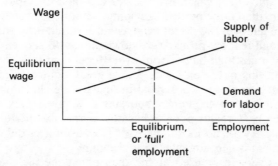

Figure 2.1   *Wage Incentives and the Supply of and the Demand for Labor*

The marginal utility/marginal productivity theory that underlies the incentive responses posited above is highly problematic, as an extensive literature attests (Harris, 1980). The problems center on the difficulty inherent in the idea of changing levels of employment with a fixed stock of capital. This includes the difficulty in measuring capital; the implausibility of varying employment while holding capital constant; the implausibility of diminishing returns, if capital is allowed to vary with employment; the consequent impossibility of measuring the marginal product of labor in order to set it equal to the real wage. Moreover, by assuming Say's Law, the supply-siders ignore the key influence on hiring: can you sell the output? So this theory of the demand for labor is flawed. Furthermore, the work/leisure choices for workers are strongly influenced by the availability of jobs, by the need to survive and reproduce, and by their customary life-styles. So this theory of the supply of labor is limited.

The tax and social spending cuts proposed by supply-siders and enacted by the Reagan administration were meant to rearrange the monetary incentives described above. By taking from the poor and giving to the well-off these measures were meant to spur the poor to work more and harder, the rich to save and invest more. But increased incentives in the form of greater income inequality had not boosted economic activity in the past, or in other industrial countries. Most European countries have higher taxes, larger government and less income inequality than the US, yet their economies perform no worse, indeed often better, and they would score much higher on almost any index of social well-being (less crime, better public services, cleaner streets and parks, fewer beggars and homeless, etc.) (Thurow, 1980).

The experiment with supply-side policies in the US has failed. Between 1980 and early 1983, investment dropped 7 per cent in real terms. Employment was down 0.2 per cent and unemployment was up by more than three percentage points – from 7 to over 10 per cent. Sales were flat over the period, capacity utilization dropped below 70 per cent, and real net profits were down almost 40 per cent. Inflation slowed by more than half – from over 10 per cent to less than 5 per cent – and this has been claimed as a great victory by the supply-siders. But it represents a typical business cycle slowdown in inflation. All the other economic theorems of supply-siders have been proved empty. Greater poverty has not spurred people to work harder, for there were no jobs to be had. Tax advantages did not trigger an investment boom, for sales were declining.

Supply-siders recognized at the outset that the income effect of changes in take-home pay partially offsets the substitution effect. The income effect involves a family's 'target' income or life-style. A fall in wages may force the family to work more hours in order to pay bills and maintain living standards. The substitution effect – leisure becomes cheaper when wages fall, so leisure is substituted for work – may be irrelevant to a family trying to make ends meet. Similarly, when wages rise, the target life-style is achieved with less work, and overtime and moonlighting may be cut back. The question is, which effect is stronger?

Supply-siders wriggle out of this problem in two ways. First, Laffer points out that workers will not work for zero wages, and they will work for some positive wage: 'Therefore, over the entire range of possible wages, the supply of work effort is unambiguously increased by a total increase in take-home wages' (Laffer, 1981a, p. 41). Secondly, Laffer supposes that the change in taxes (take-home pay) is matched by an equal change in transfer payments, which constitute a disincentive to work. The income effect will thus wash out: 'If you tax $100 from Jones, thus forcing him to work harder (income effect) and give $100 to Smith, Smith is required to work less to achieve his desired level of wealth.'

There are obvious problems here. First, Laffer supposes that the supply curve is straight. He has two observations, and can plot it as shown in Figure 2.2. However, we could easily say the line encompasses Laffer's two observations but has the shape shown in Figure 2.3.

A second problem concerns transfer payments, which might as well be covered here. In true Reaganite fashion, Laffer believes that transfer payments – Aid to Families with Dependent Children, food

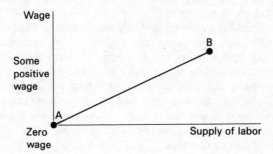

Figure 2.2   *Laffer Plots Two Points (A, B) and Makes a Line*

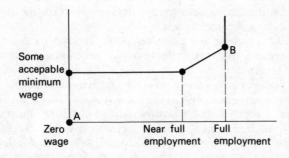

Figure 2.3   *Rinder Plots Two Points and Makes a Squiggle!*

stamps, unemployment insurance – constitute principally a disincentive to work. Since payments rise with family size, they are also an incentive to fertility. Since only the poor can qualify, it 'pays' to be poor. Not very lordly sums, to be sure – $370 per month in 1979 for a family of four in New York State, one of the most generous. In the absence of these payments, Laffer feels that wages would entice more people to seek work. The large majority of welfare recipients are mothers with young children, however. Who is to care for those children while their mothers work? This is an unsettled question. However, in the supply-side view, these women, having no visible means of support, ought not to have had those children in the first place. And, while punishing these helpless innocents is not a stated objective, the need to work would prove a clear disincentive to poor women against irresponsibly having further children.

In sum, the high taxes on wages that are a disincentive to work have a mirror image – transfer payments, which are both a disincentive to work and an incentive to fertility. This allows the supply-siders to assume that the income effect of a tax cut would be a 'washout', and that the substitution effect would prevail.

Cutting social spending, then, has many agreeable consequences in theory: workers work more, for taxes can be cut; the poor work more, for their disincentives to work are removed; the poor practise contraception, for their incentives to fertility are removed. Supply-siders, having assumed Say's Law, need not worry about the declines in consumption spending as cutbacks in government employment and transfer payments are absorbed in family budgets. In the real world, however, declining consumption and piling up of inventories constitute a disincentive to production and investment, no matter how low are taxes and factor costs. Furthermore, empirical data do not show the income effect of changes in real take-home pay to be a washout. Labor force participation rose sharply in the 1970s (see Figure 2.4), when real wages dropped (see Figure 2.5). So families responded more to the income effect of wage declines than to the substitution effect as leisure became cheaper.

Curiously, much of the press coverage of supply-side economics has emphasized that tax reductions will encourage savings, since after-tax returns to savings will rise. The supply-side literature, however, focuses much more on the incentives to work and to invest that they feel are embodied in tax cuts. It is true that individuals will save more if they expect a positive after-tax return, but this is not essential to their argument. Thus, the commonly offered refutation of supply-side theory (that individuals will spend their tax cuts) side-steps the question. Indeed, between the lines of supply-side economics one can almost read a Cambridge consumption function. That

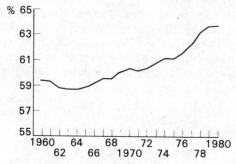

Figure 2.4 *Labor Force as a Percent of Working-Age Population*
Source: US Bureau of Labor Statistics

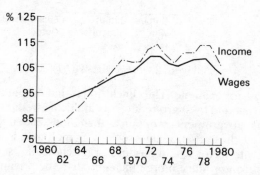

Figure 2.5 *Index of Real Wages and Real Median Family Income
(1967 = 100)*
Source: US Bureau of Labor Statistics and US Bureau of the Census

is, workers will spend their new take-home pay, which is minimal because the tax cuts are tilted to the upper brackets; and the wealthy (entrepreneurs) will save (invest) theirs.

The Tax Wedge and Government Spending

Having dealt with the incentives, Laffer then develops his 'tax wedge' model, which shows how employment and output would be higher with lower taxes (see Figure 2.6). Reduce taxes, says Laffer, and the cost of labor to the firm drops, causing increased demand for labor; and the after-tax wage of labor rises, causing increased supply of labor. Output is considered, for simplicity's sake, to be proportional to employment. The larger the wedge, the lower society's output.

This implicitly assumes that government provides no services, and that the taxes constitute a drain on the economy, a complete waste.

Thus you can both raise wages and lower costs without subtracting from anything! Further discussion shows that some parts of government spending do provide services – public goods such as highways and armies – while others provide no services or even dis-services – transfer payments and regulation of industry, with their production

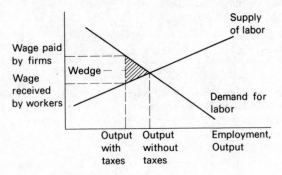

Figure 2.6   *The Tax Wedge*

disincentives, for example. The conclusion is that output could be significantly expanded by sharp reductions in the tax wedge, first cutting dis-servicing government programs, then non-servicing ones, and leaving intact those that benefit society, namely goods and services that the private sector would produce or purchase on its own but that government can produce more efficiently than the private sector.

The question of the amount and the reduceability of waste in government operations is highly complex. First, let me go on record as saying that the government is not the enemy of the economy. Rising government activity does not decrease private output. Indeed, government operations create most of the infrastructure – roads, education, system of rules – that the private sector uses as a base of operations. Moreover, the size of the government sector and its counter-cyclicality provide a cushion to the private economy, preventing free-fall recessions. Empirically, US economic growth has been rapid in periods of growing government activity, slower when government growth slowed. And many countries have relatively larger governments than the US, higher levels of social services and security, and perfectly respectable economic growth records. Thus the widely fostered opinion (even Democrats say it lately) that US government is too big, and that taxes and government spending are too high, is false.

On transfer payments
Without welfare, food stamps and support for the elderly, social

coherence and social peace will decline. The sense of living in a somewhat decent society is necessary to individual and social growth and
development. Neoconservatives would have it that the welfare state
has destroyed the family. On the contrary, the expansion of production necessarily shifted the focus of economic activity from home, village and clan to factory and office, to city and suburb, to unrelated
work associates. The resulting breakdown of traditional ties has given
rise to the welfare state, which is necessary to prevent social disin-
tegration (Polanyi, 1968).

Moreover, to 'cut the fat' in welfare programs may cost far more in
social workers, accountants and computers than to tolerate the occasional abuse. Standard audit procedures, already in use, minimize
costs while usually preventing large-scale fraud. Occasionally journalists will make a scoop on welfare cheats and, oddly enough, hard-
pressed electorates will always be more outraged at these poor frauds
than at richer and easier ones.

In sum, the supply-siders and other conservatives assume that welfare programs can be cut with minimal adverse effects, indeed with
beneficial results. These programs, it seems, have sprung from
nowhere, not in answer to social needs.

On regulation

The supply-siders treat regulation of industry as 'a garbage good' –
something the private sector would not by choice pay for and therefore a dead weight on the economy. Regulations increase costs to
producers, thereby constituting a disincentive to produce. While the
air may be cleaner and factories and automobiles safer, this represents no gain to society, for consumers would not have bought clean
air and safe cars by choice. And while factory workers and their families would choose safe factories, the rest of society would not, making
it an uneconomic choice.

Again, supply-siders reject the notion that regulation protects consumers and society from the consequences of unfettered operation of
powerful companies and industries, which focus on short-term
growth and earnings with little concern for long-term social and economic by-products.

On waste in general

Anyone who has worked in the private sector knows that the government has no monopoly on waste. Inefficiency in production and production of dubious goods are prevalent in private industry. However,
waste in private production is disguised. Its cost is included in the
price of goods and services. Supply-siders would be less one-sided if
they recognized private as well as public 'waste'. Indeed, waste may

be a necessary factor of production: executives may need ten useless meetings to achieve one good idea; clerical workers may need to use half their ingenuity to undermine and ridicule their martinet supervisor, to bear tedious work while retaining their ingenuity.

In sum, the drive to cut 'waste' from government operations is one-sided, often short-sighted and unlikely to succeed.

The Laffer Curve

Having postulated the tax wedge model (a tax–output tradeoff), Laffer develops his famous curve (see Figure 2.7). This iso-revenue curve is the locus of points of combinations of tax rates on labor and on capital that leave revenue unchanged. On the vertical axis of the iso-revenue curve, the tax rate on labor rises as we move up the axis; on the horizontal axis, the tax rate on capital rises as we move from left to right. To achieve some revenue – say 100 – a pair of tax rates on labor and capital will be appropriate. To change tax rates, keeping output and revenue constant, you must raise one tax and lower the other. Thus revenue can be achieved at the extreme left of the diagram with high taxes on labor and low taxes on capital, or at the extreme right with low taxes on labor and high taxes on capital, or in

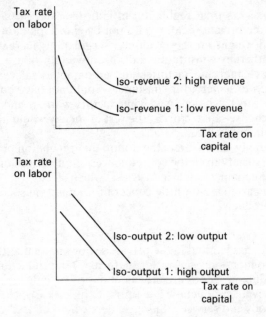

Figure 2.7   *Iso-Revenue and Iso-Output Curves*

the middle, with medium taxes on both factors. A high tax on labor depresses both supply of and demand for labor; to offset this, a low tax on capital will increase demand for and supply of machinery, and capital-intensive production will prevail. The rate of tax on labor can be reduced and that on capital raised, causing substitution of factors but keeping revenues constant. (Notice the interesting assumption that you can shift employment and capacity utilization in opposite directions. Imagine operating a factory designed for 1,000 assembly line positions using only 100 – or even 900 – workers!) A whole family of iso-revenue curves can be drawn, illustrating the effects of tax rates, abstracting from the level of output.

The iso-output curve is the locus of points linking the pairs of tax rates that hold output constant. With the same axes as the iso-revenue curve. The iso-output curve shows the appropriate pairs of tax rates that will maintain output levels. To change tax rates, keeping output constant, you must raise one tax and lower the other. Output 1 can be achieved at high taxes on labor, low on capital, or low taxes on labor, high on capital; or medium taxes on both. Note that the farther to the right the iso-output line, the lower is output. This follows from Laffer's 'tax wedge' proposition: the higher the taxes, the lower the output.

Laffer's iso-output and iso-revenue curves parallel the microeconomic techniques for developing indifference curves. They are purely theoretical constructions, do not represent any empirical data and include dubious assumptions about how people make choices and how production is organized.

We can see where Laffer is leading: for each level of revenue, there is one pairing of tax rates that maximizes output (see Figure 2.8). To

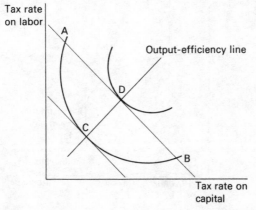

Figure 2.8   *Iso-Revenue and Iso-Output Curves Combined*

achieve revenue 1, tax pairs A, B or C will do the trick. Point C however, by providing greater incentives in the form of low tax rates to both workers and entrepreneurs, will maximize output. Points A and B are doubly unsatisfactory, for not only could the same revenue be obtained at higher output (point C), but alternatively more revenue could be obtained at the same output (point D). The Laffer curve, with a stroke of the computer, tells us that government can have its cake and eat it too! The government can continue its wasteful activities, for it can reduce taxes, so raise output and keep revenue constant. It can raise output even more by cutting taxes and accepting lower revenues.

Wanniski gives a simpler, one-factor presentation of the Laffer curve that abstracts from the substitution of factors. He states that for every revenue there are two (and only two?) tax rates that will achieve it (Wanniski, 1978, p. 97). His tax rate curve starts at 0 per cent – at which revenues are zero – and curves up to 100 per cent at which revenues are also zero, for no one will work to hand over the total product to the government. In Figure 2.9, the vertical axis represents tax rates – on any kind of income – rising from 0 per cent at the bottom to 100 per cent at the top. The rise is not necessarily proportional, however: point E, Wanniski is quick to caution, is not supposed to represent the 50 per cent tax rate, though it may. The horizontal axis measures rising revenue levels from left to right. The ellipse indicates that increasing tax rates result in increasing revenues up to some point, after which the high tax rates depress output so much that they result in a reduced tax take. Revenue 1 can be

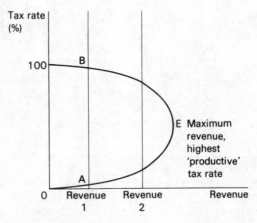

Figure 2.9   *Wanniski's One-Factor Laffer Curve*

achieved both by point A – low tax rate and high output – and by point B – high tax rate, low output.

Now what is the point of all this? Many economists concede that, where individual identification with the common good is not strong, increases in tax rates can conceivably become counter-productive. But where US tax rates stand now on this backward-bending revenue curve is a separate issue. Supply-siders feel that US tax rates are above point E in Figure 2.9, and that a drop in tax rates will stimulate effort, employment and investment. Others are dubious.

Martin Gardner's proposed neo-Laffer curve is only partially tongue-in-cheek (Gardner, 1981). He works from Wanniski's one-sector format, but takes into account the 'technosnarl' of the real world. 'Even if we could determine at which point to put the economy, it is not clear from the snarl just what fiscal and monetary policies would move the economy fastest along the curve to the nearest point E' (p. 27).

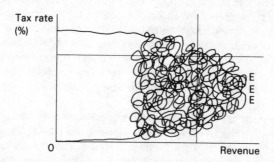

Figure 2.10   *Gardner's Neo-Laffer Curve*
From: Martin Gardner, 'The Laffer Curve and other Laughs in Current Economics'.
Copyright © 1981 by Scientific American, Inc. All rights reserved.

Summary: The Real Economy

To recapitulate the essential points of supply-side economics on the real economy:

● Say's Law holds, so there's no worry about the sufficiency of effective demand.
● Individuals respond to monetary incentives in choosing between work and leisure.
● Entrepreneurs respond to factor cost incentives in choosing production levels.
● Taxes, in raising factor costs and reducing factor rewards, constitute a principal disincentive to production (the tax wedge).

- Reducing taxes will thus result in increases in output, and tax revenues may not decline – indeed, they may rise (the Laffer curve).
- An important part of government activity is positively bad for the economy. Transfer payments and regulation of industry both represent disincentives to production, for example. So sharp cutbacks in government activity will raise output.

To summarize the critical comments:

- Say's Law does not hold in a money economy, as shown by Keynes and as illustrated by current economic conditions.
- Individuals do not exist in social isolation, and habitual life-styles and the availability of jobs are the most important influence on work/leisure choices.
- Entrepreneurs respond to the level of their sales and the running down or piling up of inventories in choosing production levels.
- Taxes finance necessary public expenditures, so the 'tax wedge' idea – to subtract from costs and add to wages – must subtract something else from the economy – government services.
- Tax reduction may cause sales to rise and stimulate increases in production, not because incentives to work are greater but because take-home pay is higher.
- Government services and programs provide some social cohesion and some protective cushioning against too-disruptive effects of economic growth and change. Red tape stems not from bureaucracy's love of intricacy, but from the gradual evolution of rules and exceptions in a complex society. These rules reflect a delicate balance of the common good and private interests. Separating the good from the bad rules is not easy. Sudden attempts to throw wholesale programs out and start from scratch will prove short-sighted and not cost-effective.

Forecast: The Results of Supply-Side Policies

Note: this forecast was written in winter 1981, when this essay was first drafted. Since then, these expected results have become reality.

1 A cut in personal taxes may increase consumption and thus stimulate production or inflation. However, since the tax cuts are aimed mostly at the rich, and spending cuts at the poor, consumption may fall (the poor spend most of their incomes on consumption). Increased investment by the rich is not likely to take up the slack,

for newly-approved investment incentives will pale into insignificance as capacity utilization drops and inventories pile up.

2　A cut in taxes on capital will be followed by capacity-enhancing investment only when sales are rising steadily. Non-productive investments – takeover wars, gold and art funds – do nothing for supply.

3　A cut in welfare payments will depress consumption and stimulate crime, alienation and misery. It will not stimulate work unless unskilled jobs and day-care centers suddenly become widely available, and then the causing agent would be the availability of such jobs and services, not the so-called incentives.

4　A cut in government regulation will stimulate pollution, factory accidents, job discrimination, etc. Investment will increase only if sales are rising – otherwise additional funds made available by fewer restrictions on by-products will be diverted into speculative investments or held for later opportunities. Again, the cause of higher investment is not availability of funds but sales prospects.

The Gold Bug

Up to now the discussion has dealt only with the real economy; but the major thrust of the supply-side program is its offer of renewed growth with price stability. Whence the price stability?

First, it must be mentioned that supply-siders – indeed most economists – treat inflation as intrinsically evil. Actually, inflation benefits some, hurts others. Normally hurt are those whose incomes are set by long-term (one year or more) contracts – workers, landlords, pensioners. Normally helped are those with some control over the demand for their products – usually large corporations – who can keep prices rising ahead of costs. Historically, price inflation in the aggregate has been associated with times of economic growth and rising living standards. Deflation and stability have normally prevailed in times of stagnation and increasing misery. It is instructive to compare current literature to economic writings of previous centuries, when economic data were scarce. In the past, *the* economic indicator was the price level, and rising prices indicated prosperity.

Perhaps the most controversial major tenet of supply-siders is that a return to the gold standard is necessary to cure inflation. Their case rests on two arguments. First, the central bankers cannot control the supply of money. By imposing reserve requirements on one kind of money, they cause another kind of money to emerge, as banks, individuals and corporations ingeniously side-step central bank controls. 'Monetary restraint is difficult to maintain in a world of shifting exchange rates, huge international flows of stateless money, and continual disagreement about what constitutes money itself', suggests Robert Mundell (*Business Week*, 1980, p. 76). Moreover, central bankers cannot be relied on to act responsibly. Political pressures could entice them to debase the currency. So gold convertibility would provide a simple, clear-cut rule for monetary authorities, easy to follow and difficult to weasel out of.

Secondly, the central bank *should* not control the supply of money, for example by a steady growth rule as prescribed by monetarists. Instead, they should match the growth of supply to the growth of demand for money. The way to do this is to assure the *quality* of money by making it convertible to gold.

Lehrman considers attempts by the Federal Reserve System (the Fed) to control money supply growth to be 'monetarist fine tuning – an effort to fine tune the money stock, according to a predetermined rule, a rule which may or may not give rise to an equilibrium level of cash balances during a given market period. . . . Open market operations, even in the hands of intelligent men of good will, are at best nothing more than poorly educated guesses . . .' (Lehrman, 1981, p. 36). Lehrman points out that the steady growth rule proposed by monetarists ignores the fact that, historically, rapid money growth has sometimes been matched by rapid growth in production, sometimes by rapid increases in prices. The key, then, is to match the growth of the money supply to the growth of production (demand for money) by the automatic mechanism of gold convertibility.

How does the gold standard work? By setting the price of gold at some fixed dollar figure – they recommend a figure in the neighborhood of $400–600 – the price level, and thus the value of currency, becomes fixed in terms of gold. If gold is set at $500 an ounce, and a loaf of bread costs $1, then bread will cost 1/500 oz of gold. If improvements in technology made bread production easier, its price would fall. If deteriorating technology or wheat crop failures made bread more expensive to produce, its price would rise. But offsetting declines in prices of other commodities would keep the overall price level fixed in terms of gold. How? If prices begin to rise (indicating that money supply is growing too fast), dollars will buy fewer goods. But, dollar holders will choose to convert to gold rather than to buy goods at inflated prices. This will reduce the supply of money and re-establish the price level to the equilibrium (at which people desire neither to acquire nor to dump gold).

A similar mechanism would prevent international disequilibrium. If a country imports more than it exports, an outflow of currency, backed by gold, pays the difference. If the import binge continues, suppliers will convert the currency to gold, draining reserves from the country. This will cut money supply and put downward pressure on prices, making domestic products more desirable than imports; as prices fall, the demand for the country's products abroad will increase, improving exports at the same time that imports are declining, thus restoring import–export balance.

Laffer feels that fixed exchange rates, maintained by gold convertibility, optimize allocation of world resources and thus maximize world efficiency. A regime of floating exchange rates, in contrast, is usually argued, in the integrated world economy, to provide some independent control over domestic money supplies, allowing countries to some extent to avoid 'importing' inflation or deflation. The equilibrating mechanism for a floating rate regime is similar to that for the fixed rate case. If imports exceed exports, an outflow of currency will be followed by a devaluation of the currency. This will reduce imports by making them more costly. In the fixed exchange rate case, the amount of money is changed, thus adjusting prices, resulting in quantity changes re-establishing equilibrium. In the floating rate case, the price of the money is changed, thus adjusting prices of goods, resulting in quantity changes re-establishing equilibrium. However, in the floating rate system, governments have some control over the timing and extent of adjustments to be made, some ability to cushion the adverse effects of the free market process. This is not considered an advantage by supply-siders, who feel that the operation of the free market will always give optimal results.

Laffer counters that the flexibility argument assumes that foreign currency is of no use except for its import-purchasing power. Thus 'flexible rates provide a complete barrier to trading in money between countries, preventing money from moving from areas of excess supply to areas of excess demand' (Laffer, 1981b, p. 391). 'The world would operate more efficiently if money were instead allowed to move freely between countries, evening its cost. Countries where the cost had been high would now use more real balances and less real resources, freeing those real resources for other, more productive uses' (p. 393). This argument reflects the 'comparative advantage' analysis, which shows that all parties necessarily benefit from free trade. A discussion of international trade is beyond the scope of this paper, but recent writings show that underdeveloped countries may benefit from trade barriers, and can be hurt by the specialization resulting from free trade (Amin, 1977).

Once gold convertibility is reinstated, supply-siders expect the public to be reassured about the quality of currency, and interest rates will collapse as investors become willing to commit funds on thirty-year maturities. When interest rates drop, by the way, the federal deficit will melt away, since a large proportion of federal expenditures is for debt service. Thus, if the federal deficit causes inflation, the cure is not only in supply-side tax cuts, which increase revenues, and in supply-side cutbacks in government activity, which reduce expenditures, but also in sharp reductions in interest rates following reinstatement of the gold standard.

Supply-siders point out that there is no need to divert extensive resources to producing and storing gold. Since the price level will be maintained, people will not choose to convert dollars to gold. Thus, a small store of gold can support a large money supply. Dependence on possibly hostile gold sources – USSR, South Africa – is therefore not a problem either. Indeed, instead of a stable price level with production, money supply and gold stocks rising 3–4 per cent per year, production could rise and prices fall 3–4 per cent, with money supply and gold stocks flat.

A key contention of gold buggers is that the gold standard worked, providing price stability for 200 years, or for many millennia in the more enthusiastic view.

> Gold has been instinctively and wisely chosen as a monetary standard by free people from all walks of life over hundreds of years – because the average rate of increase of new gold production (1–2 per cent) tends to parallel the rate of population and economic growth over long periods of time (about 2 per cent) thus preserving the purchasing power of the monetary standard – gold. (Lehrman, 1981, p. 25)

Let us examine these arguments.

It is true that the monetary authorities have limited control over the supply of money. Since formally adopting money growth targets in October 1979 as its stated policy objective, the Fed has found the growth of measured forms of money gyrating violently from quarter to quarter, paralleling (or leading to, as the monetarists would have it) the irregular growth and decline in the economy. Given modern financial institutions and the evolution of money as essentially a matter of record-keeping, what little control the Fed *does* exercize over measured money becomes irrelevant as funds are generated from non-measured and uncontrolled money. Commercial paper, money market funds and other forms of 'non-money' grew rapidly in the 1970s, reducing the influence of the central bank over the supply of money.

What *can* the Fed do, then? It can tend to keep interest rates high. While the Fed renounced control over interest rates in favor of controlling money supply as its monetary policy instrument in October 1979, the fact remains that its main method of achieving a target money growth involves pegging interest rates. Open market operations and reserve requirement changes affect the demand for money by shifting interest rates, since the system can always generate some uncontrolled form of money if the price is right. Relatively high interest rates damp real economic growth, thus slowing the growth of the money supply and of inflation as well. But this method of controlling inflation is costly in terms of forgone production, business failures and the human misery implicit in high unemployment. The Fed recognized this by returning, after mid-1982, to an emphasis on interest rates as a monetary policy instrument.

Secondly, *should* the Fed attempt to control the supply of money? It seems more important that government economic planning and programs should focus on employment, production and pricing, and let money take care of itself. This view reflects a Keynesian and post-Keynesian belief that the money supply is to a significant extent endogenous, and adapts to the needs of the trade. The Fed, then, should guarantee the integrity of the banking system. This is not as straightforward as it sounds. The changing structure of the US financial system places a growing share of bank-like organizations outside the banking regulatory framework (Sears, Merrill Lynch, American Express). Moreover, 'the changes in the financial structure have increased the proportion of speculative and Ponzi finance in the total financial structure, and therefore increased the vulnerability of the financial system to refinancing and debt-validating crises' (Minsky, 1980, p. 26). Thus the Fed has its work cut out for it – to prevent panics and bank failures and to ensure that newly emerging financial institutions operate in ways that safeguard depositors' funds.

Thirdly, did the gold standard work well? Economic history suggests that a rigid gold standard imposed periods of contagious deflation and recession among nations, causing suspension of fixed gold-backed exchange rates at numerous times and places. But Lehrman says that 'the gold standard, throughout history, has failed only because of world war, excessive protectionism, or self-centered currency manipulation' (Lehrman, 1981, p. 18).

In a way, this brings us back to the beginning. Governments do not interfere in markets out of some perverse desire to meddle, but to protect their societies and allow peaceful growth. Consider this tautological theorem of economic policy: if a program is politically untenable, it cannot be held to. No matter what the supposed long-run benefits, no constituency will, in its instinctive political and economic wisdom that Wanniski and Lehrman so go on about, accept for long programs that mean certain short-term misery. Governments will therefore be constrained in their ability to impose such programs. Why do the gold pushers think that countries repeatedly, though temporarily, suspended the gold standard? The human costs were just too high. And it is not merely a failure of steadfastness on the part of leaders, for leaders get voted out or overthrown if economies decline too severely.

So I believe the supply-siders are wrong on all counts. They are wrong on Say's Law, as 10 million unemployed Americans can attest. They are wrong on individual incentives, for people are complex creatures of habit, and the economic 'rationality' assumed by standard economics is a stilted view. They are wrong on business incentives, for managers look not at tax advantages but at sales prospects. They are wrong on government activity, for it provides not dead weight but needed public services and necessary social cohesion. They are wrong on the poor, who need not a crackdown on laziness and fertility but infusions – in supply-side terms – of human capital, in the form of goods, services and kindness. And they are wrong on gold, for, with apologies to William Jennings Bryan, the rigidity of the gold standard sacrifices too much well-being on the altar of price stability.

REFERENCES

Amin, S. (1977) *Unequal Development*, New York: Monthly Review Press.
Business Week, (1980) 'A guide to understanding the supply siders', December.
Gardner, Martin (1981) 'The Laffer curve and other laughs in current economics', *Scientific American* (December).
Gilder, George (1981) *Wealth and Poverty*, New York: Basic Books.
Harris, Don (1980) 'A postmortem on the neoclassical production function', in E. J. Nell, *Growth, Profits and Property*, Cambridge: Cambridge University Press.
Keynes, J. M. (1936) *The General Theory of Employment, Interest and Money*, New York: Harcourt Brace.
Laffer, Arthur (1981a) 'Supply side economics', *Financial Analysts Journal* (September–October).
Laffer, Arthur (1981b) *International Economics in an Integrated World*, Glenville, Ill.: Scott, Foresman & Co.
Lehrman, Lewis (1980) 'Monetary policy, the Federal Reserve System, and gold', New York: Morgan Stanley Investment Research.
Lehrman, Lewis (1981) 'The case for the gold standard', New York: Morgan Stanley Investment Research.
Minsky, Hyman (1980) 'Finance and profits: the changing nature of American business cycles', US Congress, Joint Economic Committee, *The Business Cycle and Public Policy, 1929–1980*, Washington, DC: US Government Printing Office, November.
Nell, Edward (1978) 'The simple theory of effective demand', *Intermountain Economic Review*, No. 9 (Fall).
Polanyi, Karl (1968) *The Great Transformation*, Boston: Beacon Press.
Thurow, Lester (1980) *The Zero-Sum Society*, New York: Basic Books.
Wanniski, Jude (1978) *The Way the World Works*, New York: Basic Books.

3 Monetarism: Conservative Policy and Monetary Theory

This chapter is actually one continuous argument, although the four sections can be read separately. The first develops the point that the critique of interventionist policy, especially the natural rate hypothesis, depends on the relation between changes in the money supply and the resulting effects on the real variables of the economy. This doctrine in turn rests on the 'crowding out' critique of fiscal policy, which is the subject of the next section, where it is shown that the conservative case is based on an incoherent concept of wealth and 'wealth effects'. Then, in the third section, the relationship between real and monetary phenomena in neoclassical theory is explored, and it is shown, first, that the 'real balance effect' overcomes the problem of the 'invalid dichotomy – it provides a coherent connecting mechanism – but, second, that it introduces a host of new problems, which are explored in connection with an examination of the basic model of mainstream macroeconomics. Finally, the last section examines Friedman's work, which rests largely on the mainstream model but without the real balance effect. His work therefore contains the invalid dichotomy and a number of other problems as well. The conclusion is that neither monetarists nor mainstream economists have a valid theory of the relationship between the monetary and the real aspects of the economy.

I THE CONSERVATIVE CRITIQUE OF INTERVENTIONIST POLICY

At first sight the conservative position on the role of government in the economy is paradoxical. On the one hand, the government cannot affect the real equilibrium levels of output and employment, so it cannot achieve its policy goals; on the other hand, by intervening in activist fashion, it can and does cause real and measurable damage. Why, if the government apparently *can* affect real variables, can it do so only in a deleterious manner?

This sounds a complicated mistake, based on ideology, but it actually follows quite simply from the basic assumptions of orthodox economics. These hold that all prices and quantities of goods and services are determined in markets by interacting supply and demand curves. Supply curves are derived from the production possibilities provided by technology, plus the availability of natural resources. Demand curves follow from individual or household preferences, together with ownership of natural resources. If markets are competitive, these prices and quantities will be the most *efficient* ones, and will satisfy peoples' preferences to the greatest extent possible – they will be optimal, in a technically exact sense. So, to cut a long story short, if the free market, unaided, determines an optimal position, interference by the government can *only* make things worse.

The conservative argument is usually expressed in five propositions (bearing in mind that any such summing-up must necessarily oversimplify):

1   Since the total amount of lending is determined by supply and demand, fiscal policy financed by borrowing simply results in 'crowding-out', transferring some lending from the private to the public sector. So there are no aggregate effects in the long run, and only minimal ones in the short run. Fiscal policy financed by money creation, on the other hand, has the effects of money creation.
2   Money creation is the result of deliberate government action. The money supply is not market determined, but is exclusively determined by actions of the central banking authorities, who do not respond to economic incentives, but who do respond to economic conditions and political pressures.
3   In the long run, changes in the quantity of money have no effects on real output and employment, which are wholly and exclusively determined by the market forces of supply and demand; monetary changes affect only nominal variables – prices and money wages.
4   In the short run, however, chiefly as a result of misperceptions by various categories of economic agents, changes in the stock of money *can* affect real output and employment. Such effects, however, will prove temporary and will evaporate once the agents' misperceptions have been corrected.
5   Partly because they are based on misperceptions, and partly because of the inevitable accompanying inflation, these temporary effects of monetary policies turn out to involve costly and often cumulative mistakes. (New policy shifts are required to correct the results of earlier policies, or the effects of the old policies wear off; these, in turn, induce new mistakes, which when eventually realized, bring reversion, requiring further policy shifts.)

Different writers develop different emphases, but the most commonly cited arguments in support of the above are the following, and they illustrate how the conservative position rests on the most literal-minded interpretation of basic textbook price theory:

1 Deficit spending, financed by government borrowing, amounts to an increase in private sector wealth, which raises the private sector demand for money. This, in turn, raises interest rates, choking off private borrowing. This effect, in turn, is held to be strong enough to offset the initial stimulus provided by the government spending. So these two cancel.

2 Government's net effect on the economy, if any, must come through the monetary system, which is controlled by the central bank, since that institution determines the 'monetary base' – high-powered money – and the relation between the monetary base and other components of the money supply is supposedly highly regular. (In fact, it is not.)

3 Money is not produced in the way food, clothing and shelter are. But changes in the money supply have only temporary effects on employment and output. Once again this is because equilibrium in the labor market results from the interaction of supply and demand schedules, which relate *real wages* and employment.

4 The real wage rate is the ratio of the money wage to the general price level. Thus if an increase in the money stock pushes up prices, this will lead firms to offer more employment, since if the money wage is unchanged, the real wage will be lower. Workers, not yet having taken in that all prices are up, will offer to supply more work, and real output and employment will rise – temporarily.

5 Once the workers catch on, they will withdraw the extra labor, and output will fall back to the original level, as determined by supply and demand. But prices and money wages will both be permanently higher. The temporary position of the economy was one of disequilibrium, which involved a misallocation of resources, and so represented waste or inefficiency. Attempts to bring unemployment down below the 'natural rate' thus cause both inflation and inefficiency.

So fiscal policy has no effects (deficits crowd out private spending), the money supply is controlled by the central bank, relative prices and quantities in every market are set by supply and demand, operating in competitive markets, and the labor market in particular is governed by demand curves based on marginal productivity interacting with supply curves based on marginal disutility.[1] Unemployment is thus either a matter of 'searching for a (better) job', or of 'preference for leisure'. That is, given an equilibrium real wage, people would rather look for a better job, or stay at home than work. In general, the lower the real wage, the higher will be unemployment for these reasons. But, for conservatives, there is no such thing as '*involuntary unemployment*'.

Over the years these propositions have been subjected to intensive criticism of basically two kinds, which might be called practical and theoretical. Practical criticism accepts the proposition as fundamentally reasonable at the level of pure theory, but mildly or substantially inaccurate in practice. Very broadly, it is difficult to control the money supply for many reasons. Conditions are not competitive and, even when they are, markets often respond sluggishly; the labor market, in particular, is highly imperfect. Moreover, technology does not exhibit smoothly diminishing marginal products, nor do workers have either preferences or information of the kind postulated. The monetarist argument in short is a theoretical curiosum; interesting, perhaps, but quite inapplicable to the world, and outrageous as a practical basis for policy.

Monetarists will readily agree that their assumptions are 'unrealistic'. Market conditions are not always competitive; both business and households frequently respond to non-economic incentives, often at the expense of their economic interests; human errors and delays can cause failures of markets to adjust. In short, at any given time the monetarist case can be faulted for being out of touch with the facts. But, the monetarists reply, *over time* they are right. Over time, both businesses and households will keep their economic interests foremost – and those that do not will lose out to those that do. So in the long run, prompted by scarce dollars and common sense, markets will work, and the monetarists' conclusions will be verified, even though, at any given moment, their assumptions may seem unrealistic or even false.

The theoretical criticism asserts not merely that the propositions are inaccurate in practice, but that *they are wrong as a matter of pure theory*.

Starting from the orthodox framework, contemporary economists have arrived at three different and, for the most part, mutually inconsistent theories of how monetary changes affect the real economy; we shall dub these the Keynesian, the monetarist and the neoclassical mainstream. Of course, each has a number of variants, and there are strong disagreements between economists whom we would place in the same camp. Nevertheless each settles on a characteristic and defining account of what can be called the 'transmission mechanism' connecting real and monetary phenomena. Taking them in reverse order:

● *Mainstream* Changes in the stock of money do not affect the long-run equilibrium values of real output and employment, or the real rate of interest or relative prices. Only nominal magnitudes are affected. But changes in the stock of money *will* affect the disequilibrium adjustment paths of real variables, and therefore will affect the short-run position of the economy. In general these effects can be stabilizing, if policies are chosen wisely.

● *Monetarist* Changes in the money stock will not affect the long-run equilibrium values of real variables; only nominal magnitudes are affected. But short-run real variables are affected, because of misperceptions and money illusions. In general, these effects will be destabilizing.

● *Keynesian* Changes in the money stock can affect the long-run equilibrium values of real variables, but need not, and likewise may or may not, affect the economy's short-run position. If there are such effects, they can be made stabilizing by correct choice of policy.

Let us look, in simplified terms, at the rationale for each of these in turn, taking the mainstream position first. Households and businesses are supposed to demand 'real cash balances' (that is, sums of money in real terms) for various reasons, mainly because they provide convenience in making regular or unexpected payments in the course of normal business. The demand for real balances depends largely on the level of real activity (GNP) and perhaps on the rate of interest (the higher the rate of interest, the more the earnings forgone by holding non-interest-bearing cash). The demand for *nominal* balances, on the other hand, will clearly rise with the price level: a higher price level means more money will have to be held to make the regular and probable unexpected payments for the same real output. If the money supply is increased, so that households and businesses find themselves with larger *real* balances than they need (e.g. the Federal Reserve Bank buys bonds so businesses and households have more cash and fewer bonds), they will spend, thus bidding up the money prices of goods and services. Cash balances will fall and prices will rise until the desired level of *real* balances is restored. Relative prices, however, will remain unchanged (provided the process of introducing the increased money supply into circulation has not changed the relative wealth positions – the 'endowments' – of the various individuals and firms in the system). Hence, when the process has worked itself out, money prices will all be higher, relative prices will be unchanged, and real balances will be the same. But during the adjustment period the real values the variables successively take will all depend on the quantity of money (among other things, of course).

The pattern of movement will – it is usually assumed – be towards restoring equilibrium at a higher general price level.

The monetarist argument proceeds by involving a broad conception of the quantity theory understood as an account of the demand for money. The money supply is determined by the central bank. Demand for money depends on income and interest rates, as in Keynesian and mainstream theory, but, perhaps most significantly, it depends on a broadly defined idea of wealth. A rise in the money supply, by increasing wealth, leads both to substitution among assets and to a shift between holding assets and current spending. (Such wealth effects are central to the case against fiscal policy.) An increase in current spending chiefly affects prices rather than output, for reasons largely unexplained as we shall see. As prices increase following an increase in the money supply, workers and/or firms are fooled into thinking that the *real wage* has changed, so that employment in the labor market will be increased. As already suggested, employers may think the real wage has fallen because prices are up, while workers think it has risen because money wages are up. There will thus be a temporary – and inefficient – increase in employment and output. Once workers and firms realize their mistake, employment will fall back to the equilibrium level, but with nominal wages and prices permanently higher.

Keynesians take a different tack altogether. An increase in the supply of money (e.g. the Fed buying bonds from the public) will mainly show itself in bidding up the price of bonds, thus lowering interest. This will stimulate investment, assuming it is responsive to interest rate changes, which will raise employment and output through the multiplier. Effects on prices will come only as employment and output approach their full capacity levels, so that shortages and bottlenecks appear. These effects may be either cost-push or demand-pull, or both. Below near-capacity levels prices are not responsive to changes in demand, being largely cost determined. Keynesians and post-Keynesians, however, do not consider real balance effects important, first because neither prices nor money wages respond readily to demand changes, but secondly – and more important – because inflation of prices and money wages has a much more significant impact: it changes the *burden of debt*. When all money prices (including wage rates) go up, creditors are paid back money of less purchasing power than they loaned. Inflation benefits borrowers and harms lenders, while deflation has the opposite effect. Real balance effects, if they exist at all, are minor compared to changes in the burden of debt. Thus for Keynesians and post-Keynesians, the equilibrium levels of output and employment may be affected by changes in the quantity of money. (However, in contrast to the others, Keynesians would not refer here to the 'long-run', for that phrase normally designates the *growth path* of the economy. 'Long-run equilibrium' refers to a balance between the growth of demand and of capacity, an extension of the usual macroeconomic problematic.)

Yet many Keynesians want to stay in the fold. Keynes himself, after all, held that, at full employment, the traditional economic theory 'came into its own again'. It was a *special* case because its results were true only at the point of full employment; but, as an analysis of the optimal allocation of fully employed resources, he saw no reason to object to it. Moreover, he accepted the marginal productivity curve as giving the short-period demand schedule for labor[2]. Nor could he have done otherwise, even though in the *Treatise* (1930) he had already outlined an alternative theory. For the neoclassical theory of distribution – factor pricing – is simply the reflection of the theory of marginal costs. Accepting price theory implies acceptance of the correlative theory of distribution. Moreover, since neoclassical price theory relates *relative* prices to *absolute* quantities, it leaves the absolute price level undetermined. The basic market processes and the fundamental data on which they are based – tastes, technology and initial endowments – do not determine the money price level. Money seems to be exogenous to the market system – its supply determined by the monetary authorities, its demand by the convenience arising from its use, perhaps including its use for speculative purposes. In short, Keynes' claim that neoclassical theory 'comes into its own again' at full employment entails the Keynesian acceptance of the basic framework as theoretically valid, as the proper foundation for any economic analysis.

This, of course, creates an obvious and well-known problem for, on the face of it, neoclassical price theory seems inconsistent with the multiplier. If quantities of goods and employment are determined by supply and demand, how can the multiplier work? Keynesians are thus reduced to claiming that the basic framework is correct theoretically, but unsound empirically, at least for the short run. Prices and money wages, for various 'practical' reasons, are inflexible downwards. This is simply an unexplained matter of fact, the result of 'friction' or something like it. However *ad hoc* the point may be, Keynesians contend that it is true, and, as a consequence, that changes in money will affect interest rates and that the resulting changes in spending will affect quantities, rather than prices, with the result that employment can change even without changes in the real wage. Moreover, if prices and money wages are inflexible downwards, unemployment will not cause them to fall. This is crucial since, if they did fall, real balances would rise and, according to mainstream thinking, this would stimulate spending, pushing the system back towards full employment. Thus, with flexible money wages and prices, the system would 'automatically' tend to full employment – in theory. But with 'sticky' wages and prices there will be no real balance effects to bring about full employment automatically. *The assumed 'stickiness' of wages and prices thus arises from the need to reconcile the Keynesian acceptance of the basic framework (which is used to define full employment and to analyze the labor market) with the multiplier transmission mechanism, the centerpiece of Keynesian theory.*

Making such an assumption, however, has left Keynesian theory open to counter-attack from the Right. Without the stickiness of wages and prices, markets would work as theory says: full employment would be automatically ensured, monetary policy would leave real variables unaffected, and there would be neither call nor room for Keynesian policies of demand management. A great deal thus hangs on a proposition for which there is no theoretical grounding at all.

The mainstream has therefore abandoned wage-price stickiness and accepted the real balance effect – and wealth effects generally – as a major connecting link between the real and monetary sides of the economy. This also involves conceding the tendency of the economy to move automatically towards full employment, the very point Keynes attacked. But the mainstream argues that in actual practice this tendency is weak and unreliable. Policy can achieve the same end more quickly and reliably, with much lower social cost. To this monetarists reply that fiscal policy is inherently ineffective because of the very wealth effects on which the mainstream relies, while monetary policy, which is effective, acts with an unpredictable lag and so may prove destabilizing.

To see the debate between conservatives and mainstream economists more clearly, let us look closely at one of the chief conservative claims: that the effects of a government deficit may be offset by the impact on interest rates due to the borrowing required to finance it. This will illustrate the important role of wealth effects, and will also give us a chance to examine what is meant by 'wealth'.

II   WEALTH EFFECTS AND THE GOVERNMENT BUDGET CONSTRAINT

In recent years it has been widely argued that a stimulative fiscal policy is inherently ineffective unless accompanied by an expansion of the money supply. The reason is that the government deficit must be financed by borrowing, that is, by open market sales of new government bonds to the private sector, thus raising the private sector's wealth. Since the demand for money is widely held to be an increasing function of wealth, this will raise demand with a fixed money supply, and so will bid up interest rates for all levels of income, counteracting the stimulus to spending provided by the deficit. The new equilibrium is likely to be at about the same level of income, but with a higher level of interest rates.

A Standard Approach

Figure 3.1, adapted from Blinder and Solow (1973), illustrates the argument. Let S=saving, I=investment, M=stock of money, L=demand for money, and E=equilibrium. Y will be aggregate income, and i the indicator of the complex of interest rates. Starting

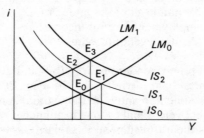

Figure 3.1

from less than full employment income, deficit spending shifts the IS curve from IS_0 to IS_1. This requires financing by a new bond issue, which shifts the LM curve up from LM_0 to LM_1, which would lead to a small *decline* in income. But the new bonds, representing new *wealth*, cause a further shift of the IS curve to IS_2, with the resulting equilibrium, E_3, slightly above the original level of income. (These shifts will be the subject of the following analysis.) Perhaps not everyone would agree that a new issue of government bonds to the private sector (new borrowing from it) represents 'new wealth' of such a sort as to stimulate additional spending in the current short period. But there is general acceptance of the view that deficit spending financed by bonds entails a parallel outward shift of the IS curve, partly or wholly offset by a parallel upward and inward shift of the LM curve. By contrast, when the deficit is financed by money creation, the LM curve shifts out, and continues to shift so long as the deficit lasts.

One conclusion frequently drawn is that fiscal policy is not independent of monetary policy; another is that fiscal policy, on its own, is ineffectual. It is monetary policy that rules the roost. I shall argue that these conclusions are wholly unjustified because the original argument and most of the subsequent discussion have misunderstood the relationship between the public and private sectors implied in the 'goods market equilibrium' of the simple Keynesian model, and have drawn uncritically on an incoherent concept of wealth.

A Simple Model

Consider a simple Keynesian *IS–LM* model in linear form (a model we will criticize later):

$$S = a+bY+ci \qquad a<0,\; b,c>0$$
$$I = d+eY+fi \qquad d,e>0 \quad f<0$$
$$L = \alpha+\beta Y+\gamma i \qquad \alpha,\beta>0 \quad \gamma<0$$

i_T = minimum, or 'liquidity trap', level of the interest rate
i_e = equilibrium level of the interest rate
Y_F = full employment level of income
Y_e = equilibrium level of income.

Here, the equilibrium conditions are: $I=S$ and $L=M$, where M is fixed by the central bank. Briefly, a is dissaving at zero income; d is autonomous investment; b and e are the marginal propensities to save and invest, respectively; c and f show the influence of interest rates on saving and investment (presumably c is relatively weak, while f, bearing on the marginal efficiency of capital, is significant); α is autonomous demand for money; β is transactions demand for money; and γ is the speculative demand for money.

Solving,

$$i_{IS} = \frac{d-a}{c-f} + \left(\frac{e-b}{c-f}\right)Y \qquad \text{goods market flow equilibrium}$$

$$i_{LM} = \frac{M-\alpha}{\gamma} - \frac{\beta}{\gamma}Y \qquad \text{equilibrium in holding the money stock}$$

$$Y_e = \frac{(c-f)(M-\alpha)-\gamma(d-a)}{\gamma(e-b)+\beta(c-f)} \leqslant Y_F$$

$$i_e = \frac{(b-e)(M-\alpha)-\beta(d-a)}{\beta(f-c)+\gamma(b-e)} \geqslant i_T$$

Provided $b>e$, and given the usual assumptions, the model can be drawn as in Figure 3.2. Now let us introduce the government. To the investment equation we add G, the government's spending, and to the savings or withdrawals equation we add taxes, in the form tY, where t is the fixed rate of income tax. This yields a new 'injection–withdrawal' (*JW*) equation,

$$i_{JW} = \frac{G+d-a}{c-f} + \left(\frac{e-b-t}{c-f}\right) Y,$$

or, rearranging,

$$i_{JW} = \frac{G-tY}{c-f} + \frac{d-a}{c-f} + \left(\frac{e-b}{c-f}\right) Y.$$

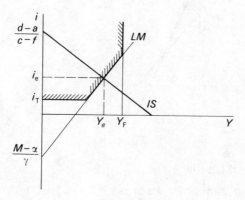

Figure 3.2

(These equations could be written so that saving or both saving and investment depend on disposable income, $Y-tY$, rather than on income. In the first case, then,

$$i_{JW} = \frac{G+d-a}{c-f} + \left[\frac{e-(b)(1-t)-t}{c-f}\right] Y$$

and, in the second,

$$i_{JW} = \frac{G+d-a}{c-f} + \left[\frac{(e-b)(1-t)-t}{c-f}\right] Y.$$

The intercept remains the same, but the slope is steeper than when saving and investment depend on income.) Call this the JW locus. Clearly when $G=tY$, $i_{JW}=i_{IS}$, $Y_{JW}=Y_{IS}$. When $G>tY$, $i_{JW}>i_{IS}$, and when $G<tY$, $i_{JW}<i_{IS}$. The two lines can be graphed. They will cross when $Y=G/t$; for lower levels of Y, the government budget will be in deficit, and for higher it will be in surplus. The further Y from G/t the

larger the deficit – or surplus. Adding the government raises the intercept and steepens the slope. When government is in deficit, of course, the private sector will have an equivalent surplus; while a government surplus implies a private sector shortage of savings.

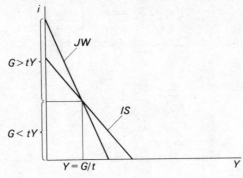

Figure 3.3

Borrowing and Lending

The argument from which we began is that a government deficit must be financed either by money creation or by borrowing, i.e. issuing new government bonds. Let us ignore money creation. Hence, writing ΔB for new bonds, with subscripts 'g' and 'p' to denote 'government' or 'private', and using a subscript 'F' to indicate 'finance required' for G and I, respectively, we can write that government spending is financed by taxes and borrowing from (lending to) the private sector:

$$G_F = tY + \Delta B_g$$

(If $\Delta B < 0$, the government is lending its surplus.) If the government borrows, the private sector must lend. Hence we have the corresponding condition, which states that finance for private investment equals private saving plus borrowing from (lending to) the government:

$$I_F = a + bY + ci + \Delta B_p.$$

Whatever is borrowed must be loaned:

$$\Delta B_g = - \Delta Bp$$

hence, adding and assuming that the 'required finance' is actually spent:

$$G + I = tY + a + bY + ci = T + S,$$

where T is total taxes. This is the condition that defines the JW locus; derived here from the assumption that withdrawals will be loaned to finance injections.[3] So we see that the government's deficit or surplus is financed *at every point by the equivalent private sector surplus or deficit*. The multiplier re-spending process generates the required *flow* of funds; there is no need to disturb the *stock* equilibrium represented by the LM locus. Changes in Y of course, mean the system will move along the LM to maintain monetary equilibrium.

Wealth Effects and the LM Locus

Surely the issuing of new government bonds to the private sector counts as raising wealth and hence the demand for money, thus shifting the LM locus in and upwards? Let us accept this for a moment and explore the implications of this doctrine. First consider an LM line cutting JW at the point at which JW intersects IS (see Figure 3.4).

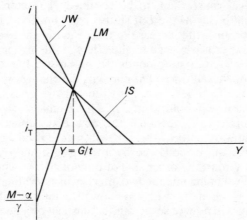

Figure 3.4

(This is purely arbitrary; however it makes it easy to consider both deficits and surpluses on the government's account.) At this point $Y = G/t$ – the government budget is in balance and private savings exactly cover investment. There is no outstanding government debt. Suppose some exogenous and temporary disturbance in the supply of money causes LM to shift in and up; a deficit will emerge. This deficit will have to be funded and, accordingly, private sector wealth will be permanently increased by the new bonds issued to cover the government deficit. Hence the initial temporary disturbance of the LM locus will be compounded by a further shift in the same direction. But this shift in turn will further increase the deficit, leading to still further open market operations, and so on. The economy will contract without limit.

Suppose, now, that the exogenous disturbance causes LM to shift out and down; a surplus will emerge. Instead of borrowing, the government now will be lending in the open market. By symmetry, such lending – buying bonds from the private sector – must *reduce* private sector wealth, and so will also reduce the private sector's demand for money. Hence the LM curve must shift down and out. But each such shift of the LM locus will further increase the surplus, leading to yet another shift, so the economy will expand to full employment, or until i has fallen to i_T, whichever is reached first. Hence there is only one possible equilibrium point, namely, $Y = G/t$, and any slight deviation from this level of income will set up forces driving the economy either to zero employment or to full employment.

If there is initially an outstanding government debt (a quantity of bonds, B), then a change in the level of the interest rate as the LM locus shifts will cause them to be revalued. To determine the *net* change in wealth (say as the LM shifts in and up from an initial zero deficit equilibrium), the increase in the deficit leading to an issue of bonds will have to be reduced by the effect of the higher interest rate on the value of the existing bonds. If the outstanding debt is small enough and/or the JW locus flat enough, the change in the value of existing bonds will be less than the issue of new bonds, and the previous conclusions will hold. But if B is large and JW steep, then the revaluation effect will outweigh the new issue effect, so that an inward and upward shift of the LM will *reduce* total wealth. Hence the initial shift will be followed by a downward and outward shift, taking the system to the other side of the point from which it began. At this new level of income the two effects will assert themselves once again, but working in opposite ways now. The interest rate has fallen, so revaluation will now raise wealth, but instead of a deficit there is a surplus, so bonds will be retired, reducing wealth. Since the revaluation effect outweighs the issuing effect, the net result will be a new inward and upward shift of the LM locus. Clearly this process can either converge back towards or progressively diverge from the initial equilibrium, depending on how strongly the revaluation effect outweighs the issuing effect.

Further Wealth Effects

Now let us return to the case considered at the outset, where there is no outstanding government debt, and the government budget balances, but where wealth effects shift the IS and JW loci, as well as the LM. Rewrite the equations, adding a wealth term, ω:

$$S = a + bY + ci + x\omega \qquad x < 0$$
$$I = d + eY + fi + y\omega \qquad y > 0$$
$$L = \alpha + \beta Y + \gamma i + z\omega \qquad z > 0.$$

Then, solving, introducing G and t as before:

$$i_{IS} = \frac{d-a}{c-f} + \left(\frac{y-x}{c-f}\right)\omega + \left(\frac{e-b}{c-f}\right)Y$$

$$i_{JW} = \frac{G+d-a+(y-x)\,\omega}{c-f} + \left(\frac{e-b-t}{c-f}\right)Y =$$

$$\frac{G-tY}{c-f} + \frac{d-a}{c-f} + \left(\frac{y-x}{c-f}\right)\omega + \left(\frac{e-b}{c-f}\right)Y$$

$$i_{LM} = \frac{M-\alpha}{\gamma} - \frac{z}{\gamma}\omega - \frac{\beta}{\gamma}Y.$$

Here $(y-x)/(c-f) > 0$, and $-z/\gamma > 0$, so the *IS*, the *JW* and the *LM* loci all shift upwards with an increase in wealth.

Wealth is defined in the literature as money plus bonds plus real capital, a definition with serious problems, as we shall see shortly. Accepting it for the moment, however, we take both the money stock and the stock of capital as fixed. Hence

$$dW = dB = G - T = t(Y_B - Y_E).$$

The change in wealth is equal to the budget deficit, which in turn equals t times the difference between the balanced budget level of income, Y_B, and the equilibrium level, Y_E (where *LM* cuts *JW*).

Now compare the *IS* and the *JW* equations: $i_{IS} = i_{JW}$ if and only if $G = tY$, i.e. iff $Y = G/t$, regardless of the level of wealth! Hence if wealth increases it will shift both the *IS* and the *JW* loci by the same vertical amount (leaving Y unchanged), since both contain the identical wealth term, which raises the balanced budget rate of interest by that same vertical distance – equal to $(y-x/c-f)\,\omega$ (see Figure 3.5).

Start from a balanced budget equilibrium, as illustrated in Figure 3.6. The *LM* locus cuts the *JW* locus where it intersects *IS*; hence $Y = G/t$ and the interest rate is the balanced budget rate. Suppose now some initial disturbance in the money supply shifts *LM* upwards. A budget deficit will emerge and wealth will rise as bonds are issued to finance the deficit. So both the *LM* and the *IS* and *JW* loci will shift upwards. If the vertical shifts are exactly equal (i.e. if $-z/\gamma = (y-x)/(c-f)$), then after the initial disturbance is corrected a balanced budget equilibrium will be established at the same level of income but

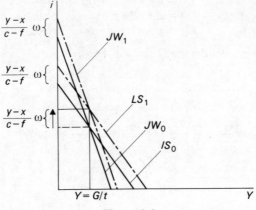

Figure 3.5

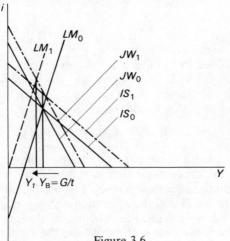

Figure 3.6

with a higher interest rate, reflecting the influence of the higher level of wealth. But if the *LM* locus shifts upward *more* than the *JW* and *IS* do, (i.e. if $- z/\gamma > (y-x)/(c-f)$), then the new equilibrium will be established at a level of income, Y_1, *below* $Y_B = G/t$; thus a new deficit will emerge, which will persist even after the initial disturbance has been corrected. This new deficit requires a new issue of bonds, hence further increases wealth. This brings another set of shifts, in which again *LM* will shift upward more than *IS* and *JW*; the new intersection will be at a level of income $Y_2 < Y_1 < Y_B = G/t$. The deficit will again be increased, and the process will repeat itself until income has fallen to zero.

An exactly similar story can be told starting from an initial expansion of the money supply, shifting *LM* down. In this case a surplus will emerge if the *LM* shift is greater than that of *JW*. Each time, therefore, wealth will be reduced, but, since the reduction shifts *LM* further, income will progressively expand and the interest rate fall until either the full employment level of income or the liquidity trap level of interest is reached.

Next suppose there is some disruption that causes actual income, Y, to fall below the initial balanced budget equilibrium (i.e. from Y_B to Y_0), thus creating a deficit, but that the wealth effects are such that the subsequent upward shift of the *LM* locus is *less* than that of *JW* and *IS*, i.e. $- z/\gamma < (y-x)/(c-f)$. The new equilibrium will now be to the right of the new intersection of the *JW* and *IS* loci, that is, the new level of income $Y_1 > Y_B = G/t > Y_0$. The government will thus be running a *surplus*, and so will retire bonds, which will reduce wealth. Both the *LM* and the *IS* and *JW* loci will now shift down, but the shift of the *JW* and *IS* will be relatively larger. There are now three cases, depending on whether the surplus equals, is less than or is greater than the initial deficit, $t(Y_B - Y_0)$. If the surplus equals the initial deficit, $|t(Y_b - Y_1)| = |t(Y_B - Y_0)|$, then the downward shifts of both *JW* and *LM* will exactly reflect the initial upward shifts and the original balanced budget equilibrium will be restored in one stroke. If $|t(Y_B - Y_1)| < |t(Y_B - Y_0)|$, then the downward shifts of both will be less than required to restore the initial equilibrium, and at the new intersection there will still be a surplus, but it will be smaller. Hence there will be further shifting (possibly including overshooting) until equilibrium is reached. If $|t(Y_B - Y_1)| > |t(Y_B - Y_0)|$, then the downward shift will overshoot the balanced budget equilibrium, creating a deficit, but a smaller one than initially existed. Hence there will follow an upward shift of both loci, but smaller than previously, resulting in a smaller surplus, which, in turn, will produce downward shifts to an equilibrium that will yield a deficit, but a smaller one than before. The oscillations will continue back and forth, eventually converging upon the balanced budget equilibrium.[4]

Two points stand out. First, the borrowing or lending consequent upon a deficit or surplus takes time; thus the movement towards or away from balanced budget equilibrium will take place over a substantial stretch of time – certainly not within one 'short period'. This virtually eliminates the possibility of 'short-run equilibrium' or of determinate short-run adjustment processes, since wealth effects will be causing income–expenditure changes all the time. Second, the model is completely arbitrary. If wealth effects on consumption and investment are relatively weak or non-existent the model is radically unstable. If wealth effects on consumption and investment are strong relative to such effects on the demand for money, the model is stable, though it will not adjust within a short period. But there are no intuitive or institutional reasons by which to explain such a conclusion. It rests on nothing but mechanics.

The Basic Error

In fact, no such instability exists; it is a sign that something has gone wrong in the analysis. The error comes in thinking that government borrowing or lending necessarily affects the *stock* equilibrium in the holding of assets. What we actually have is a flow equilibrium between injections and withdrawals. The total finance required will have to cover investment plus the government deficit, if any; the total finance currently available will consist of savings plus the government surplus, if any. For any feasible level of income, in equilibrium, the total finance currently demanded will exactly equal that currently available. Hence moving from one point to another on the *JW* locus (*or*, 'considering the difference', to stay within the bounds of comparative statics) does *not* require a shift of the *LM* locus. The latter shows the levels of income and of interest rates necessary to ensure the holding of the entire money stock. Changes in the public/private mix of borrowing and lending do not affect the transactions, precautionary or speculative demands. But such changes do not affect the money supply either, for the government's borrowing draws down the banking system's deposits by just the amount that the surplus savings of the private sector had increased them.[5] Hence, on the one hand, the government deficit can be financed by borrowing the flow of new savings created by the expenditure multiplier, and, on the other, the monetary stock equilibrium locus is not affected, either on the demand or on the supply side.

The Concept of Wealth

But what about the claim that new issues of government bonds constitute an increase of private wealth, which in turn increases the demand for money as a consequence of portfolio readjustments? This is the heart of the matter, and is a point on which both monetarists and mainstream Keynesians agree. I shall argue, by contrast, that government issues of bonds do not, as such, constitute an increase in private wealth. They are one of several forms in which wealth can be held. But private financial wealth is accumulated from period to period as a function of savings, regardless of the form in which the savings are held, that is, whether as private securities or as government bonds.

Consider, the new bonds are bought with new savings. It is surely strange to count the *bonds* as the addition to wealth, rather than the savings, for the bonds are just the form in which the savings are held. In mainstream thinking, government bonds count as new wealth, for they are held to involve no liability to the private sector. (Yet the interest on them will have to be paid out of future taxes, unless the government engages in actual production. Such taxes would presumably reduce the value of private sector wealth in proportion to the size of the government debt. But we will ignore this point.) In any case government bonds are treated as a net asset for the private sector. Corporate bonds, however, are held to be a liability; business's dissaving in selling the bond must be set against the household saving which buys it. So there is no *net* private sector saving. But this forgets that business borrowed in the first place in order to invest, i.e. to acquire new capital goods. Business dissaving is offset, in turn, by its real asset accumulation. So we can count either the real investment by business or the act of saving by households as the net addition to wealth, in the case where the wealth is held in the form of corporate bonds.

But if private sector wealth is a function of total private savings, or of total bond purchases, private and public, then the effect of wealth on the demand for money will not be a function of the government deficit; it would be a function of the level of income and the case against fiscal policy must vanish.

This raises the question of what is meant by 'wealth' here. Keynesians and monetarists seem to agree that total wealth, W, can be written:

$$W = M + B + K$$

where M is the money stock, B is the outstanding stock of interest-bearing government bonds and K is the total capital stock. Private bonds and equities are not included because they are claims against K, so to include them would be to double count. In the short period, it is argued, it is customary to take K as fixed, but M and B can be varied.

This conception of wealth contains serious problems. Money is generalized purchasing power that stores value, but is itself neither productive nor useful. If K were to disappear or to diminish substantially, then M would exchange against fewer (or in the limit, no) goods; hence prices would rise, and the real value of M would fall more or less in proportion (assuming a given capital–output ratio and a given degree of utilization). If M were to disappear, however, this would not affect the value of K in terms of the output it can produce, although, by making transactions less convenient, it would raise the costs of circulation. Similarly, if K were to disappear or diminish, the bonds of the government would become worthless or problematical, since the tax base would be gone or eroded. But if B were to disappear or diminish, there would be no effect on K. Thus both M and B depend on K; their value reflects that of K, which, however, is independent of them. Adding the three together to get total wealth therefore cannot be valid.

There is also a problem in connection with the stock of capital. The justification for taking it as fixed in the short period is that it takes time to produce and install new plant and equipment – *capital goods*. But portfolio analysis is chiefly concerned with *capital funds*. The accumulation of capital goods requires investment to be completed, which takes time, whereas the accumulation of capital funds requires only saving to be performed, and this certainly takes place within the short period. Hence the growth of portfolio wealth should be identified with current savings, which will then be divided between money and bonds and other assets. This is clearly an issue for growth economics: just as capital funds are growing, so must the stock of money and bonds, since the demand for money will clearly be expanding, but the shift in this demand will not be a function of the government deficit.

Wealth and Money

Even if wealth did increase as a result of the sale of bonds to the private sector, it is not clear why this should raise the demand for money. Why should the private sector demand more money just because it has more government bonds? Is it for transactions reasons? Look at it another way: just before the private sector bought the bonds it had the savings on hand with which to buy them; why did portfolio managers not make the optimal division of these savings between money and bonds at the moment of purchase? (Why do they not also demand more money as a result of, or in connection with, their purchases of private bonds?) But why should this optimal division lead to higher cash balances? Surely if the ordinary transactions, precautionary and speculative motives are satisfied, there is no further reason to add to non-yielding balances.

Finally, if the money supply is itself partly endogenous, the LM locus will be relatively flat. Let the money supply function be

$$M = \bar{m} + mY + ni, \quad m, n > 0.$$

Here $\bar{m}$ is determined by the central bank, m is the coefficient showing the creation of money in response to aggregate demand (e.g. by shifting funds from time deposits or short-term securities to demand deposits, or by activating previously negotiated lines of credit), and n is the coefficient showing the creation of money in response to the level of interest rates (e.g. the introduction of new media of circulation). Then

$$i_{LM} = \frac{\bar{m} - \alpha}{\gamma - n} + \left(\frac{m - \beta}{\gamma - n} \right) Y,$$

which will have a positive slope if $\beta > m$, but will be flatter than the previous LM locus. Hence a given government deficit will have a larger effect. If a wealth term is now added to the demand for money, we could argue symmetrically that the endogenous supply of money could also respond to wealth – just as it does to income. As wealth increases, the banking system creates money to fund it. Thus, even if the wealth effects discussed above made sense, and even if they caused a rise in the demand for money, this could be partially or wholly offset by endogenous money creation.

Conclusions

The wealth effects that supposedly result from the government's financing of its deficit make the *IS–LM* equilibrium implausibly unstable. On closer inspection these 'wealth effects' turn out to be based on an arbitrary and invalid conception of wealth. Moreover, it is not clear that a rise in wealth would necessarily raise the demand for money, or that, if it did, such an increase could not be offset by an endogenous increase in the money supply. Every link in the anti-fiscalist chain of reasoning is suspect.

Appendix

The JW–IS–LM diagram can be used to examine other policy questions, dropping all reference to wealth effects. Consider a 'supply-side' tax cut, lowering t from t_0 to t_1, first with G constant. According to received supply-side doctrine, this should lead to an increase in savings, lowering interest rates, so raising investment, and expanding income, perhaps enough to generate sufficient new tax revenue to offset the cut in rates and balance the budget. Now, look at Figure 3.7. Start from a balanced budget equilibrium. The lower tax rate t_1 swings the *JW* locus out from JW_0 to JW_1. The new intersection with the unchanged *LM* locus therefore occurs at a higher level of income but also at a higher rate of interest. Since JW_1 intersects *IS* at a much lower i and higher Y (compared to JW_0's intersection with *IS*), the new equilibrium involves a substantial government deficit, with a corresponding excess of private saving over investment. Investment is higher, but savings have risen even more. So the supply-side analysis is wrong on three counts: the new interest rate is higher, the government is in deficit, and savings have increased more than investment.

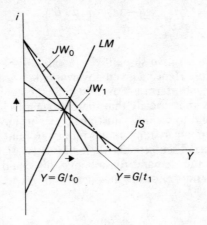

Figure 3.7

Next, if G were reduced in proportion to the tax cut, the JW locus would rotate around the initial (balanced budget) equilibrium point, staying within the angle made by JW_0 and IS, and there would be *no* effect on either interest or income.

III   THE REAL BALANCE EFFECT IN NEOCLASSICAL THEORY: MICRO AND MACRO

The monetarist arguments endorsing 'crowding out' have been shown to rely upon an incoherent conception of wealth, which is alleged to produce effects of an implausible kind, while the entire anaylsis mixes up stocks and flows in a most confusing way. But this is not an isolated case; it will become apparent that neoclassical theory has no generally agreed-upon theory of the relationship between monetary and real variables. In the modern literature, this issue appears in the guise of arguments over the nature of the 'transmission mechanism'. In a somewhat earlier, but still post-war, literature, it took the form of arguments over 'valid' and 'invalid dichotomies', between real and monetary aspects of the economy, to which we shall now turn. Our argument will be first that monetarists have never successfully addressed the question posed in that dispute, and hence have *no* account whatever of the causal connections between monetary changes and the real economy. Secondly, we shall contend that, for related reasons, both mainstream and Keynesian approaches are also inadequate.

The Dichotomy

The problem is both simple and deeply rooted. Neoclassical theory determines the equilibrium of supply and demand for commodities, in one, a few or all markets together, as a function of *relative prices*. So the general price level is indeterminate on the basis of supply and demand for goods. This seems to leave room for another market, one for money, in which supply and demand will then determine the general price level. The equation of exchange, $MV=PY$ (where M is the money stock, V is velocity of circulation, P the general or average price level, and Y real output), has often been interpreted as such a market balancing, or 'excess demand' equation. (Excess demand functions show demand minus supply at various prices, with the equilibrium price being the one at which excess demand is zero.) Given an exogenously fixed M, with Y determined by the supplies and demands for goods, which also determine V (since V simply reflects the simplification by money of a predetermined pattern of barter), the price level follows straightforwardly.

But there is a hitch – indeed, worse, a contradiction. The quantities – not the relative quantities, but the absolute amounts exchanged in equilibrium – are functions of relative prices, which means that if *all* prices were, say, doubled or halved the equilibrium quantities would be unaffected, since no *relative* prices would be changed. (Technically, this is expressed by saying that the excess demand functions are homogeneous of degree zero). But the equation of exchange will be thrown out of balance if, from an initial equilibrium, all prices are doubled or halved. The equation of exchange, in fact, is homogeneous of degree one. Yet, according to Walras' Law for multi-market equilibrium, if $n-1$ markets of an $n-$commodity system are in equilibrium, the nth market must also be.

This had better be explained: it follows from the fact that, in the aggregate, total demands must equal total supplies, since the demand for any good is always an equivalent supply of another and saving is supplying capital funds. To put it another way, in a neoclassical market system, every purchase by a given agent implies an equivalent sale by that same agent, since goods are purchased with goods (for these purposes, money is just another commodity that has to be purchased with, for example, labor services). Hence excess demand anywhere implies equivalent and offsetting excess supply somewhere; alternatively, in the aggregate excess demands/supplies always sum to zero.

Returning to the argument: if the equation of exchange is an excess demand function of the same character as the others, then, if all markets for goods are in equilibrium, so must the money market. But we have just seen that this is not so; if all prices were doubled, equilibrium in the goods markets would be preserved (since no *relative* prices would be changed), but the money market would be upset. Is the equation of exchange different, then? Or perhaps Walras' Law does not hold for monetary economies? Or perhaps the supply and demand equations for goods are mis-specified?

The first two possibilities have to be dismissed if the analysis is to stay within the traditional framework. When the equation of exchange is written in the Cambridge form, $M=kPY$ (where $k=1/V$ is the proportion of the real volume of planned transactions to be held as cash balances), it can be seen to be a supply and demand equation. It should therefore enter the system on the same footing as any other. Hence Walras' Law should continue to hold when the money market is taken into consideration, just as it would if any other market were added to the system. The difficulty comes about because the general price level is really a weighted average of individual money prices, and money prices have no influence on supply and demand.

Consider an imaginary experiment, in which there is a doubling of the price level – regardless of how it comes about. If there were equilibrium in holdings of real balances before such a change, there cannot be afterwards. It might be argued that such a change could not come about except by a doubling of the money stock or of the velocity or some combination of the two, and that therefore the whole question is moot. In other words, given equilibrium in outputs and relative prices, the price level can change only if M or V or both change, and then only in the same proportion. In that case the preceding difficulties disappear, but only because we have ceased to interpret the equation of exchange as an equilibrium condition for the money market. Instead it would be interpreted as an identity defining the general price level. But the general price level is the inverse of the value of money and, in neoclassical theory, 'value' is determined by the interaction between preferences and scarcity, taking place in competitive markets. Thus the value of money should be determined by its quantity, given the demand for it, which will depend on the level of economic activity, on the one hand, and the average institutional practices of payment on the other. The first of these will be given by Y, the second by V, although a more sophisticated analysis would have to include the interest rate, and perhaps the yields of other assets, too. Then the equation of exchange would express the *equilibrium condition* determining the price level at which excess demand for money becomes zero. This is clearly the only interpretation consistent with the neoclassical approach. Since an equilibrium condition cannot be an identity, we cannot accept the above objection that our imaginary experiment could only come about through a doubling of *M* or *V* or both. The problem stands: according to Walras' Law, if all goods markets are in equilibrium, the money market necessarily should be also, if the value of money is determined by scarcity and preferences. But our thought experiment shows that money market equilibrium does not follow.

Blind Alleys

There have been attempts to escape from this bind. Petri (1982), for example, argues that the relative money balances of agents cannot be among the given endowments with which the analysis begins. Long period equilibrium requires that the agents have the right money balances to sustain their equilibrium activity levels; hence these balances will have to be established in the process of moving towards equilibrium. By contrast, Patinkin and others treat initial money endowments for each agent as among the data of the system. Even so, once an equilibrium is established, a uniform change of money prices upsets the money market, but not the goods markets. Nor does Petri tell us how supply and demand lead each agent to obtain the correct money balance for equilibrium. The agents must start with *some* balances, even if they are not the final ones, but he nowhere explains the path that will be followed. So the difficulties remain.

Jurg Niehans (1978) proposes a complicated revision of Walras' auctioning system. A 'compensation fund' must be established that will lend to those short of cash, and to which those with cash surplus must contribute. Then, starting with some price fixed arbitrarily in money equilibrium, relative prices are determined. These relative prices are then frozen, and in the second stage, returning everyone to their original cash balances, the arbitrary price level is varied until monetary equilibrium is reached. First, this procedure is impossibly cumbersome, and runs counter to economic incentives. Why should those with surplus cash pay it into a 'compensation fund'? Secondly, Niehans nowhere addresses the issue of how the correct distribution of cash balances is to be brought about – the issue, that is, of the correct relative size of cash holdings, the point that Petri considers central. Otherwise the compensation fund will have to be permanent. Finally, once the equilibrium price level is disturbed, the contradiction re-emerges, even in Niehans' world.

The Real Balance Effect

The favored way out of this impasse has been to re-specify the supply and demand equations for goods so that, besides relative prices, supply and demand functions contain *real cash balances*. Real balances yield utility to consumers because they permit the bridging of gaps between sales receipts and purchases, and enable individuals to take advantage of unexpected opportunities (Patinkin, 1965, pp. 14, 78, 80). For exactly the same reasons, they yield productive services to firms. Individuals are enabled to consume more easily, firms to produce more easily, the larger are their real balances. In other words, higher real balances lead to greater spending. As a result, a change in the general price level, or in the supply of nominal money, will have effects that show up in the adjustments of supplies and demands for goods, as well as in the money market. A doubling of prices will therefore *not* leave goods markets undisturbed; since it will halve real balances, supplies and demands for goods will have to adjust. Both goods and money markets will be disturbed, and both will have to readjust, a process in which they will interact. So the contradiction disappears.

At first glance the argument seems to work out very nicely. At the macro level the real balance effect provides the grounds for contending that a perfectly, or even a reasonably, competitive economy, one with sufficient wage and price flexibility, would always tend towards full employment equilibrium. This, of course, while true in theory, would be modified in practice, since market imperfections would prevent downward wage and price flexibility in many areas, and even where such flexibility existed the adjustment processes might prove too slow or too painful. There would therefore exist good *practical* grounds for Keynesian policies, while at the same time the theoretical optimality of the competitive market system could continue to be upheld, ideological implications intact. The causes of unemployment and inflation are in the system's imperfections, not in the system itself.

At the micro level the argument looks equally attractive. For the long run, the 'neutrality' of money could, it seemed, be affirmed: a rise in the money supply would raise the real value of money balances, increasing spending. If the levels of output and employment were initially in equilibrium, the effect of extra spending would not affect outputs but would increase the price level in proportion to the increased money supply. This, of course, is crucial to neoclassical theory's claim for both the efficiency and the optimality of market equilibrium: relative prices and quantities must reflect only resource scarcities, technological possibilities and relative preferences. Individual choice is constrained by the niggardliness of nature; money is a mere veil – monetary changes have no real long-term effects on equilibrium. Hence *government policy* has no such effects. If money *did* affect long-term equilibrium, then it would be impossible to argue

that such an equilibrium represented the highest achievement of preferences subject to constraints imposed by nature, or that prices
reflected relative scarcities – for both relative prices and quantities
would vary with government monetary policy, which normally has
nothing to do with consumer preferences or with natural scarcities.

So, according to proponents of this line of argument, the real
balance effect does not upset the long-run 'neutrality' of money. To
put it another way, the static comparison of two equilibria would not
reveal the real balance effect at all, for 'in [full equilibrium] comparative statics the real balance term may immediately be removed from
the functions without making any difference whatever to the solution
of the system' (Patinkin, (1965) p. 17), 'but the dynamic adjustment
process would depend fundamentally on it' (Patinkin, 1965, p. 57).
This means that when equilibrium has changed, or indeed whenever
the system is out of equilibrium, the real balance effect will propel the
system toward the equilibrium. Suppose there is unemployment:
prices and money wages will fall, raising real balances and stimulating
spending. Suppose there is excess aggregate demand: prices and
money wages will rise, real balances will fall and spending will be curtailed. Thus the real balance effect helps to guarantee the stability of
markets although it leaves the traditional conclusions of the quantity
theory largely intact – resting them on somewhat more stringent
assumptions (e.g. starting from equilibrium), but providing them
with a precise grounding in individual maximizing behavior.

A Problem: Money and Debt
A closer look reveals some flies in the ointment. First, the real
balance effect requires money holdings to consist of 'outside' money,
that is, money that is a medium of exchange and store of value but is
not at the same time some other agent's debt. However, most
'money' is in fact precisely that: obligations of banks, the government, financial intermediaries, and so on. Only gold and silver are
truly outside monies. When money is entirely or largely 'inside
money' – debt – a change in the real value of an agent's money
balances implies an equal and opposite change in the value of some
other agent's obligations. Each effect may be supposed to provide an
opposite stimulus; it is difficult if not impossible to state on *a priori*
grounds which will be the stronger. Nor are these easy to measure
empirically.[6]

The problem might be avoided by assuming that inside money consisted of obligations of the financial sector (and the government), and
that these will change their spending very little in response to a
change in the value of their obligations. Thus, although a change in
the price level will alter the value of the obligations of financial inter-

mediaries (a fall in *P* will raise the real value of what they must repay) and will lead them to change their portfolios (a matter the analysis already accounts for), it will have a negligible effect on their spending since such institutions do not spend much. (Most of their expenses are fixed costs.) The only effects will be on households and businesses, and the system will behave *as if* all money were outside money.

This leads to a second general point: no account has been taken of the fact that both households and firms have financial obligations and claims holding over time that are denominated in money. Generally, businesses are net borrowers, households net lenders. Deflation increases the burden of debt to business. When, with output constant, both prices and variable costs fall in a certain proportion, profits will fall in the same proportion; so they decline in relation to *fixed* costs denominated in money, which, of course, increases the risk of bankruptcy. Given the higher burden of fixed costs and increased risk of bankruptcy, prudent firms should clearly cut back on new projects, and prudent banks should refuse them credit if they do not. On the other hand, for exactly the same reasons, households, being net creditors, will find themselves receiving a higher real value of debt servicing payments, and thus will be stimulated to increase their consumption expenditures.

The usual observation at this point is that, while the debtors' losses equal the creditors' gains, there is no way of saying, in general, whether or not the negative stimulus of loss will outweigh the positive stimulus of gain (although that would probably be the implication of diminishing marginal utility in a Marshallian approach!). Since we cannot really say what the net financial effect will be, we cannot rule out the possibility that it will outweigh the positive stimulus of pure cash balances, particularly if the holders of large cash balances have a low marginal propensity to consume and/or tend to switch from cash into non-produced stores of value.

So everything is up in the air. This unsatisfactory state of affairs, however, results from an inadequate picture of the financial system of corporate business. Firms are not 'family firms', run by an owner-operator who borrows the savings of other families – owners or workers – through the mediation of a bank. Instead corporations are *legal persons*, with limited liability, who own their buildings and equipment and other assets outright. Holders of the corporation's equity are not the 'owners' of the corporation, in the way the family head owns the family firm. Owners of a public company's stock are entitled to a share in its earnings and to vote for its directors. That is all. So when a company's burden of debt rises because of deflation, we can expect to find its stock collapsing.

Households, besides holding bonds (having lent to business) also hold equity in business. Indeed, any well-managed portfolio should contain a balanced mixture of bonds and stocks and cash. In a deflation, bonds and cash will rise in real value, but stocks will fall and, as businesses near the bankruptcy point, will fall precipitously. Thus a deflation will have a negative effect on business, while its effect on households will depend on the composition of their portfolios, which may well be different for different classes of households. But if the deflation goes far enough so that businesses approach or reach the bankruptcy point, then not only will the value of equity fall precipitously, but also bond prices of endangered firms will collapse. Thus the effect of a sufficiently pronounced deflation on households must also be negative. Failure to see this is simply the result of failing to distinguish between stocks and bonds, equity holdings and contractual lending.

Given inside money and/or money-denominated contracts, therefore, there are problems in the short-run adjustment that the real balance effect is supposed to provide. It is simply not possible to argue that in general, if unemployment emerges in a competitive market economy, real balance effects will correct it. If there is inside money this will not necessarily be so, and if investment loans are denominated in money – as, of course, they are – the net effects of wage and price flexibility are likely actually to exacerbate the slump.[7] Since all modern capitalist industrial economies operate in large part with inside money and denominate contracts in money, there is very little left of the vaunted claim that real balance effects will, in theory, stabilize the system and keep it at full employment.[8]

A Further Problem: Demand Theory

What of the claim that in long-run analysis the real balance effect enables neoclassical theory to overcome the contradiction between the monetary excess demand functions and the demand functions for goods and services, while preserving the 'neutrality of money', the essential conclusion of the traditional quantity theory?

Here we can only summarize the results of a complex argument. Since the price level is a weighted average of all prices, *any* price change must have a real balance effect when utility is a function of real balances. But it has been shown by Cliff Lloyd (1964), and admitted by Patinkin (1965), that, apart from the case of *all prices changing equi-proportionally*, the real balance effects associated with ordinary price changes are of indeterminate sign and size. Theoretically, such effects could even swamp substitution effects for normal goods.

Consider a good, x, the consumers of which are highly sensitive to the value of their real balances, and another good, y, where consumers are insensitive to real balances. Then let a non-proportional price rise take place, with x rising very little or not at all, while y and other goods rise substantially. The relative value of x will therefore have fallen, and we should expect the demand for it to increase. But because the consumers of x are highly sensitive to their real balances, which have fallen, they will cut back their spending, whereas the consumers of y, being insensitive, will not. Thus sales of x may fall, in spite of the substitution effect in its favor. If real balance effects are strong enough to ensure full employment, they are strong enough to influence the relative demands for various individual goods in ways that undermine the conclusions of conventional demand theory. Patinkin's 'integration of real and monetary theory' results in an indeterminate theory of demand at the micro level.

Implications

If fiscal policy is ineffectual because of offsetting monetary reactions, then neoclassical equilibrium can be grounded on the real forces of productivity and thrift-technology and preferences, independently of the state. This requires showing that equilibrium depends only on real factors, i.e. that the money supply determines only nominal values. But this arguement results in what mainstream thinkers have termed the 'invalid dichotomy' between real and monetary phenomena. Moreover, it creates serious problems in specifying the 'transmission mechanisms' by which monetary changes influence real values.

Mainstream economists overcome these problems by relying on real balance effects to make the connection. A difficulty immediately arises, however, over the effects of changes in the burden of debt, since 'inside money' is debt. Moreover, when price changes are not universally equi-proportional – and they never are – real balance effects can swamp substitution effects, leaving the microeconomic theory of demand indeterminate.

Thus real balance effect overcomes one set of problems only to introduce others. This is especially true in macroeconomics, the arena in which the most intensive fighting between monetarists and Keynesians has occurred. Since both sides agree that the *IS–LM* system provides a useful general model – though they disagree on exactly how it works – we had better examine the role of the real balance effect in such a system.

Macroeconomics

Beginning with Patinkin, real balances were treated as entering into household or consumer preference functions, just like commodities. An increase in real balances increases 'utility', but at a diminishing rate. However, if real balances provide convenience in purchasing for consumers, they surely do likewise for business firms, so they should enter into production functions. This seems straightforward enough, but the consequences are unsettling. In orthodox theory, real balance effects have been confined to product markets in which businesses supply and households demand. There is no justification for this; if real balances enter into utility and production functions, then they affect household *supply* and business *demand* as well. However, these effects upset the usual results. Let us examine this.

Let us start with the most widely accepted model of modern macroeconomics. It can be represented by a three-quadrant diagram (see Figure 3.8). In the lower left are the labor supply and demand curves, derived respectively from the households' work/leisure choice and

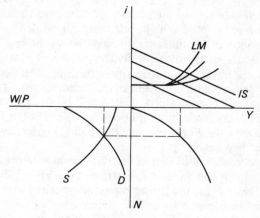

Figure 3.8

from the firms' profit-maximizing, subject to the production function, which itself is drawn in the right-hand quadrant. In this, the most usual representation, there are no real balance effects in the labor market. No reason is given for this arbitrary exclusion. In the upper right quadrant, then, are the sets of *IS* and *LM* curves, respectively defined for each possible price level. Real balance effects appear here, but only here. Because of real balance effects, lower price levels are associated with *IS* curves positioned higher and to the right; for each level of the interest rate, investment and savings balance at higher levels of income because the greater monetary wealth associated with lower prices stimulates both consumption and investment spending. Lower price levels are also associated with a rightward positioning of the *LM* curve, since demand and supply of money will balance at higher levels of income for each interest rate, owing to the lower transactions requirements when the price level is lower.

Solutions

There are several ways of illustrating the solution to this system graphically. We will adopt the one that best exhibits the Keynesian–neoclassical disagreement. First, we derive the relationships between the price level and real output for the *IS* and *LM* functions above, holding interest constant. That is, for a given interest rate we construct the locus of combinations of P and Y that equate investment and savings, and the demand for and supply of money, respectively. For a given interest rate, a lower price level implies higher real balances, hence more of both real consumption and investment; thus a higher level of real income will be required to generate the greater offsetting savings required. Thus the price level and real income will be inversely related along such a locus. For a given interest rate, a higher price level implies a higher demand for money; with a given supply, determined by the central bank, this requires a lower real income to equate demand to supply. Moreover, it is reasonable to assume that the lower real income must be equi-proportional to the higher price level, since both reflect the same nominal transactions demand. Thus the relationship – LM_p – will be a rectangular hyperbola, with PY a constant. It can, however, be cut either from above or from below by the *IS* price-level (IS_p) locus. Figure 3.9(a) and (b) illustrates the two cases.

Alternatively, we could derive the relationships between P and i, respectively, from the *IS* and *LM* curves (see Figure 3.10). For a given Y, a lower P means higher monetary wealth, so greater consumption and investment spending. Hence a higher i will be needed to encourage saving and discourage investment, in order to equate them. So P and i are inversely related in the *IS* market. In the money market, the i,P relationship for given Y will be the same as the i,Y relationship for given P. We have a replica of the usual *LM* curve. Putting the two together, we can determine i and P for given Y. Higher levels of Y shift the *IS* curve inward and the *LM* curve outward.

Now look back at the original three-quadrant diagram. In the labor market, equilibrium employment, N, and the equilibrium real wage, W/P, are determined. From the production function and N, we obtain full employment output, Y. Then with a given Y we can select the appropriate *IS* and *LM* loci in (i,P) space, and their intersection will determine the full employment rate of interest and price level. Finally. we substitute the price level into the real wage to find the

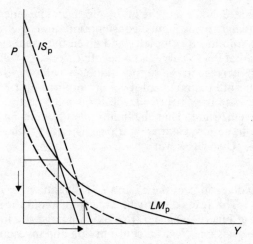

Figure 3.9(a) *Case A*

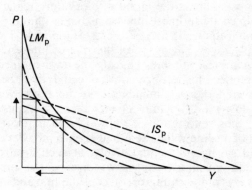

Figure 3.9(b) *Case B*

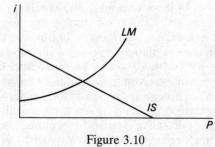

Figure 3.10

money wage rate, and using the interest rate and income level we can calculate savings investment, consumption and the demand for money. The solution is complete, and given the usual assumptions – in particular that the *IS* curve has a negative slope – it will be unique.[9] Note that an increase in the supply of money will not affect the labor market or the full employment level of output, but it will lower the interest rate and raise the price level, for it will shift the *LM* curve in (i,P) space to the right. Thus the 'neutrality of money' is confirmed – with respect to employment and output. The case with regard to stability is not so clear, however.

Stability

There are two versions of the *IS* and *LM* diagram in (P,Y) space, as seen above.[10] This leads directly to a question about the system's stability. Look at Figure 3.9 again. In Case A a large rise in P, lowering real balances, has an effect on consumption and investment that can be offset by a small fall in Y. In Case B just the opposite holds.

Now suppose that, at the initial rate of interest, the level of real output at which these lines intersect is below the full employment level. By implication, the rate of interest is too high. The excess output will imply excess savings, and the rate of interest will fall.[11] A lower rate of interest will shift the LM_p line inward, since a lower rate of interest implies a higher speculative demand, there being less to be divided between the two influences on the transactions demand. Similarly a lower rate of interest increases both consumption and investment, thus shifting the IS_p upward and to the right, since a higher level of income will be required at each price level to generate the required savings; or, alternatively, at each level of income, a higher price level will be necessary to lower real balances enough to offset the effects of lower interest on consumption and investment. In Case A the results are unambiguous: both movements lower the price level and increase income. The outcome will therefore be a tendency towards full employment income at a lower price level. In Case B things are not so agreeable: both movements lower the balancing level of income; but both movements also *raise* the price level. So the overall movement is *away* from full employment income, while the effects on the price level are inflationary. In this case the real balance effect tends to create 'stagflation'.

Case B makes it clear that the real balance effect, by itself, is not enough to ensure stability. Even in Case A, Keynesian arguments can be made, even after accepting the contention that, when income is below the full employment level, interest rates will fall. For when interest falls, the speculative demand for money increases. When bond prices rise high enough, the speculative demand will absorb all available cash, so that interest rates will decline no further. So for large discrepancies between actual and full employment income, the movement to full employment will depend on the IS_p locus shifting when interest rates decline. If this response is weak and the speculative demand strong, then full employment may not be reachable in Case A. This is possible even though prices are flexible and the real balance effect is alive and well. Hence, it must be assumed, in addition, that the speculative demand for money is weak or non-existent and that the investment–saving locus is strongly interest-elastic. In short, the claims for the stability of full employment equilibrium simply have no basis.

Real Balances Again

Now let us go back to the basic model. We noted that real balance effects appeared only in the goods markets, although real balances were assumed to enter into household utility and business firm production functions. Logically, they should also affect households' labor supply and business' labor demand decisions. In neoclassical theory, especially in general equilibrium theory, decisions are interdependent. The decisions to demand goods and to supply labor are not separate decisions; they are part and parcel of the same utility-maximizing problem. The same holds for business decisions to supply goods and demand factors; again, they are two aspects of the same maximizing process. If real balances enter into one part of the problem, they must enter into the other. A rise in real balances, for example, should reduce the supply of labor for every level of real wages. Since households are wealthier, they can consume more, hence, will opt for more leisure and less work. Furthermore, a rise in real balances should increase the demand for labor at every level of the real wage, since it enhances productivity.[12] So, holding the real wage constant, we can define a direct functional relationship between the price level and labor demand. On normal assumptions these two curves will intersect in a unique point, determining the equilibrium price level and employment. A change in the real wage, on the other hand, will shift each curve – higher real wages being associated with an inward shift of D and an outward shift of S (see Figure 3.11). Each shift lowers P, but the effect on N is indeterminate. It could go either way, or, in the extreme case, remain unchanged if two influences were to offset each other exactly.

Leaving this special case to one side, there will no longer be a unique 'full employment' level of N; nor will there be a uniquely corresponding Y, since to every level of N there will correspond many Ys, depending on the level of real balances. But the preceding line of argument depended on comparing the full employment income with the actual or initial level of income. If $Y<Y_F$, then interest (or, in most textbook accounts, the price level) would fall, setting off the equilibrating movements. When real balances enter into utility and production functions and influence labor demand and supply, the equilibrating process will itself cause the 'full employment' level of income to change. The process can no longer work.

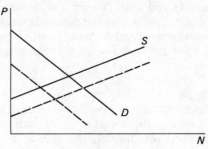

Figure 3.11

More technically, as we have already seen, without real balance effects (that is, with fixed labor supply and demand curves), the system could always be solved and the solution would normally be unique. But when we add two new functional relationships, between employment and the price level, derived from real balance effects in the labor market without any new variables, we have an overdetermined system, which will normally end up generating contradictions. For example, starting from a given labor market situation – which implies a given level of real balances, and so a given price level – we can calculate as before; whereupon we determine P and i together, for full employment Y. But the initial labor market situation *already implied a price level*, since without it the level of employment would not be determined. It would, however, be a remarkable accident if this were the same price level that cleared the product market. In general they will be different. Hence the system is self-contradictory.

In other words, when we take the real balance effect *fully* and *properly* into account, far from 'integrating real and monetary theory', it engenders an overdetermined, self-contradictory system, even apart from the issues of inside money and the burden of debt.

Income
Finally, what about the empty quadrant? Doesn't something belong there? It almost cries out to be filled. And there is, in fact, an important relationship between i and W/P, which derives from

$$PY = W/N + iKP,$$

which is the expression for the distribution of total money income between the money wage bill and the money returns to capital. Here i represents interest on money capital, and it is assumed that capital values will be adjusted in the stock market, so that the rate of dividends plus capital gains on shares will be equalized to the prevailing rate of interest on bonds. (Alternatively it may be assumed, as Patinkin does explicitly, that all capital is borrowed. Hence the only form of security traded will be bonds.) It may be objected that the condition that the rate of interest be adjusted so that $PY = WN + iKP$ is 'long run', whereas only 'short-run' questions are at issue. It is hard to see what this means. Money income *has* to equal money wages plus money returns to capital; those are the only two possibilities the model allows. Money income has to be paid out in the 'short run', because it finances expenditure. It should be added that the rate of interest determined by the income equation will equal the marginal product of the capital stock, if the production function is first degree homogeneous. From the above we derive,

$$i = \sigma - \frac{W}{P}n, \quad \text{where} \quad \sigma = Y/K, n = N/K.$$

This is a straight line with intercepts $W/P_{max} = Y/N$, $i_{max} = Y/K$; and slope equal to N/K. It states that, given the stock of capital, the full employment labor force and full employment output, the equilibrium real wage implies a corresponding full employment rate of interest. This rate of interest is necessary in order for total capital earnings plus total wages to add up to the total money value of output. If this condition is *not* met, then the spending of full employment income *cannot* purchase all and only full employment output at the going price level. This equation is a precondition for short-run equilibrium and is frequently taken for granted. But once it is written down explicitly, it is easily shown that the system is overdetermined and therefore, except by accident, inconsistent, as can be seen from Figure 3.12.

Rewrite the *IS* and *LM* loci in terms of i and P, for the full employment level of income, Y_F. This results in the loci of (i, P) that equate full employment saving and investment, IS_{Y_F}, and full employment demand for money to the given supply, LM_{Y_F}. The intersection will determine the full employment rate of interest and price level. The full employment money wage follows from this price level and the real wage. But the equation for the payment of income in conjunction with the real wage fixed in the labor market determines the interest rate that will ensure that capital income and money wages jointly exhaust the total value of output. There is no reason why this interest rate should equal the one determined by the *IS–LM* functions. Except for accidental cases, then, the system will be contradictory; it will determine two inconsistent levels of the interest rate (see Figure 3.13). Yet this is the basic model that has been employed by both sides in the debate between monetarists and Keynesians, and, as we shall now see, it is the model that Friedman himself uses.

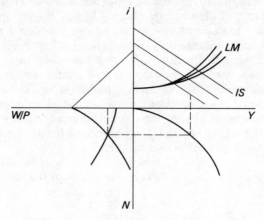

Figure 3.12

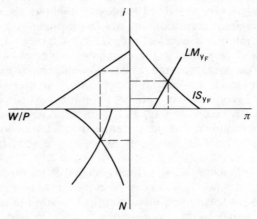

Figure 3.13

IV MILTON FRIEDMAN'S MONETARY THEORY

The preceding section has made it clear that neoclassical theory as a whole, not only monetarism, still faces substantial unresolved problems in relating its monetary theory to its basic supply and demand analysis of prices and outputs. If it simply proceeds by way of determining relative prices and quantities from the data of preferences, production possibilities and initial endowments, and then introduces a quantity equation, it engenders a contradiction. This is the procedure dubbed by neoclassicists themselves the 'invalid dichotomy'. But if it introduces a 'real balance effect' in order to overcome this, it can generate the desired conclusions for aggregate analysis (full employment, neutrality of money) only if it confines its analysis to pre-modern and implausible monetary systems – no inside money and no money contracts. Furthermore, when we consider the disaggregated system in detail, the neutrality of money is lost except in the unusual and implausible case of all prices changing in exactly the same proportion. Nor does the argument support the often-repeated claim that full employment equilibrium is stable. But much worse, most writers, following Patinkin, consider real balance effects only in the product markets. When they are introduced, as they should be, into the labor markets, the resulting model is overdetermined and contradictory.

The Monetarist Strategy

Faced with these, from their point of view, depressing conclusions from two decades of rigorous work, monetarists have proceeded in the most straightforward and effective way imaginable. They have simply ignored all the modern work. By and large, they have not changed the basic questions and neither have they challenged or replaced the modern answers. They have simply shouted the old ones louder.

Of course, it will be argued, this is not really quite fair. Serious and important work has been done and new approaches have been developed. Perhaps, but a very great deal of what has been taken to be new is nothing but the old flock of sheep herded forward in fine new wolf-garb. Lest we be thought to be criticizing scarecrows rather than shepherds, we shall take as our illustration the work of the chief shepherd himself, Friedman.[13] We will begin by showing that his arguments repeatedly – in various forms and contexts – embody the 'invalid dichotomy', to which he has never given an adequate response. In particular, it is because he implicitly assumes the invalid dichotomy that he finds it unnecessary (or impossible?) to give an explicit account of the 'transmission mechanism' by which an increase in the stock of money principally affects prices rather than, as Keynesians have always argued, outputs and employment when the economy is below full capacity. Outputs and employment are 'ground out by the Walrasian system of equations' (Friedman, 1956, p. 15), that is, by the Walrasian equations, *not including real balances and/or wealth in the form of obligations denominated in money*, because if these are included, the results (long run as well as short) will not be those of the traditional quantity theory. But if the Walrasian equations depend only on relative prices, then the quantity equation determines the price level, and the 'transmission mechanism' is trivial. However, as seen, the model is then inconsistent as a whole.

Although Friedman is attracted by the simple quantity theory, he proposes an alternative version, which he calls the 'monetary theory of nominal income', in which the supply and demand for money determine nominal income, that is, PY. Real output is determined through the labor market and the production function, thus fixing employment and so 'the natural rate of unemployment'. However, as we saw earlier, false expectations may at times be generated in the labor market, leading to temporary deviations from equilibrium employment and output levels. As workers and employers learn to form their expectations more adequately, this will happen less frequently and be corrected more rapidly. Thus in equilibrium the monetary theory of nominal income can be put together with the natural rate of employment/unemployment, and the equilibrium price level simply follows. However, Friedman has simply bypassed the determinants of aggregate demand: there is no reason to suppose that this price level is the one that would generate the full employment level of aggregate demand through the real balance effect.

The Phillips Curve and Irving Fisher

It is convenient to start an examination of Friedman's position by looking at his interpretation of the Phillips curve, which he claims to base on Irving Fisher's work. Phillips viewed the relationship between output and employment as a problem in Marshallian equilibrium analysis in a Keynesian world. Output and/or employment are the independent variables, with prices tending to adjust any resulting shortages or surpluses. Prices, or money wages, are clearly the dependent variables. Wages (or the rate of change in wages) are determined by conditions in the labor market as measured by the rate of unemployment. Fisher (1930), on the other hand, writing in a pre-Keynesian framework, drew on a Walrasian approach. Price is the independent variable, of which the offer and demand curves for labor are functions. Thus, he poses the question of what is likely to happen to output and employment in the face of a general increase in wages and prices. Fisher argues that though wages (variable costs) and business receipts may rise proportionally since a substantial fraction of costs are fixed in money contracts, total costs will rise less than pro-portionally. Resulting windfall profits ought to increase employment. Higher inflation, in other words, reduces unemployment.[14]

It is important to note that, though these windfalls may be tempor-ary because the contracts will eventually be renegotiated, they are not *illusory*. Friedman's version of the Phillips curve, on the other hand, presents a very different picture, one that is actually incon-sistent with Fisher's approach. For while he takes from Fisher the concept of price as the independent variable, he totally ignores the question of lags in the process of adjustment, and substitutes the stimulative effects of various illusions for the stimulative effects of real and permanent transfers of wealth. He argues that the equilib-rium level of employment, or the 'natural rate of unemployment', or 'the level that would be ground out by the Walrasian system of general equilibrium equations' (Friedman, 1968), is determined by the offer and demand schedules for labor for a real wage:

$$N = N \frac{(W)}{P}$$

$$\frac{1}{P} \cdot \frac{\mathrm{d}P}{\mathrm{d}t} = \frac{1}{W} \cdot \frac{\mathrm{d}W}{\mathrm{d}t}$$

From this equation we see that a change in money wages (W) and prices (P) does not result in any change in real wages (W/P); moreover, if there is no change in real wages, the equation shows there should be no change in employment (N). Thus, a change in absolute price that is not a change in relative price will not result in any changes in the equilibrium quantities, i.e. these will depend only on the given supply and demand equations. Any shifts in the curves can be due only to traders misinterpreting the data, i.e. capitalists mistakenly believing that $1/P \cdot \mathrm{d}P/\mathrm{d}t > 1/W \cdot \mathrm{d}W/\mathrm{d}t$, and workers mis-takenly believing the reverse. Since he tacitly assumes that changes in the rates of fixed costs to revenue have no consequences for employ-ment, Friedman is quite correct in arguing that any change in the equilibrium level of employment from such errors in calculation can only be temporary. 'You can fool some of the people some of the time, but you can't fool all the people all the time', says Friedman in his most statesmanlike mood (Friedman, 1973, p. 27). Traders will base their behavior either on experience or on 'rational expectations' of price changes 'on the basis of a correct economic theory'. Once they have corrected any misperceptions, there will be no effect on employment from price inflation; in other words, the Phillips curve will be vertical. There is, therefore, a unique natural rate of unem-ployment and the government can push the system away from this level only by 'fooling people' – and they will soon catch on. But note that this approach determines output *entirely* from the 'supply side'. Nothing has been said about whether or not there is sufficient real aggregate demand to ensure that this output – no more, no less – can be *sold*. This was the original question for the Keynesians, and Friedman simply ignores it.

Nor is he even true to Fisher. There is a difference between employment changes due to windfall profits, as in Fisher, and employment changes due to miscalculation of costs and revenue. In Fisher's model there is no reason for employment to revert to its original position, for it was not due to a disequilibrium. Employers and workers were not fooled, and the increases in their offers were based on real factors. Friedman changed the nature of Fisher's argument by totally ignoring the whole question of fixed costs. His approach resembles Fisher's only in the choice of the price level as the independent variable. For the rest, his argument assumes a simple old-fashioned labor market in which supplies and demands depend on the real wage. There are no real balance effects, although in the *text* he repeatedly suggests that prices begin to rise because of an increase in the supply of money. This is what sets off the inflationary process during which the various agents misperceive or miscalculate. He assumes the validity of his 'monetary theory of nominal income', but, as we shall see, it does not deal with demand.

Moreover, if there are no real balance effects, how does Friedman propose to avoid the inconsistency? He refers to a 'Walrasian general equilibrium', so Walras' Law must hold; if it does, the quantity equation cannot be tacked on to the rest. As already mentioned, the point holds equally for micro and for macro models, as we shall shortly show. But Friedman is silent on the subject.

The Transmission Mechanism

Let us approach the subject from another point of view. Friedman supposes that an increase in the supply of money will raise prices. These price increases will then be misperceived, etc., by various agents who will adjust their supplies and demands. Keynesians, by contrast, would expect an increase in the supply of money to lower interest rates rather than raise prices, and then, as a result of lower interest, investment spending might increase, which if the increase were large enough might push up prices. The Keynesian account of the 'transmission' of effects through the economy is quite detailed. Friedman rejects the Keynesian account and holds that changes in the money supply *directly and immediately* affect prices, How? What is his alternative account of the transmission process?

In 'The Quantity Theory of Money: A Restatement', Friedman attempts to integrate monetary theory into the general framework of neoclassical value theory. To a utility-maximizing individual, the demand for money is determined in the same way as the demand for any other commodity or asset – a combination of income and substitution effects. The demand for money is part of a portfolio equilibrium decision: 'To the ultimate wealth-owning units in the economy, money is one kind of assets, one way of holding wealth' (Friedman, 1956, p.4). As such, its demand will be determined by the level of wealth and the return on alternative assets and their expected rate of change. Friedman defines the following symbols (in addition to the ones we have used before):

Let r_b = rate of return from bonds (fixed in nominal terms)
r_e = rate of return from equities (fixed in real terms)
w = ratio of 'non-human' to 'human' wealth
u = variables that affect taste and preference
P = price level or the implicit return from goods.

Then, first writing a demand for money in nominal terms and dividing through by P, we get a demand for real cash balances:

$$L = f\left(r_b, r_e, \frac{1}{P}\frac{dP}{dt}; w; Yu\right).$$

This equation describes an individual wealth holder. The aggregate function is derived by aggregating over all relevant individuals. The questions as to who these are, and what should be the aggregation weights, will come up in a moment.

According to Friedman, the quantity theorist is distinguished from other economists in holding that:

1 This demand for real cash balances is highly stable.
2 The supply of and demand for money are independent, i.e. there are important factors affecting the supply of money that do not affect the demand.
3 The liquidity trap is not important; quantity theorists reject the doctrine that the demand for money becomes perfectly elastic at very low rates of interest.
4 Quantity theorists interpret wealth and the spectrum of assets more broadly than conventional economists.

All this may be interesting but it does not add up to an account of the transmission process. Friedman was satisfied to end his restatement with 'the proof of the pudding is in the eating' (1956, p. 17). But puddings, no matter how tasty, should be eaten only for dessert. For an entrée it would be reasonable to ask to be shown why a stable demand for money function when linked to an increase in the supply of money would lead to *price* rather than *output* change. In other words, we need a theory of the determinants of spending in the process of short-run adjustment. Finally, in his 'A Theoretical Framework for Monetary Analysis' (1970), Friedman attempted to come to grips with this problem, as well as to try to specify the difference between his monetary framework and the Keynesian system.

Asset Choices

Friedman couches his explanation of the transmission mechanism in an asset choice framework so as better to contrast it with what he believes to be the Keynesian challenge and, surprisingly, the argument is essentially the same as the approach of Patinkin. (The reason for surprise is that if he accepts the real balance effect, he must accept the results that go with it – and these do not square with the conservative position. Specifically, Patinkin's approach provides an important role to aggregate demand, and so to government.) Let us see what he says.

Money is regarded as one of a spectrum of assets, yielding a service similar to other assets and having similar properties of diminishing marginal utility. An increase in the quantity of money in an economy initially in asset equilibrium induces a disequilibrium in the structure of asset holding; that is, there is excess supply relative to a stable demand for real cash balances. This induces a generalized substitution from money to other assets, driving down their rates. The fall in rates on assets raises the implicit, non-observable rates of return on consumer durables. At the same time, the price of current consumption in terms of forgone future consumption (Marshall's 'reward for waiting') has fallen, which, in principle, ought to increase the demand for non-durables as well (Friedman, 1970; in Gordon, 1974, p. 28).[15] We therefore have an increase in money expenditures generated by the increased money supply due to the constant demand for real cash balances. But the excess supply of money is not eliminated by simply being passed around like a hot potato. Friedman and the Keynesians both agree that one person's expenditure is another person's receipt. To restore equilibrium it is necessary for the real value of cash balances to be restored to what the public desires to hold.

It is here that monetarists and Keynesians part company. Friedman argues that the equilibrium will be restored by inflation, which will reduce the value of money until real cash balances are returned to their equilibrium level, while Keynesians would argue that increased expenditures would stimulate employment, which will increase the number of individuals holding cash balances. Taking his cue from Leijonhufvud (1968), Friedman reduces this difference to one of adjustment velocities. Which adjusts faster, prices or quantities. It is important to emphasize this point. While Keynes has been accused (many would argue falsely) of achieving his results by assuming fixed prices, for Friedman to derive *his* transmission mechanism from money to prices, he must assume fixed employment. Though he admits 'there is nothing in the logic of the quantity theory that specifies the dynamic path of adjustment, nothing requires the whole adjustment to take place through *P* rather than through [real variables]' (Friedman, 1970; in Gordon, 1974, p. 17), he does not offer a satisfactory solution as to which it will be. It is not sufficient to claim, as he does, that this is an empirical question; the empirical results are contradictory, as is well known.

Even more seriously, his empirical work raises questions for his theory. In *A Monetary History of the United States* (Friedman and Schwartz, 1963), the claim is that the *long-run* changes in the quantity of money have a negligible effect on real income, so that non-monetary forces are all that matter for changes in real income. For shorter periods, changes in the supply of money will be reflected in all three variables, velocity, price level and real income. But if in the short run a change in the money supply will change real income, presumably it will also change employment and therefore the aggregate amount of money the public wishes to hold, since the total demand for money function is specified in terms of individual demands, which must then be aggregated. If the disequilibrium condition initiated by monetary expansion is solved by employment changes, the aggregate demand for real money (the foundation of the transmission mechanism for long-run price changes) must shift since the number of individuals overs which aggregation takes place and the weights accorded them will have to change with changes in employment.

Friedman's attempt to deal with the problem of the missing mechanism through analysis of asset adjustment is wholly unsatisfactory. The details of such a transmission mechanism are hard to pin down. Variations in money income are made up of fluctuations in both real income and prices, and Friedman has given us no grounds on which to explain their relative magnitude. Furthermore, as Laidler points out,

> Although the practice of treating the determination of variation in money income as a problem prior to and separate from that of breaking such variations down between real income and prices

would, as Friedman (1971) argued, greatly simplify macroeconomics, the premises [for doing so] are factually wrong. How much money income will change in response to a given change in the quantity of money depends upon how much of that change comes in real income and how much in the price level. (Laidler, 1978 , p. 162)

This approach will not provide Friedman with his transmission mechanism. First, the basic model, being Keynesian, strongly suggests that changes in money will affect interest rates and output initially and prices only later. Worse, if real balance effects are excluded, the model is inconsistent; but if they are included, Friedman's simple labor market analysis of the Phillips curve must be rejected, for the reasons advanced earlier.

The Monetary Theory of Nominal Income

These and related objections were advanced from many quarters and Friedman finally took up the challenge to present his complete theory, showing exactly how the monetary theory of nominal income differs both from standard Keynesian theory and from earlier, presumably inferior, versions of the quantity theory. He begins by presenting 'A Simple Common Model' that '. . . would be accepted alike by adherents of the quantity theory and of the income–expenditure theory' (Friedman, 1970). Let us look at this carefully.

Using our previous notation, but now designating the interest rate by r, to indicate that it is defined in Friedman's sense, the model is:

$C = \mathrm{f}(Y, r)$, where C is consumption
$I = \mathrm{g}(r)$
$Y = C + I$ or $S = Y - C = I$
$M^{\mathrm{d}} = P.\mathrm{l}(Y, r)$, or, if elasticity of the demand for money with respect to Y equals unity: $M^{\mathrm{d}} = PY.1\,(r)$
$M^{\mathrm{s}} = h\,(r)$, or later $M^{\mathrm{s}} = H.m\,(r)$ where H is high-powered money and $m\,(r)$ is the money multiplier
$M^{\mathrm{d}} = M^{\mathrm{s}}$

This is a system of six equations with seven unknowns: $C, I, r, P, M^{\mathrm{d}}, M^{\mathrm{s}}, Y$.

Two comments immediately come to mind:

1   Friedman's investment function is a great simplification of Keynes' investment function, but the idea of separating expenditures into induced (C) and autonomous (I) is correct in spirit.

2   Most *IS–LM* models treat M^s as an exogenous policy-determined variable. To do so, however, requires an assumption that policy is unaffected by changes in the other variables, i.e. the central bank ignores P and r when deciding on changes in M. To Friedman such a state would be desirable (the Fed on automatic pilot), but he recognizes that as an assumption of actual M^s it is unwarranted.

Friedman then states (in Gordon, 1974, p. 31), 'There is a missing equation. Some one of these variables must be determined by relationships outside the system'.[16] He proceeds to consider:

1   The simple quantity theory: hold Y constant. Friedman admits that to do so 'is the essence of what has been called the classical dichotomy' (p. 32).
2   The simple income–expenditure model: hold P constant.

Friedman admits (p.44) that both of these assumptions lack grounding in theory and are not well supported by evidence. He rejects both of these therefore and puts forth his own, third alternative, which he describes as a combination of Keynes and Fisher.

Yet, amazingly, since his account of the Phillips curve is based on it, Friedman has simply ignored the labor market! That market, of course, consists of three substantive equations (ignoring the equilibrium condition) – labor demand, labor supply and the production function – while introducing only two new variables, the money wage and employment. The complete model therefore has nine equations and nine unknowns. Indeed, the model is, in all essentials, precisely the one we analyzed in the preceding section. There is no 'missing equation'. How could Friedman have overlooked this?[17]

Moreover, and crucially, when we add the labor market to his 'Simple Common Model', determining full employment output, the invalid dichotomy is present and the contradiction discussed earlier is implicit. Further, it can easily be explained in macroeconomic terms. Assume inside money and no real balance effects. Start from full employment and then assume an increased money supply. This must involve the banking system buying bonds, i.e. lending more, so lowering interest rates. Hence aggregate demand will rise above the full employment level, creating an inflationary gap, so that the price level begins to rise. With a higher price level, bank deposits will rise, making available a larger supply of loanable funds. But with a higher price level, the funds needed to finance investment will have to be larger. Both demand for and supply of bonds therefore rise in the same proportion. The same thing happens in the commodity markets:

earnings are up in the same proportion as costs. Hence in these markets no check exists to the rise in the price level. In the money market, by contrast, the implication is that the increase in income due to the fall in the rate of interest shifts the demand for money schedule by a definite amount so that it intersects with the new supply at a definite price level (see Figure 3.14). But as Walras' Law implies, the money and bond markets are simply *alternative* ways of expressing the same relationships. They cannot give different answers. Hence this formulation of macro theory is inconsistent.[18]

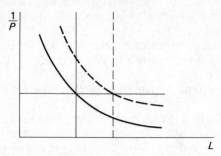

$\frac{1}{P}$

L

Figure 3.14

By contrast, when a real balance effect exists, it acts to check the rise in the price level in both the commodity and the bond markets. As prices rise, real balances fall; hence demand will be cut back in the commodity markets. Falling real balances will similarly require portfolio adjustments, cutting back the demand for bonds. The real balance effect therefore eliminates the inconsistency noted above.

Friedman does not explain why he believes such a contradiction can be avoided, however; he simply presents the model and claims that the real balance effect 'is not significant empirically' for short-run analysis. He does not explain how the *theoretical* problems can be overcome. Is the 'invalid dichotomy' acceptable in the short run? Why? As far as we can tell, he never discusses these problems. Does he or does he not accept the Walrasian analysis of markets? If he does not, why does he continually appeal to the equations of general equilibrium? If he does, what happens to Walras' Law in short-run equilibrium?

He claims at one point that wealth effects ensure that the long-run equilibrium position will always be a full employment one: 'There is no fundamental "flaw in the price system" that makes unemployment the natural outcome of a fully operative market-mechanism' (in Gordon, 1974, p. 16). So evidently he accepts the real balance effect for the long run. But notice that he is talking about the 'price system' here, not about steady growth. In replying to critics of his approach, he states, '. . . for the most part I was concerned with the short run . . . and I have never believed that the real balance effect is of much empirical significance for the short run' (Friedman, 1974, p. 175). This would seem to imply that he accepts the 'invalid dichotomy' for the short run, which means that Walras' Law would not hold for a short-run equilibrium in which the monetary theory of nominal income was combined with the product market side of the economy. Why this should be acceptable is never discussed. Nor is it clear that this is what he actually intends, since his discussion of the 'transmission mechanism', which is clearly a Keynesian- type short-run linkage, is indistinguishable from a real balance analysis. Why is the real balance effect sometimes treated as 'long-run' and other times as 'short-run'?

Friedman's Theory of Interest

Finally, let us look at Friedman's own approach (1970; in Gordon, 1974), which he describes as a combination of Keynes' interest rate (determined by expected future rates) and Fisher's distinction between the nominal rate (r) and the real rate (ϱ)[19]:

$$r = \varrho + \left(\frac{1}{P} \frac{dP}{dt} \right).$$

This equation must be viewed as an identity rather than a theoretical statement. Though one could say that the true 'burden of debt'

$$\varrho = r - \left(\frac{1}{P} \frac{dP}{dt} \right),$$

this is an *ex post* concept. When the debt is contracted, only r is known. The rate of change of prices over the life of the debt is not known, and therefore cannot be calculated until the debt has been repaid. As Keynes pointed out, however, decisions must be made even in the face of uncertainty. Using * to denote expected values, Friedman's equation reads

$$r = \varrho^* + \left(\frac{1}{P} \frac{dP}{dt} \right)^*.$$

The nominal rate equals the real rate plus the rate of change of the price level. Or the true 'burden of debt' equals the nominal rate minus the rate of inflation.[20] This has a Fisherian flavor, but, to repeat, it is well defined only as an *ex post* concept. Since $Y = PY/P$, this can be written:

$$r = \varrho^* + \frac{1}{PY} \frac{\mathrm{d}(PY)^*}{\mathrm{d}t} - \frac{1}{Y} \frac{\mathrm{d}Y^*}{\mathrm{d}t},$$

or

$$r = \varrho^* - g^* + \frac{1}{PY} \frac{\mathrm{d}(PY)^*}{\mathrm{d}t}$$

where g^* is the expected rate of growth of real output, and

$$\frac{1}{YP} \left[\frac{\mathrm{d}(YP)}{\mathrm{d}t} \right]^*$$

is the rate of growth of money income.

Next Friedman argues that the difference, $\varrho^* - g^*$, designated by k_0, is both constant and small, so that

$$k_0 = \varrho^* - g^*,$$

and even if k_0 changes,

$$k_0 < \frac{1}{P} \frac{\mathrm{d}P}{\mathrm{d}t}.$$

Hence, he concludes:

$$r = k_0 + \left[\frac{1}{YP} \frac{\mathrm{d}(YP)}{\mathrm{d}t} \right]^*.$$

He then writes:

$$M^{\mathrm{d}} = PYl(r)$$
$$M^{\mathrm{s}} = h(r)$$
$$M^{\mathrm{d}} = M^{\mathrm{s}}.$$

Since he claims (Gordon, 1974, p. 38), 'At any point in time $(1/YP$ $[\mathrm{d}(YP)^*/\mathrm{d}t])$, the "permanent" or "anticipated" rate of growth of nominal income is a predetermined variable . . . based partly on past considerations outside our model . . .'. With r determined this way, the supply and demand for money determine nominal income, PY.

Now we can see quite plainly what Friedman has done. The level of nominal income so determined is nothing more than the level of nominal income that equates the supply of money to the demand for it, at the fixed interest rate. There is no reason to suppose that this is the level of income that will actually prevail in the economy, since nothing has yet been said about *spending*. It is through spending that goods are sold and prices and outputs actually realized, and Friedman has not yet told us about consumption and investment. He has done nothing more than determine which level of nominal income will establish equilibrium in the holding of money for the given rate of interest, as determined by expectations of future rates and of price changes. If these expectations are not realized in the present period, they will very likely change. Friedman's determination of r^* depends upon expectations being realized, that is, upon goods being sold in the anticipated quantities at the anticipated prices. But there is no reason for this to happen, since there is no way to reconcile the consumption and investment side of the 'Common Model' with the rest of his analysis. This can be seen in Figure 3.15. Friedman's monetary theory of nominal income determines r^* and the LM_{P_1} locus, which together with the labor market and the production function determine equilibrium in the following way: the labor market determines W/P and N; from the production function we obtain Y_F; then from the LM locus, given Y_F and r^*, we obtain the price level, P, which substituted in the equilibrium real wage determines the money wage, W. Since we know r^* and Y_F, we can substitute these values in the consumption and investment functions to determine C and I. But *there is no reason to suppose that the* C *and* I *so determined will add up to* Y_F! If the *IS* locus – the set of points for which $C+I = Y$ – is in the position shown, they will add up to less than full employment Y_F.

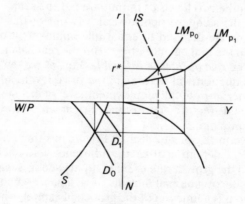

Figure 3.15

There is plainly a contradiction here; it seems that unemployment could perfectly well be a natural outcome of the market system, conceived this way.

One way of analyzing this result proceeds by arguing that the *effective* demand for labor must be shifted down, reflecting the inability to sell the product. Thus employment is adjusted to sales. The new effective labor demand curve, D_1, reflecting under-utilized capacity, cuts the supply curve at a lower real wage and level of employment, corresponding to the output that can be sold. (Whether this is an adequate theory of labor market adjustment is another question. But if no adjustment takes place we simply have a contradiction.) Now we see a remarkable and wholly counter-intuitive implication of Friedman's theory. To re-establish equilibrium in the supply and demand for money at the given interest rate, the price level must *rise*, to take up the slack created by a lower real output. Correspondingly, given a higher price level, the money wage must fall substantially, both because the real wage must be lower and because the price level must be higher. Thus excess supply (or potential excess supply) causes money prices of goods to rise but the money price of labor to fall and, indeed, to fall sharply. This makes no sense at all. Of course, defenders of Friedman might reply that they do not believe the labor market adjusts its current demand for labor to current sales or sales expectations – but then they have to explain what happens when the *IS* curve fails to intersect the *LM* curve at the full employment level of real output.

To put the argument briefly: Friedman's monetary theory of nominal income can be combined either with the *IS* curve to determine output and the price level, or with the supply-side equations. But it cannot be combined with both without an explanation of what happens when the two levels of output are not the same.

Of course, the standard neoclassical way out of this impasse – a failure of aggregate demand to equal full employment output – has been to rely on the real balance effect. But the real balance effect will only work if the *rate of interest is flexible*. For, as we saw earlier, the real balance equation will determine the price level and the rate of interest together, for the full employment level of income. Hence this approach would require jettisoning Friedman's 'Keynes–Fisher' theory of the rate of interest.

There are good reasons to dismiss Friedman's theory. The crucial step comes in the definition of k_0 (the difference between the real rate of interest and the growth rate of real output) and its separation from the growth rate of nominal income. Friedman contends that the growth of output is a function of the growth of capital, which will only change slowly over time through the accumulation of savings. But for

Keynesians and mainstream economists generally, the growth of capital depends on its actual productivity (and its actual profitability), and this in turn depends on its rate of utilization, as determined by aggregate demand. Utilization and demand will also affect the price level. For these reasons the actual nominal rate at any point in time may differ from the expected nominal rate that Friedman's equations depend on. (That is, both the actual rate of growth of real income and the actual rate of growth of nominal income may differ from the 'permanent' or 'anticipated' rates, because of fluctuations in aggregate demand.) In other words, Friedman has simply divided off the real forces, productivity and thrift, which in his view determine real growth, from monetary forces, which determine the growth of prices. But this is arbitrary. Once we allow that real growth may be influenced by monetary developments and that the growth of prices may be affected by real forces, then Friedman's equation for the nominal rate no longer holds and his simple quantity theory result – that supply and demand for money determine nominal income – cannot be derived. Once again Friedman's conclusions depend on an illegitimate dichotomizing of real and monetary forces.

Rates of Growth

Finally, another peculiarity of Friedman's approach should be considered. The variables with asterisks are interpreted as 'permanent' or 'anticipated' rates of growth. Presumably, then, they are growth paths along which supply and demand are balanced – 'warranted' rates of growth in Harrod–Domar terminology. If the economy's transmission mechanism involves quantity adjustments and the multiplier, then a deviation of the actual rate of growth of either real or nominal income from its warranted or permanent level will set up a cumulative movement increasing the divergence between the two. This is the familiar Harrod–Domar result.[21] But in his discussion of the adjustment process, Friedman nowhere explains why he neglects this problem.

Let us consider this point a little further. Like Friedman, Harrod (1948) assumes a fixed interest rate, which, he contends, means that the capital–labor ratio will stay fixed. Under these circumstances, he argues that the warranted growth path is unstable, and that it will be unlikely to equal the growth rate of the labor force. So, in the long term, there will be a tendency to instability and unemployment. Does Friedman accept these conclusions? Presumably not, but he nowhere discusses them.

The by-now standard neoclassical answer is given by Solow (1970), who allows the capital–labor ratio to vary. Hence the warranted rate of growth will adjust to the natural, i.e. to the rate of growth of the labor force plus technical progress. According to Friedman (1970), however, the growth rate of nominal output will adjust to the growth rate of the money supply. If the growth of real output were determined by the growth of labor plus technical progress, then the growth of the money supply would determine the rate of inflation, and we would have a long-run version of monetary neutrality (see Gordon, 1974, pp. 56–7). But can the interest rate be unaffected by the rate of growth of the money supply? If interest *is* affected, then will not the rate of interest affect the rate of accumulation? Monetary growth would then have effects on real growth.

The problem becomes even more complicated when we take account of the fact that saving out of profits is usually much greater than saving out of wages. The distribution of income between profits and wages therefore matters, so that the effects of monetary changes on distribution should be considered. Friedman nowhere discusses these questions, nor do most mainstream economists.

The conclusion we reach is in some ways a startling one, in this age of monetarism. It is that neither monetarists nor mainstream neoclassicals have an adequate theoretical account of money or, consequently, of the role and impact of the state. Monetarists, exemplified by Friedman but by implication including all who accept the NRH, are committed to what mainstream discussion agreed upon years ago as the 'invalid dichotomy', and they have so far failed to show why their models should not be rejected on these eminently Walrasian grounds. But mainstream economics itself is also in trouble, for its integration of monetary and value theory has inherent defects, first in its adoption of an incoherent concept of wealth and 'wealth effects'. Indeed, except in the unlikely case of uniformly proportional money price changes, real balance effects in the product market result in indeterminate demand changes, upsetting traditional results. Secondly, difficulties arise from the inadequate way it considers the effects of changes of the price level on money contracts. Finally, its generally inadequate aggregate model fails to include real balance effects in labor supply and demand decisions, and fails to include an expression for income, i.e. wages plus profits. The conclusion must be that the basic framework is defective. The theory that relates monetary and real economic phenomena will not rise on these foundations.

The consequence is therefore that conservative economists have no grounds for holding that government interference with the free market will result in damage to the economy. The claim that the free market system will tend towards full employment cannot be sustained, since the 'real balance' models, on which it rests, prove to be contradictory. Nor does the real balance effect work for modern monetary systems with contracts and inside money. Indeed, since neoclassical economics has no adequate theory of money, it cannot have an adequate theory of economic policy. The most basic tools of neoclassical theory actually prevent modern economists from understanding the role of the state in managing the economy.

NOTES

1 The short-run demand curve for labor is normally interpreted as the first derivative of the aggregate production function, '. . . showing diminishing marginal returns – as the capital stock is spread over more and more workers' (Branson, 1979, p. 96). The supply of labor is derived from the individual's work/leisure decision: '. . . a worker can allocate hours to work, thus earning real income . . . or to leisure' (p. 104). Then '. . . we can sum all the individual labor-supply curves to get the aggregate labor supply curve for the whole economy' (p. 106). The labor demand curve considers additional workers joining an established workforce; it shows the demand for a varying number of workers, each working a fixed work day, as they join the established pattern. But the supply curve shows the supply by a fixed number of workers (all those over whom the aggregation took place) of a *varying* number of hours per day. The two curves are dimensionally inconsistent. Dennis Robertson once wrote to Keynes, 'Has "classical" theory, in *any* sense, ever tried to apply the notion of marginal disutility in connection with the numbers of work people? It seems to me appropriate in connection with the amount of work done by an individual, but not in connection with the numbers . . .' (Keynes, 1971–, Vol. XIII, p. 500).

2 However, Keynes changed his mind in the light of Dunlop's finding that real wages and employment rise and fall together rather than moving inversely, as neoclassical theory asserts. See Keynes (1971–), Vol. XIV.

3 The government need not lend its surplus by buying new private sector bonds. Instead it could retire old government bonds held in private hands. Either way the funds required by the private sector to finance its investment spending are made available to it.

4 To complete the analysis, the new issuing effects just discussed should be compared with the revaluation of existing government bonds, due to changes in the rate of interest. But this will not change the central point. As on page 52, the outcome will depend on the relative strength of the two effects, which is altogether arbitrary. If the outstanding government debt is small and other conditions are appropriate, the conclusions above hold; otherwise the result may be a convergence back to the initial equilibrium, or a divergent oscillation about it. But whether the system is stable or not does not seem to depend on any plausible economic rationale. In any case it makes little sense to introduce a stable quantity of 'existing government bonds' into a model in which the issuance of those bonds would have provoked violent instability.

5 Perhaps this point about finance can best be seen by separating the multiplier completely from the monetary system. Assume a simplified Kalecki-Robinson system, where I is wholly independent of i; all I is financed by retained earnings, all profits are saved, and all wages consumed. Here the injection–withdrawal condition will be: $G+I = T+P$, where $T = tY$ and $P = Y-wN$. Further, let $I = d+eY$, as in the text. It then follows that $Y = (G+d)/[1+t-wn-e]$, where $n = N/Y$, and is assumed constant as the level of utilization varies. Under these circumstances, a government deficit will

always be exactly matched by the excess of private sector profits over private sector investment (deficits are good for profits), and this will be brought about by the multiplier. Such a *JW* locus would be vertical in (*i*, *Y*) space, and would therefore affect the interest rate without being affacted by it.

6   Patinkin (1965, p. 298) considers the case where inside money moves equi-proportionally with outside, and shows that real balance effects still work under these very special conditions.

7   Even in a pure outside money system there is a problem. For the same reasons that firms and households hold transaction balances, they also hold inventories of goods. A price change that increases their real balances alters the value of their inventories in the opposite direction. There are other problems as well. Pigou and Patinkin held that the wealth effect would result chiefly in spending on regularly produced consumer goods; Friedman and Schwartz argue that the effect might take place first or chiefly as a switch from money to *durables*, including, but not confined to, consumer durables. But, of course, if this latter 'portfolio adjustment effect' involves switching from money to *non-produced assets* – antiques, land, Victorian houses, vintage automobiles – the only extra employment generated, if any, will be among the salesmen and refurbishers of such items. Keynes' essential contention is that, when the value of money rises, there will be no switching to *produced* goods; hence no employment will be generated by a general deflation.

8   Tobin (1980) argues that in the short run, with a given debt structure, the effects of changes in the burden of debt will always dominate real balance or Pigou effects. But in the long run, there is a Pigou Effect, since, he contends, allowing for opportunities to renegotiate debt, an economy with a lower level of prices and wages, but with the same nominal monetary base at every point in time, would have a higher level of activity than an otherwise identical economy with higher prices and money wages. (Pp. 11–12). This is difficult to understand. If the period is long enough for debts to be renegotiated, it is long enough to adjust the supply of 'near monies' to the needs of trade. If prices and money wages are low then the effective money supply will be contracted; if they are higher it will be expanded. Or does Tobin wish to argue that in the long run, there is a rigid relationship between the effective money supply and the monetary base? Neither evidence nor theory supports this. Of course, an expansion of 'near monies' on a given monetary base may cause interest rates to be higher, which might constrict investment, but this would not in any sense be a Pigou Effect. Tobin does not believe 'long run Pigou Effects' are of any practical importance, in any case.

9   When the *IS* curve has a positive slope, which it easily might in a boom period, multiple solutions are possible, and either fiscal or monetary policy will be destabilizing. See Nell (1974), pp. 66 – 90.

10 The origin here is defined by the minimum level of real income and the minimum price level – the bottom point of the trade cycle. So the rectangular hyperbola that approaches the true zero axes asymptotically will appear here as a curve with an intercept on each axis. In this way we eliminate a second but irrelevant intersection of the IS_p line with the LM_p curve. (Even so, a special case can be imagined in which there are two intersections.)

11 This, of course, is just what pure Keynesians deny, as Patinkin (1965) agrees. The excess output will never be produed, for firms will not hire labor, regardless of the real wage, if the output from that labor cannot be sold. This is the origin of the so-called 'disequilibrium school', now represented by Malvinvaud and Clower.

12 More precisely, when real balances have risen, at every level of employment additional labor could produce more additional output, since the higher balances make transactions easier, quicker, etc. Thus the marginal product curve will be shifted up, which implies that for every level of real wage, more labor will be demanded.

13 An important reason for choosing Friedman is that his work provides one of the

earliest, and perhaps the canonical, statement of the 'natural rate hypothesis' (NRH), upon which later work builds. The rational expectations school, which takes its cue from Friedman, draws even more extreme free market conclusions. But the analysis of the rational expectations is built upon the foundation of NRH models, which in turn rest upon the invalid dichotomy. For rational expectations simply states that economic agents will *expect and plan their responses to economic stimuli in the light of what the best available theory predicts*. This assumes, first, that economic actions are planned responses, planned by maximizing methods, to accurately or inaccurately perceived economic stimuli, and, secondly, in many applications that the best models are uniformly known to be the neoclassical models that generate the NRH. The first is a necessary assumption of the method.

14 But Fisher does not actually argue the converse case, that lower inflation will increase unemployment. The stimulating effect of transferences of wealth from passive (creditors) to active (debtors) members of society has been discussed in a long tradition from Hume to Keynes.

15 A similar account of the transmission of monetary effects is given by Laidler (1978), who attributes this view to Tobin, Meiselman, Brunner and Meltzer as well. Note, however, Davidson's (1974) contention that a produced good cannot effectively serve as a store of wealth unless there is an organized spot market for it. If no such markets exist, it is not liquid, and so cannot function as a substitute for money.

16 He adds the footnote: 'Of course this is speaking figuratively. It is not necessary that a single variable be so determined. What is required is an independent relation connecting some subset of the seven variables with exogenous variables, and that subset could in principle consist of seven variables' (Friedman, 1970; in Gordon, 1974, p. 31).

17 Both Patinkin (1965, p. 119) and Tobin (1974, pp. 81 – 3) point out that there is no missing equation when the labor market and the production function are properly taken into consideration. However, only Patinkin points out that this requires Friedman to confront the issue of the invalid dichotomy.

18 Yet this is precisely the form in which Friedman presents his 'Simple Common Model'. His equations 9 – 13 show:

real consumption a function of real income and interest,
real investment a function of nominal interest,
real demand for money a function of real income and interest,
real income equals real consumption plus investment,
demand for money equals supply,
supply of money exogenous or depends on interest.

19 In his reply to Tobin, Friedman calls attention to the fact that his own feelings towards this third approach are ambivalent. Tobin makes the point that by fixing the real interest rate, Friedman ensures that monetary changes will influence prices by shifting the *LM* locus; but the corollary is that deficit spending both increases output and employment and lowers the price level. Friedman replies that he regards the model's treatment of savings and investment as 'unfinished business' (Friedman, 1970; in Gordon, 1974, p. 40). Nevertheless, more than a third of his paper is devoted to analyzing his 'monetary theory of nominal income' or comparing it to other approaches. Since he presents nothing else, it is a fair inference that, unfinished or not, this is where he takes his stand. However, our criticism, unlike Tobin's, does not primarily concern savings and investment; rather our concern is with the connections between real and monetary variables, where once again we hold that Friedman has introduced the invalid dichotomy.

20 This may not really be adequate, for with higher rates of inflation the degree of

certainty attached to the expected value may decline, raising the risk, which would require a larger gap between r and ϱ to compensate.

21   Let s be the average (equals marginal) saving ratio, and v be the capital output ratio. Then aggregate demand is I/s and aggregate supply K/v. Hence $g = I/K = \triangle K/K = s/v$, is the warranted growth rate, along which aggregate demand just equals aggregate supply. Suppose now that $I/s > K/v$; i.e. that $g > s/v$. The demand will be outstripping capacity; with shortages everywhere, businesses will increase their investment, so that $I^* > I$; hence demand will rise still further above capacity. Similarly, if $g < s/v$, business will cut back on investment, and the slump will deepen.

REFERENCES

Blinder, A. S. and Solow, R. M. (1973) 'Analytical foundations of fiscal policy', *Brookings Papers on Economic Activity*.

Branson, W. (1979) *Macroeconomic Theory and Policy*, 2nd edn. New York: Harper & Row.

Davidson, P. (1974) 'A Keynesian view of Friedman's theoretical framework for monetary analysis', in Gordon (1974), pp. 90–110, esp. p. 95.

Fisher, I. (1930) *The Theory of Interest*, New York: Macmillan.

Friedman, M. (1956) 'The quantity theory of money – A restatement', in *Studies in the Quantity Theory of Money*, Chicago : University of Chicago Press.

Friedman, M. (1968) 'The role of monetary policy', *American Economic Review*, Vol. 58 (March), 1–17.

Friedman, M. (1970) 'A theoretical framework for monetary analysis', *Journal of Political Economy*, Vol. 78, 193–238; reprinted in Gordon (1974) pp. 1–63.

Friedman, M. (1971) 'A monetary theory of nominal income' *Journal of Political Economy*, Vol. 79, 323–37.

Friedman, M. (1973) *Unemployment and Inflation*, London: Institute of Economic Analysis Occasional Paper.

Friedman, M. (1974) 'Comments on the critics', in Gordon (1974), pp. 132–77.

Friedman, M. and Schwartz, A. (1963) *A Monetary History of the US*. Princeton, NJ: Princeton University Press.

Gordon, Robert (ed.) (1974) *Milton Friedman's Monetary Framework*, Chicago: University of Chicago Press.

Harrod, R. F. (1948) *Towards a Dynamic Economics*, New York: Macmillan.

Keynes, J. M. (1930) *A Treatise on Money*, London: Macmillan.

Keynes, J. M. (1971–) *Collected Writing of John Maynard Keynes*, London: Macmillan for the Royal Economic Society; Vol. XIII, 1972; Vol. XIV, 1973.

Laidler, D. (1978) 'Money and money income: an essay in the transmission mechanism', *Journal of Monetary Economics*, Vol. 4.

Leijonhufvud, A. (1968) *On Keynesian Economics and the Economics of Keynes*, London: Oxford University Press.

Lloyd, Cliff (1964) 'The real balance effect and the Slutsky equation', *Journal of Political Economy*, Vol. 72 (June).

Nell, E. J. (1974) 'Established en modelos Keynesianos simples', *Cuadenos de Economica*, Vol. 2, no. 3 (April), 66–90.

Niehans, J. (1978) *The Theory of Money*, Baltimore, Md.: Johns Hopkins Press.

Patinkin, D. (1965) *Money, Interest and Prices*, 2nd edn, New York: Harper & Row.

Petri, F. (1982) 'The Patinkin controversy revisited', *Quademi dell' Instituto di Economia*, no. 15, Siena.

Robertson, D. H. (1948) *Money*, 4th edn, London: Pitman.

Solow, R. (1970) *Growth Theory: An Exposition*, London: Oxford University Press.

Tobin, James (1974) 'Friedman's theoretical framework', in Gordon (1974), pp. 77–89.

4 Rational Expectations: Radical Assumptions and Conservative Conclusions

The three papers collected here criticize the rational expectations school on three different grounds. Kregel takes up their inadequate understanding of Keynes, and consequently of monetary equilibrium, arguing that the chief difference is not in the notion of expectations but in the underlying model. Cherry, Clawson and Dean show that natural rate of unemployment models all rely on *ad hoc* assumptions about differential rates of response to economic changes, as between different groups of economic agents. Their assumptions have no foundation in theory, but are essential to the conclusions. Finally, Handa shows that a more reasonable rational expectations approach would allow for differences in theoretical understanding of the economy. Some groups would expect the economy to behave according to neoclassical theory, others according to post-Keynesian or Marxist, etc. Under these circumstances, the conservative conclusions would not follow.

I EXPECTATIONS AND RATIONALITY WITHIN A CAPITALIST FRAMEWORK[1]

Although expectations have long been an integral part of economic theory (see Lachmann, 1976; Kregel, 1977), they have recently been given especial emphasis in certain interpretations of Keynes' *General Theory* (e.g. Shackle, 1973) and by the 'New' Chicago school or the 'rational expectations' (RE) approach. While the approach to expectations in economic theory has never been uniform, the most interesting aspect of this renewed interest is that the two approaches that have given them special emphasis produce diametrically opposed policy conclusions. The present paper seeks to compare the use of expectations in the two approaches. It concludes that, while there is substantial similarity in the use of expectations, their contradictory conclusions stem primarily from differences in the analysis of 'real' factors in the economy.

Keynes, Expectations and Interest Rates

Keynes considered a crucial point of difference between his own *General Theory* and that of the 'Classical' economists to lie in the method of analysis adopted, in particular, to deal with the rate of interest. Following what he considered common business practice, Keynes defined the rate of interest as the 'percentage excess of a sum of money contracted for forward delivery . . . over what we may call the 'spot' or cash price of the sum thus contracted for forward delivery' (1973, p. 222). Rather than equilibrating the supply of current savings and the demand for investment, the rate of interest was seen to be the price that equated the supply of and demand for money for *future delivery*. It was thus very clearly seen to be a forward price determined by expectations of uncertain future market conditions, i.e. the rates expected to rule at future points in time. This formulation brought Hicks' characterization of the rate of interest as hanging by its own bootstraps (Hicks, 1939, p. 164).

Hy Minsky has frequently summed up Keynes' close association with the real world problems of business and finance by calling his work the economics of 'Wall Street', rather than that of the village market-place (e.g. Minsky, 1980). While this representation is conceptually to the point, it is also relevant to recall that Keynes was an economist of the 'City', and in the 'City', unlike the 'Street', the finance of international trade and primary commodity markets took precedence over internal finance. Indeed, one of Keynes' first theoretical contributions was the formulation of what has now come to be known as the 'interest rate parity theorem'. According to this theorem, the market is willing to pay a premium for contracts for future delivery of a particular currency when the return on deposits in that currency is at a premium over the interest rate payable on deposits in other currencies. In ideal conditions this premium equals the forward discount on the spot price of the currency.[2]

Applying this analysis to a closed economy, the interest paid on money could be described as the premium to be paid for parting with it, i.e. for a contract for the future delivery of money. This premium could then be considered as a measure of the preference for holding money. It thus provided the basis of what came to be the theory of liquidity preference. This formulation meant that future rather than spot rates were primary factors determining interest rates. Just as commodity traders make forward contracts with respect to their best expectation of future spot prices, money and financial markets considered the best expectation of future interest rates.

Interest Rate Parity and the Rate of Interest

Keynes' approach to the rate of interest can thus be traced directly to his previous analysis of money and commodity markets. In 'The Forward Market for Forward Exchanges' Keynes defines the premium or discount of future over spot prices in foreign exchange transactions as the preference the market expresses for holding funds in a particular currency in its home market: 'If dollars one month forward are quoted cheaper than spot dollars to a London buyer in terms of sterling, this indicates a preference by the market, on balance, in favour of holding funds in New York during the month in question rather than in London, – *a preference the degree of which is measured by the discount on forward dollars*' (Keynes, 1922, p. 12; 1923, p. 123; italics added).

Keynes then goes on to show how dollar holders can earn a return equal to $(p_f - p_s)/p_s$ by selling dollars spot for pounds at p_s dollars per pound and selling the pounds thus acquired forward at p_f, a premium over spot pounds; the difference represents the return to holding pounds and the measure of what the market is willing to pay for its *preference* for holding dollars in New York. International interest rate differentials are identified as the determinants of this market preference:

> The most fundamental cause is to be found in the interest rates obtainable on 'short' money. . . . If by lending dollars in New York for one month the lender could earn interest at the rate of 5½ per cent per annum, whereas by lending sterling in London for one month he could earn at the rate of 4 per cent, then the preference observed above for holding funds in New York rather than London is wholly explained. That is to say, forward quotations for the purchase of the currency of the dearer money market tend to be cheaper than spot quotations by a percentage per month equal to the excess of the interest which can be earned in a month in the dearer market over what can be earned in the cheaper, (1922, p. 12; 1923, p. 124)

This relation can be written: $(p_f - p_s)/p_s = i_\$ - i_\pounds$ = forward discount on dollars, which can be recognized as the interest rate parity theorem.[3] Putting it another way, the theorem says that the return on funds in different financial centers will be brought into equality by means of adjustment in forward rates (and/or interest rate differential) such that in equilibrium $i_\$ (-f_\$) = i_\pounds + f_\pounds$, where f is the forward premium on sterling (and $f_\$$ is zero when the dollar is the standard of comparison and vice versa).

It was this framework that Keynes applied in the analysis of the rate of interest in the *General Theory*. If, instead of dollars and sterling held in New York and London, we substitute by analogy immediate and deferred command over future consumption (liquidity vs. illiquidity), liquidity (dollar) holders would be faced with a situation in which illiquidity is at a forward premium. The preference of the market for holding funds in liquid form is thus given by the size of the return the market is willing to offer holders of liquid funds to sell their positions spot against a discount for the delivery of future liquidity (it may be easier to think of the price of a unit of liquidity (dollars) expressed in units of illiquidity (sterling) being lower for future delivery of liquidity and thus yielding a future discount on liquidity, or requiring a premium in liquidity terms for future illiquidity). Thus, expressing prices in terms of liquidity (i.e. 'money terms', the equivalent of the indirect quotation in 'dollar terms' in Keynes' example), the holder of liquidity sells his liquid position spot, p_s, against future delivery at price, p_f. The market's preference for liquidity is then given by $(p_f - p_s)/p_s$, which represent the return from holding contracts for future liquidity or for being illiquid (in sterling).

This is precisely the way that Keynes defines the rate of interest on money, the most liquid asset, in the *General Theory*: the percentage excess of a sum of money contracted for forward delivery over the cash or spot price of that sum. Thus, the difference between the price of spot and forward liquidity per cent is the money rate of interest that represents the preference of the market for liquidity in terms of what it is willing to pay holders of liquidity to become illiquid. Since the sport price of the unit of measure is unity, the purchases and sales that determine the liquidity premium are in terms of sums contracted for future delivery: borrowers offer to supply quantities of future liquidity and lenders demand future liquidity. An increase in the demand for loans increases the supply of future liquidity relative to demand, which increases the discount and thus the premium for illiquidity. The interest rate on money could thus be described as being predominantly determined by conditions in the forward market for liquidity, i.e. by 'uncertainty as to the future of the rate of interest' (1973, p. 169); for the willingness to enter into contracts for the future delivery of any asset depends on the expected future spot prices for the periods of time preceding and succeeding the term of the contract.

Up to this point, liquidity and illiquidity could just as easily have been money and bonds. If the analysis stopped at this point it would indeed appear as if the rate of interest had been left hanging by its bootstraps, just as the premium on foreign currency would have been left hanging without the addition of the parity theorem. In the same way as Keynes tried to isolate the fundamental factors determining the exchange market's preference to holding funds in international money markets, he had to explain the factors that determined both the existence of a preference for money over any other asset capable of preserving command over future consumption, as well as the size of that preference. In the analysis of foreign currencies he had appealed to differentials in interest rates on the various national currencies. Could an equivalent be conceived for durable stores of value?

The Rate of Interest and Own Rates of Interest

In his 1932 criticism of Hayek's *Prices and Production*, Piero Sraffa draws on this previous analysis of commodity futures markets to develop the concept of 'commodity rates of interest'.[4] This was accomplished by extending the calculation of the rate of return on holding a national currency. In Keynes, this calculation shows the currency's premium measured in terms of that currency unit itself; Sraffa changes the calculation, showing the future discount or premium from the spot price of any commodity in terms of units of the same commodity. Just as the price of spot liquidity relative to future liquidity gives the market preference for liquidity the expected change in the price of wheat measured in wheat will determine the market preference for being in wheat. Keynes renames this concept the 'own rate of interest' and notes that, just as money rates of interest in national currencies vary across countries, so will the own rates of own interest for different durables. Just as international interest rate differentials are brought into equality by forward discounts and premiums when taken in terms of a common currency unit, the own rates should also be equalized when calculated in terms of a common unit of value. In short, the parity theorem can also be applied through the use of own rates of own interest to the demand for durable stores of value when their returns are in common units.

As in the case of national currencies, it makes little difference what is chosen as the standard, although Keynes notes that because of the possibility of changes in the value of the standard it would be best to have a composite commodity of constant value (1973, p. 255). (Some twenty-five years later, Sraffa proposed for another purpose, a standard commodity which appears nonetheless as a response to Keynes' desired composite.) It was thus necessary to convert all 'own rates' to a single standard, to 'money rates', since the spot and forward prices quoted in commodity markets and that enter the calculation of own rates are in money terms in any case.

Thus, as in Keynes' example of the own rate of wheat interest in the *General Theory*, the money rate of interest is 5 per cent, the forward price of wheat is £107 per 100 bushels. The owner of 100 bushels can thus sell spot for £100 and cover forward at a cost of £107 for 100 bushels for future delivery. Since his £100 will buy £105 for future delivery, he is out of pocket £2 for a loss of 2 per cent. (Alternatively, he could have 'bought' $105/107 \simeq 98$ bushels forward for a return of $(98-100)/100 = -2$ per cent.)

Following the analogy, the market expresses its preference for positions in money to the extent it is willing to offer a wheat premium (sterling premium) in terms of money (dollars) of $(107-100)/100 = 7$ per cent, which in equilibrium is corrected by the -2 per cent own return to yield the same 5 per cent return as could be obtained on money: $i_{money} = i_{wheat} + $ premium.[5] Thus, 'the difference between the "future" and "spot" contracts for a commodity, such as wheat, . . . bears a definite relation to the wheat rate of interest, but, since the forward contract is quoted in terms of money for forward delivery and not in terms of wheat for spot delivery, it also brings in the money rate of interest' (1973, p. 223).[6] This relation is, of course, applicable to all durable assets in the system and provides a perfectly general theory of the demand for durable assets and their returns. There is nothing to indicate that it was meant only for money and bonds. Nor is it left hanging by its bootstraps any more than the parity theorem.

Own Interest Rate Parity

This reformulation of Wicksell's natural rate analysis provided the framework for Keynes' criticism of Say's Law. Keynes believed this alleged law to be in error because it postulates 'that the owner of wealth desires a capital asset *as such*, whereas what he really desires is its *prospective yield*' (1973, p. 212). This is, of course precisely the basis upon which the parity theorem allocates command over future consumption across durables according to their prospective yields or the own rate corrected for the premium or discount. This implies that both existing and newly produced assets compete in satisfying wealth holders' desires for the highest possible prospective yield. Keynes generalized the concept of 'own rates' by identifying three components: q, the prospective yield due to a position in the asset; c, the costs associated with maintaining a position in any asset in order to receive q, and l, the liquidity premium. The return considered by investors would then be composed of $(q-c)+l$ in proportions that would be determined by the nature of the durable in question. For purposes of comparison the rates for the various assets had to be converted into common units: 'money terms'. This Keynes did by introducing a, 'the expected percentage appreciation (or depreciation)' in the relative price of the asset in money terms. The rates that must be compared are thus composed of two elements, the 'own rate', r, and a or $\pm a + (q-c) + l$, which, in equilibrium, should be driven to equality with the return on any other durable. As in the interest parity theorem, the premium or discount, a, in money plus the own rate in money equals the rate of interest on money. Dealing with two currencies (as we argued above, p. 99), the relation is $i_\$ = i_\pounds + f_\pounds$ (with the dollar as standard). This becomes $i = r_w + f_w$ in the money and wheat case (above, p. 99), which, in Keynes' more general terminology, reduces to $i = \pm a + (q-c) + l = r + f$ with a, the discount or premium, serving to equate the difference between the rate of interest on money and the rates of interest on other assets. Thus, the determinants of the relative differences between spot and future prices of the system are the differences in the own rates of return of the assets under consideration.

Own Rates and the Level of Output

Keynes thus identifies own interest rate differentials as the basic factor in the determination of the discount or premium for durable assets. This raises the question of the determinants, first of the own rates and then of the process of adjustment to equilibrium. It is in the responses to these questions that Keynes' theory differs fundamentally from that of Wicksell:

> Put shortly, the orthodox theory maintains that the forces which determine the common value of the marginal efficiency of various assets are independent of money, which has, so to speak, no autonomous influence, and that prices move until the marginal efficiency of money, i.e. the rate of interest, falls into line with the common value of the marginal efficiency of other assets as determined by other forces. My theory, on the other hand maintains that this is a special case and that over a wide range of possible cases almost the opposite is true, namely, that the marginal efficiency of money is determined by forces partly appropriate to itself, and that prices move until the marginal efficiency of other assets falls into line with the rate of interest. (Keynes, 1937, p. 147, 1950, p. 420)

Thus Keynes puts emphasis on the role of a and r as they move into equality with i, rather than on the role of i and a in adapting to r. This adjustment process was already evident in *A Treatise on Money* (1930). The main difference from that treatment lies in the emphasis given in the *General Theory* to forward prices.

The shift of emphasis from markets that set spot prices to future market prices, joined to the analysis of the rate of investment in the *Treatise*, produced the basis for Keynes' new analysis of interest and investment:

> Entrepreneurs are induced to embark on the production of Fixed Capital or deterred from doing so by their expectations of the profit to be made.... Professor Schumpeter's explanation of the major movements may be unreservedly accepted.... Besides these we also have fluctuations in the rate of investment due to a change in the rate of interest.... A change in the rate of interest will affect the advantages of owning a particular piece of Fixed Capital so long as the income to be derived from it remains unchanged. But there will be no reason for this income to be changed until the supply of Fixed Capital has been changed relatively to the demand for it. The process of changing the supply of Fixed Capital, until the income derived from it is again in equilibrium with the rate of interest, amounts, however, to the same thing as a change in the rate of investment. (Keynes, 1930, Vol. II, pp. 95–7)

Keynes thus outlines two factors that influence investment and its fluctuations:

1 Expectations as expressed in future prices to be received for the output of investment projects;
2 A change in the supply of investment goods due to a change in interest rates, given expectations.

As Keynes notes, the two factors will be interrelated. As discussed elsewhere (Kregel, 1976a), Keynes frequently assumes implicitly in the *General Theory* that 'short-period expectations are always fulfilled' and that long-period expectations are constant. Thus Keynes' discussion primarily concerns the influence of the second effect, although change in the status of general expectation is never excluded. This is equivalent to the discussion of the effect of a change in a on the value of r, the own rate of return.

Assume that an increase in purchasing power is used to buy the asset with the highest of all available prospective yields. The initial effect will be to increase the spot price of this asset, which, given its future price, reduces a as $(p_f - p_s)/p_s$ falls. With given costs of production, this will eventually lead to conditions of 'backwardation', that is, where the suitably discounted forward (or flow supply) price lies below the spot price. This reverses the initial situation by increasing the demand for newly produced assets and reducing spot demand. Thus the increased production of the asset will lead to a lower value of q until the return on the asset (its $a+(q-c)+l$) becomes equal to that of all competing assets, which will result from the combined effect of the change in the spot price (until it exceeds the supply price) and then an increase in the supply price (due to the effect of diminishing returns on higher output) leading to a fall in q until the overall return from a position in that asset has fallen to what could be earned in any other.[7]

In conditions of equal return on all assets, on the other hand, if there is a uniform increase in the demand for all assets and the changes in the own rates are unequal due to different production conditions, then the rates of change of new output must be non-uniform and/or a must adjust to equalize the differences in yields until production can adjust.

Keynes' criticism of Say's Law could thus be completed in this framework given the assumption that there is some asset whose own rate is fixed, or that falls more slowly than any other when the demand for it increases. The own rate of return on this asset will then set both the level of total production and the level for each durable for, as long as the return on this asset falls more slowly, it will be preferred to all others – it will become, in Keynes' words, 'a sink for purchasing power'. This is simply Keynes' argument concerning the money rate of interest 'ruling the roost' because it sets the standard of return that all other assets must achieve if they are to be purchased for their return and thus the conditions in which the relation between and future prices will be such as to cause them to be newly produced. From this follows Keynes' definition of money as that durable whose return falls most slowly with an increase in the demand for it and his definition of a 'non-monetary' economy as one 'in which there is no asset for which the liquidity–premium is always in excess of its carrying costs' (1973, p. 239). For such an economy would have full employment as its natural position and Say's Law would prevail.[8]

However, in Keynes' system a fall in the rate of interest leads to a rise in spot prices, given expectations, relative to future prices or an adjustment in a. The change in spot prices relative to flow supply prices leads to new production, rising supply prices and a reduction in $(q-c)+l$, i.e. an adjustment in both a and r, irrespective of any effect on expectations.

The Efficacy of Monetary vs. Fiscal Policy

It is well known that Keynes was sceptical about changes in interest rates leading to full employment, just as sceptical, indeed, as he was about wage reductions increasing employment, for he considered one as the inverse of the other. The reason for this doubtful efficacy of monetary policy in assuring full employment is to be found in the theory of liquidity preference as given above. Since the interest rate itself is determined primarily by expectations of future interest rates (there are no technical production constraints as with physical assets), under certain conditions it might be possible that traders might believe that an increase in the money supply will be only temporary so that the demand for money will become identical with the supply. Hicks would have called such conditions 'inelastic expectations' (see Davidson and Kregel, 1980, who borrow Hicks' 1939 terminology), but they could just as easily be described as 'rational'. If the best information available does not lead the market to believe that future interest rates will move, then neither will future prices or outputs (although absolute prices may adjust).

Keynes further believed that it is possible for the own rates on durables to be so influenced by the state of general expectation that the reduction in the rate of interest that will be required to induce new production will be below that which a private enterprise profit-maximizing banking system could rationally support. He was also sceptical about market reactions (see the explanation of the determination of liquidity preference in the *General Theory*, 1973, pp. 201–3).

It would be easier to influence output and employment, Keynes argued, by acting directly on one of the basic components of own rates – expectations of future prices relative to costs. If producers are more inclined to believe their own cash box than financial market analysts' announcements about monetary policy, the most expeditious method would be direct government expenditures to increase the flow of spending. Given the multiplier, the whole process would appear to producers as an increase in the own rate of return on capital assets. With given interest rates, a must be falling with spot prices rising relative to future prices, which have a limit in discounted flow supply prices. Even considering the rise in supply prices due to higher output, the entire rise in q caused by the expectation of higher yields will not be eliminated and investment will expand. With excess capacity, the dampening effect of diminishing returns on supply prices is lessened (and to a similar extent the pick-up in new investment).

When this process works too well, however, as Hy Minsky has argued, and producers actually believe that q never stops rising, they may produce a financial structure that is adequate only to the continuance of such conditions, so that even the smallest setback brings the whole house of cards tumbling down. The method of direct intervention on the state of expectations may err in being too successful. This may lead entrepreneurs to be more prudent in their responses to what their cash box tells them about future yields – and their expectations become more important. They may become just as jaded as their compatriots in financial markets concerning the reliability of government pronouncements about expenditure. In such a context, the role of monetary policy is to prevent the construction of the house of cards and, when it fails, to try to keep the collapse as circumscribed as possible, i.e. to act to direct entrepreneurs' expectations. One does well to recall Keynes' insistence on his different method of analysis and that he was not averse to using monetary policy to temper general expectations (see Moggridge and Howson, 1974; Peden, 1980).

In summary, two aspects of the relationship between expectations and prices can be discerned in Keynes' *General Theory*. At one level prices are determined by interest rates on money, given expectations that determine future prices:

$$i = \pm a + (q-c) + l. \tag{1}$$

Here a change in monetary policy can influence prices and output only if it changes i. While Keynes accepted that it could, he was highly sceptical that it could influence i in a manner which would produce full employment. Secondly, there is the state of general expectation that determines q through the determination of the relation of future costs and prices for the output of a durable asset. Expectations enter into the determination of prices at two levels, first in the relation of spot to future prices represented in a, and second in terms of the future prices expected for the output of producers' goods relative to expected costs. In terms of the relation of future to spot prices, Keynes states:

> It must be remembered that future prices, in so far as they are anticipated, are already reflected in current prices, after allowing for various considerations of carrying costs and of opportunities of production in the meantime which relate the spot and forward price of a given commodity. Thus we must suppose that the spot and forward price structure has already brought into equilibrium the relative advantages, as estimated by the holder, of holding money and other existing forms of wealth. (Keynes, 1979, pp. 82–3)

This statement implies that

$$p_s = p_f \text{ (or } E_t(P_{t+1}) = P_{t+1}) \quad \text{and} \quad a = 0 \tag{2}$$

Condition (2) means that p_f is the correct expectation of the future spot price expressed by the given state of expectation and thus that own rates equal the rate of interest on money (the money rate equals the 'natural' rate). It is on this basis that Keynes argues that equilibrium can be established at any level of output and employment because, given the state of expectation, own rates will adjust to the rate of interest. Traditional remedies – lower wages or monetary expansion – could achieve full employment only if they could affect i or r so as to produce $i=r$ *at full employment*. Since there is a lower limit beyond which monetary policy is ineffective in reducing the rate of interest, and policies to cut wages only serve to make it more profitable to postpone production, Keynes believed that the most efficient method is direct intervention on the flow of spending to affect q by means of an impact on both spot prices relative to future prices and yield relative to cost of investment goods: i.e. to create the backwardation conditions necessary to set the multiplier process in motion.

Rationality and Price Expectation

The representation of Keynes' *General Theory* given in the preceding sections was formulated so as to allow for the treatment of the interaction of expectations, prices and output as found in what has come to be called the rational expectations (RE) approach. Before setting out on such an exercise, we shall present a sketch of what appear to be the basic foundations of that approach.

It is possible to distinguish two separate strands in the RE literature (as regards our concerns here – there are, of course, many other sub-strands). The difference is akin to the traditional separation between micro and macro theory. The first stems from Muth's (1961) explanation of the formation of expectations about variations in particular prices in commodity markets. This approach could be characterized as claiming not only that people behave *as if*, for example, the traditional perfectly competitive model of price determination were true, but that such a model actually reflects the natural order of the world and that agents eventually discover the existence of this order and base their expectations of prices on calculations of the minimum variance unbiased forecasts generated from such a model. This is appreciably more than Friedman ever claimed for 'positive economics' and comes close to providing a physio-psychological foundation for the correspondence principle. On the other hand, from a Marshallian point of view, it might be described as assuming that the prices that equilibrate the market in both the short and long period are the same. This strand has generated the work on the 'principle of efficient markets' and might be summarized as

$$P_t = E_t(P_{t+1}) \quad \text{or} \quad \Delta P_t = E_t(P_{t+1}) - P_t. \tag{3}$$

Such a description of price formation does not in any way assume or imply perfect certainty about future events, yet it does imply perfect knowledge may be gained about the structural relations of the economic system that generate these future events. What will occur, of course, need not be known if the informational input and the decision-making structure that produces the events are known.

The second strand comes from the macro explanation of unemployment known as the 'search' theories based on the natural rate of unemployment hypothesis first formulated by David Hume and popularized by Friedman in his AEA Presidential address in 1967. This development was closely related to the discussions of the Phillips curve in the mid-1960s. This approach is based on a distinction between real and nominal magnitudes such as proposed in some definitions of money illusion. It turns on the difficulty of distinguishing between changes in relative prices and changes in the nominal price level in the absence of perfect information. Only when agents correctly discount the changes in nominal prices in taking their supply decisions will they be acting rationally, i.e. in response to changes in relative prices. There is presumed to be some future date (the long run?) at which agents will have gathered sufficient information about the system to be able correctly to anticipate changes in nominal prices and thus respond only to changes in real magnitudes. It must be presumed, but it is not always specified,[9] that the structure and the behavioral functions that produce the 'rational' or 'natural' actions are the same as those employed in the micro version, i.e. the competitive general equilibrium model. This second strand may be summarized:

$$P_{t+1} = E_t(P_{t+1}) \quad \text{or} \quad \Delta P_t = P_{t+1} - E_t(P_{t+1}), \tag{4}$$

which can be written, for easier comparison with (3), $P_t = E_{t-1}(P_t)$ or $\Delta P_t = P_t - E_{t-1}(P_t)$. Given the previous hypothesis (3), which says that today's price fully reflects all available information about possible future events, (4) indicates that future prices can indeed be anticipated perfectly given time and knowledge of the underlying structure (now of the entire economic system). Of course, in the limit, if both the efficient market hypothesis and the natural rate hypothesis hold, equilibrium prices, or the future path of equilibrium prices, are given in the present, or at most should change only once from some initial value and there is then nothing that should cause them to deviate from these 'natural' values. This explains the scepticism concerning the long-run efficacy of policy intervention to shift the system from these values. Just as money is neutral in its long-run effect on relative prices in the classical monetarist scheme (so that monetary policy is destabilizing in the short run), in the full RE scheme (natural rate plus efficient markets) fiscal policy will be neutral in the long run and destabilizing in the short run, for it can at best produce only temporary displacement from 'natural' values.

Thus, the short run, where information may be imperfect or not fully perceived and money illusion is possible, may exhibit divergence from equilibrium natural values because of the possibility of what is referred to in some versions of RE as 'unanticipated' changes, i.e. what are by definition exogenous shocks or changes in the structure of the system. Indeed, the RE approach has itself suggested that policy actions may be further destabilizing in the sense that they influence the very structure of the system. If this is correct, as Keynes would have accepted for example in relation to the behavior of trades unions in money-wage bargaining, then, as long as such changes are not systematic, policy will have some long-term effect, although it may not be predictable (for example, Joan Robinson has frequently referred to 'demand management' as a 'blunt instrument'). This recognition leads to a rather different result, with stability at under-full employment; there is no tendency for the system to move to full employment, which is considered to be a highly unstable position: 'The general upshot of our argument is that the point of full employment, so far from being an equilibrium resting place, appears to be a precipice over which, once it has reached the edge, the value of money must plunge into a bottomless abyss . . . a policy of maintaining stable prices . . . is by no means equivalent to a policy of maintaining stable employment' (Robinson, 1937, pp. 189, 195). Agreement is substantial here, as both approaches accept positions of equilibrium at less than full employment and the possibility of structural change when the system is policy-induced to full employment, which neither views as a natural equilibrium.

The two strands may then be summarized as:

$$P_t = E_t(P_{t+1}) = E_{t-1}(P_t) \tag{5a}$$

or

$$\Delta P_t = [E_t(P_{t+1}) - P_t] + (P_{t+1} - E_t(P_{t+1})). \tag{5b}$$

If prices are correctly anticipated, $P_t = E_{t-1}(P_t)$ and the second term of (5b) is 0 (natural values prevail). If markets are efficient, $E_t(P_{t+1}) = P_t$ and the first term is 0, so $\Delta P_t = 0$ with $E_{t-1} = E_t$ and $P_t = P_{t+1}$. There is no reason why the first term should not be zero, nor does there seem to be any easy way of showing that it does not, while the second term may be non-zero in the case of short-period or unanticipated shocks.

Expectations and Monetary Equilibrium

As already noted above, the set of relations between expectations and prices set out in the *General Theory* may serve to produce conclusions just as pessimistic as those of RE concerning the efficacy of policy measures in producing full employment. A more basic similarity is to be found, however, in the acceptance by both approaches of the efficient markets hypothesis. As already pointed out, Keynes' equilibrium condition of $a=0$ (see also Sraffa, 1932, p. 50: 'In equilibrium the spot and forward price coincide, for cotton as for any other commodity; and all the "natural" or commodity rates are equal to one another, and to the money rate' [10]) is formally equivalent to (3), which is equivalent to the long-run solution behind the natural rate hypothesis: $i=r$. The relative prices generated by the two approaches should then be the same, except for one crucial difference. The RE approach in its natural rate guise appears to claim that there is one unique level of output and employment associated with the $i=r$ equilibrium corresponding to $E_t(P_{t+1}) = P_{t+1}$.

It will be recalled that Sraffa's formulation of the commodity rates of interest used above was in criticism of Hayek's version of Wicksell's notion of monetary equilibrium based on the equality of the natural and the money market rate of interest. Hayek had argued in favor of a 'neutral' banking policy, which is similar to the monetary 'rules' proposed by some writers on the basis of RE analysis. It was also by means of the use of 'own rates' that Keynes was led to a rejection of Wicksell's monetary rule for stability. A brief outline of Wicksell's natural rate theory and Keynes' reasons for rejecting it may thus aid in isolating the point at which the use of expectations in the two approaches diverges.

The characterization of Wicksell's theory that best suits present purposes is that given in Hicks (1977, pp. 66ff). There is an initial position in which prices are stable so $E_t(P_{t+1})=P_t$ and $E_{t-1}(P_t)=P_t$. There is an average, $\hat{r}$, of all the individual natural rates of return weighted in the same way as the price index, P, which is equal to the rate of interest, i, charged for bank lending. In Keynes' terms this position would be written as $\hat{r} = (q-c) + l$ (omitting summations and weights) with $a=0$ so $i=\hat{r}$. The efficient market hypothesis is given by $p_s-p_f=0=a$.

Now assume that i is lower at $i°< r$. To preserve equilibrium with $i°=a°+\hat{r}$, a must be lower at $a°$. Since expectations of future prices are unchanged, this is achieved by a rise in P_t (or P_s in Keynes' spot price terms). This causes $p^\circ_s > p_f^{11}$, which may dampen the demand for loans and thus stabilize p_s at the point where $i^\circ = a^\circ + \hat{r}$. Thus, what Hicks calls a 'pseudo-natural rate' may be established at i°, which exhibits pseudo price stability at p°_s. But this also implies that $E_t(P_{t+1}) - P_t^\circ < 0$ and over time there should be a revision of present period expectations of next period's prices, which should cause p_f to rise. Thus a° falls back towards $a=0$, which causes $i^\circ < a + \hat{r}$ and the same process resumes from a higher price level. Over a period of time, rational agents learn to expect price rises and a stabilizes at $a^\circ = 0$ and prices rise at a rate equal to $\hat{r} - i^\circ$. Since $\hat{r}$ is not affected by this process, output and employment are unchanged from their natural levels. This would seem to be a valid representation of the RE explanation of the natural rate in the 'long run' when a has ceased to fluctuate between $a=0$ and $a^\circ = \hat{r} - i^\circ$ and p_s and p_f both rise at a uniform rate and E is in terms of rates rather than levels, with real output and employment at their natural levels.

Keynes' criticism of Wicksell starts by pointing out that if money is the standard for measuring own rates (Keynes' proxy for Wicksell's natural rates) or marginal efficiencies of various assets, then the rate of interest $i = a + l$, with l the liquidity premium on money and $a=0$ by construction. For all other durable assets the interest rate parity theorem requires $i = a - r$ and monetary equilibrium requires $a=0$, where $r = (q-c) + l$ and $p_f - p_s = 0 = a$. In the argument concerning the rate of interest on money, ruling the roost implies that an increase in the demand for any durable store of value, given the liquidity premium on money, should cause a process of adjustment that involves changes in a but no change in aggregate output or employment, irrespective of the initial level.

In the case of a lower rate of interest due to a shift in liquidity preference, however, this would produce $i^\circ = l < r + a$ and a must be reduced by spot prices rising relative to forward prices. If backwardation occurs, a combination of new production and price adjustment will take place that reduces r until $i^\circ = l = a + r^\circ$ with $r^\circ < r = i^\circ < i$ and $a = 0 = p_s - p_f$ (although both p_s and p_f may be higher). This led Keynes to the conclusion that 'for every rate of interest there is a level of employment for which that rate is the "natural" rate, in the sense that the system will be in equilibrium with that rate of interest and that level of employment' (1973, p. 242). He then goes on to redefine Wicksell's equilibrium as the 'neutral' rate 'defined as the rate of interest which prevails in equilibrium when output and employment are such that the elasticity of employment as a whole is zero' (1973, p. 243). Here a change in the rate of interest brings about the possibility of a finite rise in prices, a fall in the natural rate and a higher level of natural output and employment – the opposite of Wicksell (and RE), which Keynes considered to be a special case holding at the 'neutral rate' of interest. In this special case, with a zero elasticity of employment, both Keynes and Wicksell reach the same conclusions for a change in the rate of interest, while Keynes and RE agree that the rate of interest cannot be relied upon to produce full employment if the equilibrium is at less than full employment.

Conclusions

It would thus seem that the point of contention between Keynes' approach and the RE approach lies in Wicksell's concept of monetary equilibrium. Since the concept was first proposed, it has received widespread criticism. Robertson, for example, in a criticism that foreshadowed RE, notes that the ex-ante-ex-post formulation

> does not of itself . . . afford us a firm basis for a criterion of monetary equilibrium. For suppose, in an economy hitherto stable, the public as a whole rightly anticipates an abnormal expansion, or a contraction, in the money income stream, and expands or contracts its ex-ante savings to match; the ex-ante and ex-post savings will remain equal to one another and to realized investment in spite of the disequilibrating expansion or contraction of the income-stream. (Robertson, 1959, p. 35)

More directly, the concept of monetary equilibrium does not seem to answer the question of (a) the determinants of the rate of interest, or (b) the validity of the classical mechanism by which the interest rate equilibrates saving and investment only at a single, unique, natural rate of output and employment.[12]

The RE approach would seem, at least implicitly, to require a foundation of Robertson's productivity and thrift as the determinants of the interest rate and Wicksell's monetary equilibrium to determine the natural rate. It is in this latter point that the basic disagreement is to be found. It is interesting to note that this disagreement is in no way dependent on assumptions about expectations. In this sense, RE could be characterized as a theory that presumes that agents act as if classical economics were true. It is also interesting to note that this is exactly the result that Keynes hoped to achieve through the results of the policy implications of his own theory (see 1973, ch. 24).

The point of divergence is then to be found in the analysis of the rate of interest. Keynes believes that r is variable up to the 'neutral' rate, while for Wicksell it is fixed at that rate. It is thus possible for Keynes to assert that the rate of interest can affect the level of output yet be ineffective in producing full employment when money has a 'natural' rate that is fixed or declines more slowly than the own rate of other assets. This brings the argument back to the definition of the rate of interest as the price for the future delivery of liquidity. If the future is uncertain, and even if markets are efficient, given expectations, the interest rate may set (via the own rate parity theorem) spot and future prices such that equilibrium may emerge at a position of less than full employment, indeed at any level of employment. Rational expectations in Muth's sense cannot challenge this result. This can be done only by a demonstration that the rate of interest will always, as the result of a 'neutral' monetary policy, be such as to produce relative prices at which investment equals full employment saving. Indeed, for all the new-fangled notions about expectations, we have not come very far from the debates that exercised Robertson, Keynes, von Mises and Hayek. Having recognized what the argument is about, perhaps fruitful discussion can now take place between the two proponents of 'expectations'.

NOTES

1 I am indebted to Professor Otto Steiger of the University of Bremen for helpful discussion on the differences and similarities between Keynes' use of own rates and Wicksell's concept of natural rates and Myrdal's criticism of the idea of monetary equilibrium. An initial version of this paper was presented at the 1980 American Economic Association Meetings in Denver, Colorado, and I am grateful for comments received at that time. Related themes are treated in Kregel (1982) and Part II of Kregel (1983) in particular the articles of Kregel and Nell.

2 See Keynes (1922), p. 12: 'What Fixes Forward Rates?'. Keynes' own contributions to a series of special editions of the *Manchester Guardian Commercial* entitled 'Reconstruction in Europe' were republished in 1923 as *A Tract on Monetary Reform*. Sraffa collaborated on the series as an expert on banking and financial matters; see, 'Italian Banking Today', 7 December 1922, pp. 675–6.

3 The terminology may confuse. Keynes followed standard market practice of 'indirect' quotation when he describes the options open to a dollar holder in London, i.e. by giving the dollar price per pound sterling as the price of a dollar. Thus a dollar discount is represented by a future price in excess of spot. The standard practice for currencies other than sterling, however, is to quote in 'European' terms, i.e. per dollar. The forward premium or discount is then against dollars for forward delivery. Changing to European (sterling) terms, a dollar discount becomes a sterling premium in Keynes' terminology.

4 Sraffa's main criticisms of Hayek, who had attempted to show that a non-'neutral' bank policy would lead to divergence of rates of return between investment and consumption good production, was (a) that such a divergence could easily occur in a non-monetary as a monetary economy, for in neither is there any reason for all the own rates to be uniform, and (b) that the 'divergence of rates is essential to the effecting of the transition (from one composition of demand to another) as is the divergence of prices from cost of production; it is, in fact another aspect of the same thing' in a monetary economy that is not stationary (Sraffa, 1932, p. 50).

5   Or, identically, the discount on money. Sraffa's own formulation has the commodity rate equal to the interest rate on money plus the excess or minus the deficiency of spot to future prices, e.g. $-2\% = 5\% -7\%$.

6   It is interesting to note that in Wicksell's approach (1936, pp. 103–4) to the natural rate of interest he first assumes that it is expressed through the actions of producers who borrow, pay wages and other costs, sell and repay in kind and that the rate thus determined will be identical when contracts and all other transactions involved are assumed to be in terms of money. Myrdal (1939) highlights the weakness of assuming that money is autonomous from the real determinants of the natural rate: 'for credit is a causal factor not only for the price *level* but also for price relations, which are partly determined by the profitability of business and therefore, by the supply and demand for credit' (p. 16); 'The interest rate must obviously be of central importance to this problem since it embodies in a certain way, the *exchange relation* between commodities in general at two different points in time' (p. 23). He thus suggests that the natural rates in a monetary economy would not be the same as those in an economy that operates in kind. This may be viewed as a part of the general recognition by both Keynes and the Swedish theorists of the necessity of integrating the money and real sectors, e.g. as in Keynes' proposed 'monetary production economy'.

7   See Keynes (1930), Vol. II, pp. 140ff for a more precise formulation of the effect of excess stocks on the relation of spot to future prices and the trade cycle. Keynes' use of 'contango' and 'backwardation' as determinants of changes in the volume of output is fully explained in Davidson (1972), pp. 99ff. The combined effect of changes in future, spot and supply prices on the level of output is described in detail in Davidson (1974).

8   It is here that the specification of the essential properties of money become crucial (see the treatments in Davidson, 1972, 1980; Minsky, 1975). The argument here seeks to lend further support to the position (see Kregel, 1980; Nell, 1983) that the essential properties of money cannot be used as the basis for the reformulation of the 'demand for money', but that they must be considered within the context of the essential properties of interest; this requires an expression of liquidity preference that explains why the marginal efficiency of money is sticky or falls less rapidly than the marginal efficiencies of other assets. This is conceptually different from the traditional 'demand for money', which is simply the demand half of the market that determines the spot price of money. Keynes rather places emphasis on the theory of liquidity preference as the explanation of the determinant of the price of the future delivery of liquidity.

9   See the clear statement by Hahn (1980) as well as his doubts about the possibility of agents satisfying all the conditions required for general competitive equilibrium. It is interesting to note that Friedman (1980) responds to the Hahn-Neild (1980) challenge in *The Times* concerning the applicability of the GE model as the theoretical underpinning for his approach by suggesting that they are challenging not the quantity theory but the Phillips curve.

10 As I have suggested elsewhere (Kregel, 1976b) this may be considered as the root of Sraffa's statement (1960) that appeals to the money rate of interest as the determinant of the rate of profits in his system, for, in equilibrium, spot and future prices are equal and the own rates of return that could be calculated for a 'Sraffa system' would, in equilibrium, equal the rate of interest on money. Also see Nell (1983).

11 Hick's assumption that forward prices do not immediately adjust would seem to be supported by Wicksell's observation (1936, p. 93) that forward prices are not to be confused with the spot prices that will actually rule in the future, but that the former, once contracted, hold until the contract is met.

12 Garegnani (1978–79), in an article originally published in Italian in 1964, was one

of the first to suggest that the real point of debate concerns the analysis of the rate of interest. He argues that Keynes' use of liquidity preference is based on 'subjective' factors and thereby leaves open the way for the classical theory to re-establish itself. It seems obvious that he is referring to what is now called the neoclassical synthesis, which reaches its highpoint in the neoclassical theories of growth, but the argument also seems to apply to RE. It is interesting to note that Keynes also believes that the crucial point is in the theory of interest. In a 1937 article of much greater importance than the oft-quoted response to Viner in the *Quarterly Journal* (reprinted in Keynes, 1973, Vol. XIV, pp. 109–123), Keynes tries to isolate his differences from classical theory as well as to highlight the similarities (see Keynes, 1937, reprinted in Keynes, 1973, Vol. XIV, pp. 101–8; for an interpretation, also see Nell, 1983).

REFERENCES

Davidson, P. (1972), *Money and the Real World*. London: Macmillan (2nd edn, 1978).

Davidson, P. (1974) 'Disequilibrium market adjustment: Marshall revisited', *Economic Inquiry*, Vol. 12 (June).

Davidson, P. (1980) 'The dual-faceted nature of the Keynesian revolution: money and money wages in unemployment and production flow prices', *Journal of Post Keynesian Economics*, Vol. 2 (Spring).

Davidson, P. and Kregel, J. A. (1980) 'Keynes' paradigm: a theoretical framework for monetary analysis', E. J. Nell, ed., in *Growth, Profits and Property*, New York: Cambridge University Press.

Friedman, M. (1980) 'Monetarism: a reply to the critics', *The Times* (London), 3 March.

Garegnani, P. (1978–79) 'Notes on consumption, investment and effective demand', *Cambridge Journal of Economics*, Vols 1 and 2 (December and March).

Hahn, F. H. (1980) 'Monetarism and economic theory', *Economica*, Vol. 47 (February).

Hahn, F. H. and Neild, R. (1980) 'Monetarism: why Mrs Thatcher should beware', *The Times* (London) 25 February.

Hicks, J. R. (1939) *Value and Capital*, Oxford: Clarendon Press.

Hicks, John (1977) *Economic Perspectives*, Oxford: Clarendon Press.

Keynes, J. M. (1922) 'The forward market in foreign exchanges', *Manchester Guardian Commercial*, 'Reconstruction in Europe', 20 April, pp. 11–15; reprinted in Keynes (1923).

Keynes, J. M. (1923) *A Tract on Monetary Reform*, London: Macmillan.

Keynes, J. M. (1930) *A Treatise on Money*, London: Macmillan.

Keynes, J. M. (1936) *The General Theory of Employment, Interest and Money*, London: Macmillan; reprinted in *Collected Writing of John Maynard Keynes*, Vol. VII, 1973.

Keynes, J. M. (1971–) *Collected Writing of John Maynard Keynes*, London: Macmillan for the Royal Economic Society; Vol. XIV, 1973; Vol. XXIX, 1979.

Keynes, J. M. (1937) 'The theory of the rate of interest'; reprinted in W. Fellner and B. F. Haley, eds, *Readings in the Theory of Income Distribution*, London: Allen & Unwin, 1950.

Kregel, J. A. (1976a) 'Economic methodology in the face of uncertainty', *Economic Journal*, Vol. 86 (June).

Kregel, J. A. (1976b) 'Sraffa et Keynes: Le taux d'intérê et le taux de profit', *Cahiers d'Economie Politique*, No. 3.

Kregel, J. A. (1977) 'On the existence of expectations in English neoclassical economics', *Journal of Economic Literature*, Vol. 15 (June).

Kregel, J. A. (1980) 'Markets and institutions as features of a capitalistic production system', *Journal of Post Keynesian Economics*, Vol. 3 (Fall).

Kregel, J. A. (1982) 'Money, expectations and relative prices in Keynes' monetary equilibrium', *Economie Appliquée*, Vol. 35; No. 3, pp. 449–65.

Kregel, J. A., ed. (1983) *Distribution, Effective Demand and International Economic Relations*, London: Macmillan.

Lachmann, L. M. (1976) 'From Mises to Shackle: an essay', *Journal of Economic Literature*, Vol. 14 (March).

Minsky, H. P. (1975) *John Maynard Keynes*, New York: Columbia University Press.

Minsky, H. P. (1980) 'Money, financial markets, and the coherence of a market economy', *Journal of Post Keynesian Economics*, Vol. 3 (Fall), pp. 21–31.

Moggridge, D. and Howson, S. (1974) 'Keynes on monetary policy, 1910–1946', *Oxford Economic Papers*, Vol. 26 (July).

Muth, J. (1961) 'Rational expectations and the theory of price movements', *Econometrica*, Vol. 29, No. 3, pp. 315–35.

Myrdal, G. (1939) *Monetary Equilibrium*, London: Hodge & Co.

Nell, E. J. (1983) 'Keynes after Sraffa', in Kregel (1983).

Peden, G. C. (1980) 'Keynes, the Treasury and unemployment in the later nineteen–thirties', *Oxford Economic Papers*, Vol. 32 (March), pp. 1–18.

Robertson, D. H. (1940) 'Mr Keynes and the rate of interest', in W. Fellner and B. F. Haley, eds, *Readings in the Theory of Income Distribution*, London: Allen & Unwin, 1950.

Robertson, D. H. (1959) *Lectures on Economic Principles*, Vol. III, London: Staples Press.

Robinson, J. (1937) *Essays in the Theory of Employment*, London: Macmillan.

Shackle, G. L. S. (1973) 'Keynes and today's Establishment in economic theory: a view', *Journal of Economic Literature*, Vol. 11 (June).

Sraffa, P. (1932) 'Dr Hayek on money and capital', *Economic Journal*, Vol. 42 (March).

Sraffa, P. (1960) *Production of Commodities by Means of Commodities*, Cambridge: Cambridge University Press.

Wicksell, K. (1936) *Interest and Prices*, trans. R. F. Kahn, New York: Kelley Reprint, 1965.

II THE MICRO FOUNDATIONS OF THE SHORT–RUN PHILLIPS CURVE

In recent years a consensus has emerged among macroeconomic theorists that short-run deviations of output from its long-run rate of growth are determined by deviations of inflation from its expected rate. Once inflation is correctly anticipated by all economic agents, output will depart from its long-run or 'natural' growth rate only as a result of stochastic shocks. This view is known as the natural rate hypothesis (NRH).

The 'Keynesian' version of the NRH, most identified with the Brookings Institution (William Poole, Robert J. Gordon), contends that deviations from the natural rate may persist for a long time due to cultural and institutional constraints on the ability of money wage rates to adjust significantly and rapidly to changing inflation rates. These Keynesians suggest that the government should institute a fixed monetary rule with an activist feedback mechanism in order to reduce the size of short-run deviations around the natural rate.[1]

Macro rational expectations (MRE) models were developed to demonstrate that even this highly constrained activism was unwarranted. MRE models indicate that short-run deviations of output from its natural rate occur because at least some economic agents learn about or react to some price changes less rapidly than others. In all MRE models it is claimed that this lack of information results in a downward-sloping short-run Phillips curve, i.e. there is a temporary trade off between inflation and unemployment. However, MRE models contend that once economic agents obtain the missing information they adjust quickly, eliminating deviations from the natural rate. Hence, the long-run Phillips curve is vertical, i.e. the economy is at a natural employment level no matter what the rate of inflation. From this perspective, since deviations occur only when information is lacking, it would be impossible for the government, using known policy rules, to influence the size of deviations from the natural rate, even in the short run.[2]

MRE models have been subject to numerous criticisms. Many economists reject the assumption that labor markets are well-functioning auction-like markets (Poole, 1976; Gordon, 1976; Solow, 1980). Others claim that the rationality assumption used is inconsistent with learning models of behavior (Evans, 1978), uncertainty in historical time (Forman, 1980) and observed patterns of expectations (Katona, 1980). Finally B. Friedman (1979) and Fair (1978) contend that the rational expectations assumption that economic agents possess a complete model of the economy is unrealistic and inconsistent with optimal information models. Most questionable is the general acceptance of supply and demand theory within both the labor and the goods markets. If either market has significant non-competitive aspects then all versions of the NRH must be rejected.

This paper will criticize MRE models for different reasons. It will demonstrate that, even if we ignore the criticisms mentioned above, MRE models produce a short-run downward-sloping Phillips curve only where the models rest on *ad hoc* assumptions about asymmetrics between demanders and suppliers. MRE models have been perceived as a response to the weak microeconomic foundations of conventional macroeconomics. This paper will show that, like Keynesian models, rational expectations models must assume behavior patterns or institutional structure that are inconsistent with the perfectly competitive, auction-like markets on which orthodox microeconomics is based. Furthermore, various authors have offered strikingly different microeconomics rationales for the new macroeconomic models.

The Basic MRE Model

The central features of most MRE models are that unperceived changes in rates of inflation will change supply and/or demand in two ways. First, there is a substitution effect based on the difference between actual inflation and perceived inflation; second, there is a wealth effect (changes in perceived wealth growth rates) due to differences between actual money supply growth rates and perceived inflation rates.[3] All MRE models argue that unperceived inflation temporarily increases the growth rate of output and therefore of employment, N. Figure 4.1 represents the labor market behavior

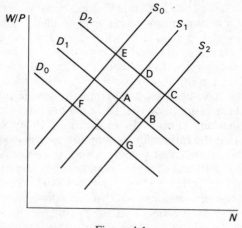

- Figure 4.1

underlying the MRE models. The vertical axis is W/P, where W and P are growth rates of wages and prices. MRE models assume that unperceived inflation shifts the supply curve from S_1 to S_2 and/or shifts the demand curve from D_1 to D_2, ending up with a temporary equilibrium at B, C or D – all of which involve higher rates of increase in employment.

One story used to explain a shift from S_1 to S_2 is that workers incorrectly perceive an increase in inflation as an increase in their real wage growth rate, so that they substitute labor for leisure. They think they are moving from A to D along the S_1 curve, but they are actually altering the terms on which they offer labor, shifting from S_1 to S_2 and moving from A to B. A story told to account for a shift from D_1 to D_2 is that the increase in money growth rates that gives rise to the unperceived increase in inflation leads households to perceive that they are wealthier, so that they demand more goods and services. A full account of the effects of unperceived inflation would consider the substitution effects on demand and the wealth effects on supply.

Throughout this paper, we have somewhat modified the typical MRE model. Since MRE models rely heavily on differences between the perceptions of workers and those of firms, we distinguish demanders' perceptions about inflation from suppliers'.[4] We have also substituted current period 'perceptions' of current period inflation $(_tP_t)$ for the conventional 'expectations' concepts used in MRE models. Since we do not discuss rational expectations per se, this substitution is costless. Moreover it has the advantage of avoiding the choice between some authors' use of last period expectations about current inflation $(E_{t-1}(P_t))$ and other authors' use of current period expectations about next period's inflation $(E_t(P_{t+1}))$. Finally, and most importantly, it allows us to distinguish between NRH models that require expectations of the future for behavioral reasons and those that do not. Also, throughout this paper we omit stochastic terms, which are crucial to disequilibrium values of rational expectations but which are irrelevant to our analysis of MRE microfoundations.

MRE Models and Wealth Effects

This section discusses the behavioral assumptions that underlie wealth effects. According to Barro (1976), when an unanticipated rise in inflation results from an equivalent rise in money growth, money-holders believe that the real value of their wealth has risen. In response, they increase their demand for goods. However, the perceived increase in real wealth also induces households to shift from work to leisure, which reduces labor supply and ultimately the supply of goods. Thus Barro notes that, if wealth effects dominate supply behavior, an upward-sloping short-run Phillips curve is possible.[5] To avoid this, some models (Lucas, 1973; Barro and Fischer, 1976) simply eliminate wealth effects from the supply side (i.e. assume $\beta_s = 0$). In this section, we exclude substitution effects from both demand and supply, focusing for analytical convenience exclusively on wealth effects. In this case, the slope of the Phillips curve depends only on the relation between suppliers' and demanders' perceptions of inflation.[6]

Barro (1976) suggests that wealth effects influence aggregate *supply* through their effects on households' preference for leisure *vis-à-vis* work and *demand* through their effect on the real value of money. But there is another channel by which wealth effects could influence producer supply and consumer demand decisions: through their impact on firms' debt and on households' holding of that debt. It is usually assumed that firms are net debtors. If, with Friedman (1975), we assume that nominal debt and the price level change independently, unperceived changes in inflation would have no wealth effects on firms. But once a rise in inflation is perceived, households that hold firms' debts will reduce their demand for goods because their net wealth is growing more slowly. Firms, realizing that their indebtedness is growing more slowly, may increase their supply, for example, if lower debt reduces borrowing costs. If and only if curtailed demand exactly offsets expanded supply would it be appropriate to ignore these wealth effects and focus exclusively on the role of money. And money must be defined exclusive of private debt, that is, as 'outside money'.

An alternative avenue is to assume, perhaps plausibly, that firms' nominal debt grows with the price level, and that both firms and households fully perceive nominal debt changes in the current period. In this case, unperceived changes in inflation *will* have a wealth effect, but perceived changes in inflation will not. Unperceived inflation increases will cause firms to believe that their *indebtedness* grows more rapidly and households to believe that their *wealth* is increasing more quickly. Again, the net outcome depends on the relative strengths of the supply and demand effects. Once inflation is fully perceived, these wealth effects will of course vanish, since real wealth is correctly perceived as unchanged.

If it is assumed that firms are neither debtors nor creditors, a wealth effect on supply might still result from changes in the perceived value of inventories when inflation is unperceived. This is equivalent to the 'accounting illusion' argument of Feldstein and Summers (1977) that firms mistake a rise in accounting profits for a rise in actual profits when using the FIFO accounting method. Firms do not realize that they must replace depleted inventories at the higher price level.

In any case, the impact of the wealth effect term on aggregate output depends on the relative strength of the supply and demand effects. The impact due to wealth effects alone of unperceived inflation on the labor markets can be seen in Figure 4.1. Workers supply less labor because they feel themselves wealthier and therefore choose more leisure, so that the supply curve shifts from S_1 to S_0. Firms may demand more labor if the demand for goods rises due to a real balance effect and/or if firms' net indebtedness is reduced. Either factor could cause the demand curve to shift from D_1 to D_2. The temporary effect of unperceived inflation would be a move from A to E. If and only if workers and firms have the same perceptions about inflation (and if β_d, $\beta_s > 0$), will unperceived inflation not change the level of employment growth, and E will be directly above A.

No convincing theoretical or empirical evidence has been presented for presuming that demand effects dominate supply effects. It is not surprising, therefore, that many MRE models exclude wealth effects altogether. Yet when they do, asymmetric assumptions about supply and demand substitution effects are necessary to ensure that MRE models disequilibrate in the right direction. It is to these assumptions that we turn next.

MRE Models and Substitution Effects

When MRE models omit wealth effects, they rely exclusively for their equilibration properties on substitution effects. Unperceived inflation works for each good like an increase in prices. Due to the substitution effect, demand falls and supply rises; for example, consumers substitute more leisure for fewer goods and producers substitute more effort for less leisure. Consider the labor market during unperceived inflation. In real wage space, the demand and supply curves shift; in money wage space, we move along the curves. The impact of unperceived inflation through substitution effects (ignoring wealth effects) would be to shift the demand curve in Figure 4.1 from D_1 to D_0 and the supply curve from S_1 to S_2. There is no *a priori* reason to believe that the new temporary equilibrium employment growth rate, G, will be greater than the old, A.

MRE models often specify only a single output equation according to which unperceived inflation raises output. These models either implicitly suppress demand or implicitly aggregate demand and supply.[7] If inventory adjustment is excluded, output changes reflect labor market adjustments. A sufficient condition for unperceived increases in inflation to raise output growth is then that a rise in the inflation rate is imperfectly perceived by workers, who therefore are willing to supply labor as before despite the fall in their real wages. Thus the labor supply schedule shifts downward in real wage space. Firms, by contrast, perfectly perceive the fall in real wages and bid up the nominal wage to attract more labor. Thus unperceived inflation causes S_1 to shift to S_2 in Figure 4.2. Workers are willing to provide the same amount of labor, n_0, at the money wage W_0. D_1 stays unchanged, implying that firms perfectly perceive the rise in inflation. The result is that firms, realizing the marginal revenue product of labor exceeds the real wage at N_0, bid up wages to W, and raise output growth from A to B.

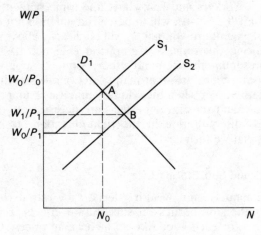

Figure 4.2

To produce this increase in employment and output growth requires asymmetric assumptions about labor supply and demand behavior that are rarely stated in the second-generation NRH models used for MRE purposes. The models implicitly assume that workers respond less to inflation in the current period than do firms.[8] Below we outline four alternative asymmetric labor market assumptions found in the NRH literature. We argue, moreover, that the goods market behavior of the typical MRE model is not a necessary consequence of the labor market behavior embodied in the first three models.

Fooled workers: asymmetric worker/firm perceptions
The first asymmetric explanation for the short-run increase in output in response to an imperfectly perceived rise in the inflation rate was

the 'fooling hypothesis' offered by Friedman (1968). Friedman suggested that workers perceive inflation changes more slowly than do firms. Thus, when price inflation increases, workers are fooled into thinking that their real wages have risen. As they realize that the inflation rate has increased, they will demand higher money wages. Firms, which know that inflation has increased, can take a temporary advantage by hiring more labor at the reduced wage rate.

To analyze this hypothesis, we specify that the growth rate of labor demand and supply depends on the difference between the wage growth rate and the perceived inflation rate. We assume that workers' perceptions respond to inflation changes less in the current period than do firms' perceptions[9] (Friedman's characterization was more bold: workers' 'expectations' respond with a lag, whereas firms' respond instantly). If the inflation rate increases, the labor supply curve will shift from S_1 to S_2 in Figure 4.1, because workers think that any given wage is worth more and so will offer more labor at that wage. If firms fully perceive the increase in inflation, the labor demand curve will not shift. This assumption of asymmetric worker/firm perceptions is sufficient to guarantee that unperceived inflation results in increased output growth. This result is independent of the responsiveness of firms and workers to changes in real wages (assuming α_s, $\alpha_d > 0$).[10]

Relative versus general prices: asymmetric worker/firm decision criteria
Friedman's 1968 fooled-workers model was criticized on the ground that there is no reason to believe that workers would be slower than firms to adjust their perceptions to changes in the inflation rate. Friedman (1975) therefore offered an alternative rationale for labor market asymmetry. Firms have different decision criteria from workers: firms care about wages relative to their product price, whereas workers care about prices in general.[11] Furthermore, information about the wage/product price ratio, in contrast to information about general prices, is instantly available.

This model works (that is unperceived inflation results in increased income growth rates) even if firms are just as myopic about the general inflation rate as are workers. The model depends on asymmetric decision criteria rather than asymmetric information or perceptions. According to the relative-versus-general prices model, an increase in inflation will not be perceived immediately by either firms or workers. Both will know, however, that the price of the firm's product has risen. Firms, seeing that the price of their product has gone up, demand more labor at each money wage while labor's supply curve in nominal wage space is unchanged.

In real wage space, the labor demand curve may stay unchanged or it may move outward if the increased demand for labor at each money wage swamps the impact of the unperceived inflation. As in the fooled-workers model, the labor supply curve in real wage space shifts rightward. We go therefore from A to B or C in Figure 4.1.

There are two unsettling ambiguities in Friedman's exposition. The first is that he contradicts himself about the relative growth rates in prices and wages. He begins by asserting that the unanticipated shock to the inflation rate applies equally to wages: 'Suppose something, say a monetary expansion, starts nominal aggregate demand growing, which in turn produces a rise in prices and wages at the rate of, say, 2 per cent per year' (Friedman, 1975, p. 20). However, the mechanism whereby firms demand more labor clearly depends on a decline in real wages (perceived by firms as a decline in wages relative to product price): 'They will initially interpret a rise in the price of their product as a rise in its relative price and as *implying a fall in the real wage rate they must pay in terms of their product*' (p. 21; emphasis added).

It seems reasonable to interpret the first quotation as a slip of the pen. What Friedman probably meant was that the exogenous shock to the demand for labor in nominal wage space is identical to that to the demand for goods. But obviously the real wage must decline once the new equilibrium is reached since the labor supply curve shifts in real wage space but the demand curve does not.

The second ambiguity in Friedman's 1975 exposition is also embodied in the second quotation above, the first half of which suggests that a rise in the product's 'relative price' must mean 'relative to the nominal wage'. If firms, like labor, are myopic about prices in general, they will also perceive a rise in the wage/product price ratio as a rise in their product price relative to the price of other products. The asymmetry of this model in no ways depends upon such price myopia on the part of firms; that is, it in no way depends upon firms' misperceptions that their prices are increasing relative to those of competing firms.

Search models: asymmetric local/global perceptions
The MRE model used in the seminal article by Sargent and Wallace (1976), in contrast, unambiguously bases its disequilibration mechanism on each firm's mistaking an increase in the price of all goods for an increase in the price of the firm's product relative to other goods (similarly for each worker and his wage):

> Unexpected increases in the price level boost aggregate supply, the reason being that suppliers of labor and goods mistakenly interpret surprise increases in the aggregate price level as increases in the

relative prices of the labor and goods they are supplying. This happens because suppliers receive information about the prices of their own goods faster than they receive information about the general price level. (Sargent and Wallace, 1976, p. 243)

Rationalization in terms of local/global price confusion derives in fact from the early NRH models of Phelps *et al.* (1970); it is neither original with nor unique to Sargent and Wallace. Phelps likens labor's behavior to that of workers on an informationally isolated island, whose 'job search' activities (involving exit from employment and canoeing to other islands) decrease or increase according as they believe their wages to have increased or decreased relative to wages on other islands.

There are two problems with these search models. The first is that some rely on relative prices rather than on relative wages, and the relative price models lack a goods market rationale to match Phelps' labor market rationale. The second is that they depend on an unstated asymmetry between the perceptions of demanders and those of suppliers. We deal with each problem in turn.

What is the mechanism whereby firms are induced to supply more if they perceive a rise in the price of their good relative to the price of other goods? The profit-maximizing firms will increase supply only when perceived marginal revenue rises relative to perceived marginal cost. If the firm is a price taker in both factor and product markets, wages and product prices can be identified with marginal cost and marginal revenue, respectively. Thus, to increase supply, firms in this 'global myopia' class of models must associate a rise in their product price relative to *prices in general* with a rise in their product price relative to the *wages* they pay.[12] In other words, if global myopia models are to apply to *firms'* (i.e. goods suppliers') behavior, they can be rationalized only by assuming that firms have incorrect perceptions about the wages they pay (so long as we stay in the world of perfect competition, the realm in which NRH models are located). It is difficult to picture a firm having incorrect perceptions of its own wage bill.

The second deficiency of the search model is its assumption that suppliers and demanders of labor are asymmetrically informed. Let us look at a labor market version of the search model with a demand side symmetric to the supply.[13] Unperceived inflation causes workers to believe their local wage has risen relative to labor costs in general. Firms will therefore reduce their demand for labor while searching for lower-cost labor. The labor supply curve will shift from S_1 to S_2 in Figure 4.1 while the labor demand curve shifts from D_1 to D_0. To produce increased growth in employment due to unperceived increases in inflation, the search models implicitly assume that firms (as demanders of labor) always perceive the global wage growth rate more accurately than do workers.

MRE model-builders who rely on the distinction between perceptions of local and global shocks rarely if ever state that they are also implicitly relying on this *ad hoc* assumption of asymmetric firm/worker perceptions. Yet this asymmetry is necessary to allow employment and output in such models to depart from their natural rates of growth. Indeed, Phelps (1970), in summarizing the pre-MRE NRH models of the time implicitly recognizes their asymmetry: 'The above models typically postulate complete information on the part of buyers about all goods prices. . . . Inducing the firm to employ more – to move down its labor demand curve expressed in wage units as it were – requires a fall of product or, more loosely, of real wage rates' (Phelps, 1970, p. 18)

Implicit in Phelps' statement is the recognition that NRH models postulate complete information on the part of buyers of labor – firms – about all nominal wages. Sellers of labor – workers – are, by contrast, subject to temporary myopia about local *vis-à-vis* global wages. Similarly to the fooled-workers model, the search models assume that unperceived inflation means that workers see any given nominal wage as an increased real wage, such that the labor supply curve shifts rightward from S_1 to S_2 in Figure 4.1. Given that labor demand is said not to change, we move from A to B, and the growth rate of employment rises.

Problems with the first three models
Thus far we have argued that three of the commonly cited NRH behavioral foundations for MRE models require asymmetric assumptions about workers and firms, that is, asymmetries beyond the conventional point that suppliers of labor respond positively to real wages and demanders negatively. Friedman's 1968 reasoning (the fooled-workers model) requires an *ad hoc* assumption that workers' perceptions of inflation are short-sighted whereas firms are not myopic. His 1975 reasoning (the relative-versus-general prices model) requires an asymmetric assumption that workers' labor supply decision is independent of the firms' prices, while firms' demand for labor is not. The labor search behavior hypothesized by Phelps and others in the search model depends implicitly on an assumption about the asymmetric availability of information to workers and firms.

In addition, all three NRH models are grounded in labor market behavior that has no goods market counterpart. The representative MRE model of output behavior[14] is a goods market model that is not necessarily consistent with the NRH models above, which are labor market models. The latter all state that *employment* departs from equilibrium growth rates whenever workers' *perceptions* of the inflation rate or of the rate increase depart from actual levels. The representative MRE model, by contrast, states that *output* departs from its equilibrium growth rate whenever *expectations* of the inflation rate depart from the actual rate.

Nothing guarantees that the MRE output model follows from the fooled-workers model, the relative-versus-general prices model or the search model. First, expectations in the sense of average expectations of inflation could conceivably be accurate if the expectations of firms were systematically in error in a compensating direction from those of workers. In this case, the MRE output model would dictate no departure from equilibrium, whereas the three NRH models would. Relatedly, the MRE output model is based on price behavior, whereas the NRH models are based on wage behavior. The two will be equivalent only if wages and prices move strictly together. However, a necessary condition for disequilibrium in the NRH models is that wages and prices do *not* move together. For employment to rise above its equilibrium ('natural') rate of growth in the three NRH models, prices must rise faster than wages. Of course, once equilibrium is restored, wages and prices are rising at the same rate again. In contrast to the expectations problem just discussed, there is no possibility of inconsistency in equilibrium but, at any point in time between equilibria, the wage/price-expectations gap will not be the same as the price/price-expectations gap.

A second inconsistency between the three NRH models and the representative MRE model is that the former can be adequately represented in terms of current perceptions of current prices, whereas the latter is formulated in terms of current expectations of next period's prices. In point of fact, MRE models could also be adequately represented in terms of perceptions to the extent that they analyze *spatial* confusion about local/global shocks. Expectations are essential, however, to MRE models, which analyze confusion about whether shocks are temporary or permanent. We therefore turn to an NRH model that depends for its operation on expectations rather than perceptions. Does it provide a superior foundation for MRE models in other respects as well?

The temporary change model: temporary intertemporal substitution
Lucas and Rapping (1969) employ an MRE model that, in the labor market, essentially states that labor supply grows more rapidly when current wages are rising more rapidly than future wages are expected to rise.[15] This model lends itself to combination with the Lucas (1972)

model, which essentially states that demand for labor depends also on current versus expected future wage growth rates. The behavioral rationale for this model has to do with intertemporal substitution between labor and leisure. When current wages rise relative to expected wages, workers will substitute current for future work; firms on the other hand will temporarily economize on their purchases of labor services.

Note that this is the only model of the four that necessarily relies for its functioning upon expectations rather than perceptions. Here, a perfectly *perceived* shock to current wages may be less than fully reflected in current *expectations* of next period's wage because of uncertainty about whether the shock is to be temporary or permanent. Suppose the shock to current wages is positive, and the expectations of workers and firms about future wages respond by the same amount but by less than the increase in the wage growth rate. In other words, workers and firms both expect future real wages to be lower than current real wages. Then the vertical shifts in the supply and demand schedules would exactly offset each other, and equilibrium employment would remain unchanged.

The upshot is that, for this model to produce a short-run Phillips curve, the model requires an asymmetry between demand and supply behavior similar to the early models. The asymmetric assumption must be just as *ad hoc* as that for the fooled workers and the search models (the relative-versus-general prices model's asymmetry has, in our opinion, more plausibility). The temporary change model must make at least one of two asymmetric assumptions: that workers' expectations respond more slowly to a shock than do firms', or that workers have inferior information.

What about the goods market version of the temporary change model? Does it necessarily result from the model's labor market behavior? Alternatively, is the analogous goods market behavior plausible in its own right?

The temporary change model, when formulated for the goods market, is simply our representative MRE model (equations (7a) and (7b)). This representative model is no more consistent with the labor market version of the temporary change model than it was with the earlier models. To the previous inconsistencies is added the probable inconsistency between wage expectations and price expectations. In fact, there is no reason to believe, as there was in the previous NRH models, that labor market equilibrium is re-established at the same time as goods market equilibrium. In the previous models, equilibrium in both labor and goods markets was contingent upon actual prices equalling expected prices, whereas in this model that connection between wage and price behavior is absent.

The temporary change model does, however, have a behavioral rationale for the goods market that is analogous to that for the labor market. Suppliers will temporarily offer more goods if current prices rise relative to expected prices, and demanders will postpone purchases. But again, any change in equilibrium output must be rationalized via *ad hoc* assumptions about asymmetric expectations formation or asymmetric information between demanders and suppliers.

Conclusions

Most economists have accepted that MRE models provide a rigorous explanation for a downward-sloping short-run Phillips curve. This paper has presented models that indicate that unperceived inflation would result in a movement from A in Figure 4.1 to B through G depending upon *ad hoc* assumptions concerning the relative strengths of substitution and income effects, the differential effects on firm and worker perceptions, and/or the differential effects on global and local prices. Thus, this paper suggests that, even when perceptions/expectations are incorporated, microeconomic theory presented in the most often referenced MRE models says little about the effect of unperceived inflation on output (and employment) unless *ad hoc* asymmetries are introduced.

The fact that heretofore rational expectations theorists have been utilizing models that have ambiguous properties is striking given their contentions that Keynesians have been lacking in having weak microeconomic foundations. Of course, it is possible that further research would provide a rigorous choice-theoretic microeconomic framework for a downward-sloping short-run Phillips curve. However, it is likely that structural and institutional factors or political factors can explain the inverse relationship between inflation and unemployment rates in the short run, as well as the inability of the Western industrialized economies to sustain permanently low unemployment rates.

NOTES

1   A fixed monetary rule with an activist feedback mechanism would be as follows;

$$M_t = a + b(Y_t - Y_t^*), b<0$$

where M_t, Y_t and Y_t^* are the percentage change in the money supply, actual output and full employment output, respectively. In these models, Y_t^* is equivalent to the natural growth rate. All variables in this paper are percent changes. To keep the exposition in the text smoother, we have sometimes simplified, e.g.

writing 'wages' in place of 'growth rate of wages' or 'percent changes in wages'. For analytical simplicity, we assume the long-term average (natural) growth rate for all variables is zero.

2   Phelps (1976) has given examples of how MRE models are capable of explaining severe economic fluctuations, in cases where the government does not follow a known rule.

3   Following Barro (1976), we can characterize demand and supply behavior as log-linear functions of the form:

$$Y_t^s = \alpha_s(P_t - {}_tP_t) - \beta_s(M_t - {}_tP_t), \qquad \alpha_s, \beta_s > 0 \tag{1a}$$

$$Y_t^d = -\alpha_d(P_t - {}_tP_t) + \beta_d(M_t - {}_tP_t), \qquad \alpha_d, \beta_d > 0 \tag{1b}$$

where Y_t^s, Y_t^d, P_t and M_t are percentage changes of output supply, output demand, the price level and the money supply, respectively. ${}_tP_t$ is the current perception of current inflation.

4   Incorporating the distinction between ${}_tP_t^d$, the current perception of demanders about current inflation, and ${}_tP_t^s$, the current perception of suppliers about current inflation, produces:

$$Y_t^s = \alpha_s(P_t - {}_tP_t^s) - \beta_s({M_t} - {}_tP_t^s), \qquad \alpha_s, \beta_s > 0 \tag{1a'}$$

$$Y_t^d = -\alpha_d(P_t - {}_tP_t^d) + \beta_d({M_t} - {}_tP_t^d), \qquad \alpha_d, \beta_d > 0. \tag{1b'}$$

5   More precisely, the short-run Phillips curve in Barro (1976) is positive if $(\beta_s \, \alpha_d) > (\alpha_s \, \beta_d)$. Barro's model does not include the distinction between ${}_tP_t^d$ and ${}_tP_t^s$.

6   When

$$\alpha_d = \alpha_s = 0, \quad Y_t = \frac{[{}_tP_t^s \, (\beta_d\beta_s) - {}_tP_t^d \, (\beta_d\beta_s)]}{(\beta_s + \beta_d)},$$

For $Y_t > 0$, it is necessary and sufficient that ${}_tP_t^s > {}_tP_t^d$.

7   For example, Sargent and Wallace (1976):

$$Y_t = \alpha(P_t - {}_tP_t), \qquad \alpha > 0. \tag{2}$$

8   Including both wealth and substitution effects and assuming that prices increase at the same rate as the money supply ($P_t = M_t$), then unperceived inflation changes the output growth rate ($Y_t \neq 0$) if and only if workers' perceptions change at a different rate than do firms' perceptions (${}_tP_t^s \neq {}_tP_t^d$). This can be seen from the solution to equations (1a') and (1b') when $M_t = P_t$:

$$Y_t = \frac{(\alpha_d - \beta_d)(\alpha_s - \beta_s)}{(\alpha_d - \beta_d) + (\alpha_s - \beta_s)} ({}_tP_t^d - {}_tP_t^s) \qquad \alpha_d, \alpha_s, \beta_d, \beta_s > 0.$$

9   Friedman's model, in our notation, is:

$$N_t^s = \alpha_s(W_t - {}_tP_t^s), \qquad \alpha_s > 0 \tag{3a}$$

$$N_t^d = -\alpha_d(W_t - {}_tP_t^d), \qquad \alpha_d > 0 \tag{3b}$$

$$\delta ({}_tP_t^s)/\delta P_t < \delta({}_tP_t^d)/\delta P_t \tag{4}$$

10 To see this, solve for W by setting $N_t^s = N_t^d$ and substituting this solution into (3a) we find that the equilibrium rate of employment growth

$$N_t = (\alpha_d\,\alpha_s)(_tP_t^d - {}_tP_t^s)/(\alpha_s + \alpha_d).$$

When α_s, $\alpha_d > 0$, $N_t > 0$, when $_tP_t^d > {}_tP_t^s$, which is guaranteed by (4). Were (3) non-linear, condition (4) would be similar but more complex, since α_s and α_d would no longer represent elasticities.

11 Assume $P_t(z) = P_t$, where $P_t(z)$ is the rate of increase in the price of product z. This model substitutes $P_t(z)$ for $_tP_t^d$ in (3b) and (4).

12 That is, good z must be supplied according to:

$$Y_t^s(z) = \alpha_s[P_t(z) - {}_tW_t^s], \qquad \alpha_s > 0. \tag{5}$$

13 Letting $N_t^s(z)$ and $N_t^d(z)$ be the percentage change in labor supply and demand, respectively, in industry z and letting $_tW_t^s$ and $_tW_t^d$ be perceptions about percent change in wages at time t by suppliers and demanders, respectively, then:

$$N_t^s(z) = \alpha_s[W_t(z) - {}_tW_t^s], \qquad \alpha_s > 0 \tag{6a}$$

$$N_t^d(z) = -\alpha_d[W_t(z) - {}_tW_t^d], \qquad \alpha_d > 0. \tag{6b}$$

14
$$Y_t^s = f_s[P_t - E(P_{t+1})], \qquad f_s' > 0 \tag{7a}$$

$$Y_t^d = f_d[P_t - E(P_{t+1})], \qquad f_d' < 0. \tag{7b}$$

15
$$N_t^s = \alpha_s[W_t - E_t^s(W_{t+1})], \qquad \alpha_s > 0 \tag{8a}$$

$$N_t^d = -\alpha_d[W_t - E_t^d(W_{t+1})], \qquad \alpha_d > 0. \tag{8b}$$

REFERENCES

Barro, R. (1976) 'Rational expectations and the role of monetary policy', *Journal of Monetary Economics, Vol. 2* (January), 1–32.

Barro, R. and Fischer, S. (1976) 'Recent developments in monetary theory', *Journal of Monetary Economics*, Vol. 2 (April), 133–67.

Evans, G. (1978) 'Macroeconomic stability under adaptive and rational expectations', unpublished manuscript (Berkeley, Calif.).

Fair, R. (1978) 'A criticism of one class of macroeconomic models with rational expectations', *Journal of Money, Credit, and Banking*, Vol. 10 (November), 411–17.

Feldstein, M. and Summers, L. (1977) 'Is there a falling rate of profit?' *Brooking Papers*, No. 1, 211–27.

Forman, L. (1980) 'Rational expectations and the real world', *Challenge*, Vol. 23 (November–December), 36–9.

Friedman, B. (1979) 'Optimal expectations and the extreme information assumptions of "rational expectations" models', *Journal of Monetary Economics*, Vol. 5 (January), 23–41.

Friedman, M. (1968) 'The role of monetary policy', *American Economic Review*, Vol. 58 (March), 1–17.

Friedman, M. (1975) 'Unemployment vs. inflation? An evaluation of the Phillips Curve', I.E.A. Lecture 2, London: The Institute of Economic Affairs.

Gordon, R. J. (1976) 'Recent developments in the theory of inflation and unemployment', *Journal of Monetary Economics*, Vol. 2, (April), 185–219.

Katona, G. (1980) 'How expectations are really formed', *Challenge*, Vol. 23 (November–December), 32–5.

Lucas, R. E., Jr (1972) 'Expectations and the neutrality of money', *Journal of Economic Theory*, Vol. 4 (April), 103–24.

Lucas, R. E., Jr (1973) 'Some international evidence on output–inflation tradeoffs', *American Economic Review*, Vol. 63 (June), 326–34.

Lucas, R. E., Jr and Rapping L. (1969) 'Real wages, employment and inflation', *Journal of Political Economy*, Vol. 77 (September), 721–54.

Phelps, E. (1970) 'The new microeconomics in employment and inflation theory', in E. Phelps, ed., *Microeconomic foundations of employment and inflation theory*, New York: Norton.

Phelps, E. (1976) 'Discussant', *Brookings Papers*, No. 2, 506–9.

Poole, W. (1976) 'Rational expectations and the macro model', *Brookings Papers*, No. 2, 463–505.

Sargent, T. and Wallace, N. (1976) 'Rational expectations and the theory of economic policy', *Journal of Monetary Economics*, Vol. 2 (April), 169–83.

Solow, R. (1980) 'On theories of unemployment', *American Economic Review*, Vol. 70 (March), 1–11.

III   RATIONAL EXPECTATIONS AND IMPERFECT KNOWLEDGE

The rational expectations hypothesis (REH) has become prominent in recent years in both theoretical and empirical studies in economics. This is particularly so in short-run macroeconomics. The information requirements of the explanation *à la* Muth of the REH are excessive by the criteria of economics as a science since they assume that the individual knows the true economic theory that will explain the non-stochastic elements of real-world observations. Section (a) looks at these requirements and rejects them as grossly unrealistic.

Economists have been aware of the excessive requirements of the REH. Walters (1971) argues for 'consistent' expectations, defining these as ones that utilize the best theory possible among several available ones. The individual chooses the 'best' theory, that is, the one that predicts better than its alternative ones, and so is the one that will maximize profits. Feige and Pearce (1976) consider the costs of acquiring information and suggest the notion of 'economically rational expectations', that is, those that are based on the individual's costs of mis-estimating future inflation and the costs of acquiring the information to make his forecasts.

This paper explores the nature of theories that do not incorporate perfect knowledge of economic processes by focusing on the errors that such theories make. We separate such errors from the stochastic ones that are usually incorporated into econometric work and are envisaged in the REH. Sections (b) and (c) assume a non-stochastic world, although we recognize that a major reason for the imperfect knowledge of economic processes is that they are stochastic. Knowledge of the economic processes in this non-stochastic or deterministic world is still assumed to be imperfect, so that theories still generally do make incorrect predictions. The errors in these predictions will be called *choice-theoretic errors*. Individuals know that these theories make errors and form expectations on these errors.

Section (b) lays the basic framework for actual and the expected choice-theoretic errors. Section (c) recognizes that there may exist several theories for explaining or predicting the value of an economic variable. There may not also exist any 'best' or 'dominant' theory in the sense that it always makes smaller choice-theoretic errors than any other available theory. There are thus several genuinely alternative theories competing with each other. The individual has this knowledge and bases his decision on a composite prediction that maximizes his utility. In general, this composite prediction will depend on more than one theory, as well as, quite possibly, on hunches, opinions of others, etc. It is only in the unrealistic and rarified world of economists who believe in the existence of a best theory that the optimal choice among theories means believing and acting on a single theory.

Section (d) extends the analysis to a stochastic world and compares the nature of choice-theoretic errors with that of stochastic errors. Since economists do not, by nature of their knowledge, have a theory on the actual choice-theoretic errors, their existence implies that regression techniques will not, in general, yield unbiased estimates. Further, the rational expectations hypothesis, defined as one that is based on the individual's optimal knowledge, is shown to imply an equation that is quite different from Muth's statement of the REH that the expected price level equals the mathematical expectation of the actual price level.

Definition of a couple of terms used in the paper would help. 'Expectations' are defined as choice-theoretic if they are based on the optimal amount of the individual's knowledge. This is what Feige and Pearce call 'economically rational expectations'. But our analysis differs considerably from theirs and focuses on the choice among theories. Our analysis is in the realm of bounded rationality and, as such, the expectations in our analysis might also be called 'bounded rational expectations'.[1]

A 'theory' is here defined as an organized body of knowledge. An economic theory is one that could be recognized as a theory in economics. Predictions of one's theories can be distinguished from hunches, guesses and the opinions of others even when such opinions are based on these others' theories, since the precise basis for such opinions may not be known to the individual.

The classification in Figure 4.3 relates the possible states of one's knowledge and theories to the possible states of the world. The REH of Muth deals with cell D – with perfect knowledge (except as to random occurrences) and a stochastic world. Our concern is with imperfect knowledge in a stochastic world. Sections (b) and (c) of the paper deal with cell E for heuristic reasons. The later sections deal with cell H, which represents the world that economists study and try to explain. (Cells B and C are empty; cells F and G should be empty, but may not be.)

	Perfect Knowledge		Imperfect Knowledge	
	Deterministic theory	Stochastic theory	Deterministic theory	Stochastic theory
Deterministic world	A SER = 0 CHER = 0	B	E SER = 0 CHER	F
Stochastic world	C	D SER CHER = 0	G	H SER CHER

SER = stochastic error
CHER = choice – theoretic error

Figure 4.3

(a) The Rational Expectations Hypothesis

The REH can be considered as having two aspects. One of these is the formal hypothesis that:

$$P_t^e = E P_t \tag{1}$$

where P_t^e is the t'th period's price level as anticipated at the end of period t–1. $E P_t$ is the mathematical expectation of the actual price level in period t.

The other aspect of the REH is the justification that Muth (1961) and others following him gave to it. This was that 'the way expectations are formed depends specifically on the structure of the relevant system describing the economy' (Muth, 1961, p. 316). Leaving aside the question of random disturbances, Muth's justification requires the exact or 'true' knowledge of the structure of the relevant system. It also requires the exact or 'true' values of the exogenous and predetermined variables pertinent to the structure of the system. The word 'true' – that is, infallible and, therefore, irrefutable – has been used to indicate that the relevant knowledge is not supposed to be merely an estimate – no matter how informed – that could be prone to error. This knowledge is also not merely knowledge of the best theory that economists have of the actual structure since theories are simplifications of reality and are refutable by their very nature (Popper, 1963).

Exponents of the REH may argue they do not assume that the economic unit always has true knowledge of the structure of the system and that he can make mistakes. But the REH proponents then assume that the economic unit will revise his theory until he finds the true one for the existing structure. If the structure changes and he does not revise his theory immediately, his mistakes will lead him to revise it until it matches exactly with the new structure. That is, the individual economic unit will eventually possess true knowledge of the actual structure of the economy. Further, if the REH is to be useful, this eventuality must occur within a short enough period, and definitely before the structure changes once again. To summarize this line of argument, the REH assumes that it is possible for economic units to achieve true knowledge and eliminate the refutability element of their theories, sooner or later.

It would be useful to separate the formal hypothesis – that is, (1) – from the justification that Muth gave to it. The former would be called the mathematical expectation hypothesis of anticipated prices (MEH). The justification given above for it will be called the full knowledge hypothesis (FKH). The assumption of the FKH is sufficient but not necessary for the use of the MEH. It is, therefore, possible to examine these two hypotheses separately.

To repeat, economic models and theories are simplifications of reality. They may or may not be valid. But they cannot be claimed to be true in the sense of being infallible or irrefutable. Only tautologies fall into the infallible category, but the relevant economic models are not tautological and cannot, therefore, be infallible – that is, 'true'. The best that can be claimed for them is that they may be valid, which in itself holds the possibility of their being invalid in some circumstances or others. The FKH asserts the infallibility of the economic units' knowledge of the relevant system, except for a random element. In doing so, it exceeds the bounds of knowledge relevant to economics or any science, which, as Popper (1963) points out, represents a collection of refutable theories. Economics cannot include theories that claim irrefutable knowledge of the behavioral structure of the relevant system. As such, the FKH exceeds the bounds of knowledge that economics as a science allows its subjects – and economists – to possess.

Muth rephrased the REH 'a little more precisely as follows: that expectations of firms (or, more generally, the subjective probability distribution of outcomes) tend to be distributed for the same information set, about the predictions of the theory (or the "objective" probability distribution of outcomes)' (Muth, 1961, p. 316). In this quote, as in the oft-quoted phrase 'the relevant theory' in the REH literature, the word 'theory', if it is used in a behavioral sense, is a misnomer for the knowledge of the structure of the economy that Muth attributes to economic units. Since behavioral theories are refutable, they do not necessarily yield such an accurate estimate of the anticipated price level that (1) will hold. Only an exact or true knowledge of that structure – except for random factors – will do so, but such knowledge is beyond the scope of behavioral theories.

Further, the FKH asserts, by implication, that while economists do not possess the true model of the economy or of a given market the public does so. Economists should then pay or bribe the public for this model, as would certainly happen in a perfect market for information,[2] so that their model would also become the true one. But that is a contradiction of the basic postulate on the nature of scientific theories.

Suppose it is assumed that the public possesses only the model or models that economists possess. But since these models may prove to be invalid for the current period, without such *a priori* knowledge, even the best of these models cannot imply (1).[3] Further, economists do not have one model. They possess several models, with different groups or schools often owing allegiance to different models. Confronted with a variety of such models and with a variety of predictions on the price level, the public cannot be reasonably and plausibly assumed to somehow average these, with appropriate weights, to arrive at the expected price level that satisfies (1). Remember also that (1) requires more than knowledge of the true model; it requires *a priori* knowledge of the exogenous variables and parameters of the model. Even economists and governments do not usually possess this knowledge. The public can hardly do better.

As a final remark, economists, being humble folk – knowingly so on the basis of their past experience and the inaccuracy of their past predictions – do not often claim that their models yield predictions that satisfy (1). Since the public considers them to be the pundits in this field, such pundits cannot in turn treat the public to be the all-seeing guru. The public's predictions need do no better than the economists' ones do. They could do worse.

(b) Choice-Theoretic Errors

Assume that the individual has a theory for predicting the price level and that the price level it predicts for period t is P_t^T. The actual price level in period t was designated above as P_t. The individual finds that, even in a non-stochastic world, his theory makes a choice-theoretic error P_t^* such that:

$$P_t^* = P_t - P_t^T. \tag{2}$$

Assume that the individual's experience over the past indicates that $\mathrm{E}P_t^*$ differs from zero. Further, this experience may also indicate that the distribution of P_t^* differs from the normal one. In short, he believes that P_t^* is not a random disturbance. P_t^* is not observable *ex ante*. It can be calculated *ex post* since P_t is known *ex post* and P_t^T is known both *ex ante* and *ex post*.

We need a name for P_t^*. There is none in the literature at present. We shall call it the choice-theoretic or non-stochastic error, or a mistake made by the theory. In the former name, the words 'choice-theoretic' and 'non-stochastic' differentiate P_t^* from the stochastic error, which we have not yet considered but which dominates empirical work in economics. The alternative term, 'mistake', seems correctly to represent the nature of P_t^* as a mistake made by the theory.

The individual is thus aware that his theory has made errors in prediction. He may, however, still continue to use it because it may be the 'best one', in a sense to be examined later, that exists or the one that is the optimal one for him to learn. The reasons why a theory that makes errors is the optimal one will also be examined at a later point when we discuss the question of choice among theories. We assume, for the time being, that the individual has one theory only and its prediction of the price level in period t is P_t^e, where period t is the next period in the future. He anticipates a non-stochastic error P_t^{e*} in this prediction. That is, his anticipated price level P_t^e, in the deterministic case, is:

$$P_t^e = P_t^T + P_t^{e*}. \tag{3}$$

The individual, not willing to throw up his hands or ignore the error that is inherent in the predictions for his theory, has to form an estimate of P_t^{e*}. His procedure or guess for reaching this estimate can be treated as itself being a theory in a wider sense. We shall not do so, having restricted the word 'theory' to a structured, consistent body of knowledge. A purely autoregressive or adaptive procedure for forming an estimate of P_t^{e*} will also not be treated as being a theory. There is no question of principle involved in this usage of the term 'theory', only a question of the definition that suits our convenience in further discussion.

P_t^{e*} may have a single value or a set of values with a subjective probability distribution. It is more likely to have the latter rather than the former since the individual does not have any hard theory or knowledge to back up his estimate of it. The set of possible values and their subjective probabilities may be based on hunches or what the individual reads in the newspapers or learns from the news media generally. It may be based on his past experience with the actual errors P_t^*. There are other possibilities also.

It is quite likely that his estimate of P_t^{e*} has a non-zero mean and a distribution that differs from the normal one. The distribution of P_t^{e*} may not even be symmetric. Further P_t^{e*} is unlikely to be independent of P_t^T, since a theory that predicts badly will lead to a larger anticipated value of the error in its predictions than a theory that has consistently predicted quite well.

(3) is rational in the sense that it is based on the knowledge and experience that the individual possesses, since he possesses knowledge of the errors inherent in his theory. Consequently, an assumption to the effect that:

$$P_t^e = P_t^T \tag{4}$$

is not rational. If the REH was defined as (4) in our present context, it would not meet its own definition of rationality.

It is likely that P_t^* is a major determinant of P_t^{e*} even though it may not be the only one. In the stationary state, the individual's experience would yield a constant value of P_t^* and also yield the knowledge that:

$$P_t^{e*} = P_t^* = P_{t-1}^* = P_{t-2}^* \dots \tag{5}$$

Outside the stationary state, P_t^* is unlikely to have a constant value and may change from period to period.

(c)   The Choice among Theories

So far we have assumed that the individual has a single theory. But economists often have several competing theories. A given individual may be aware of a number of these and use the predictions of several theories. These theories may yield different predictions, with the prediction of the i'th theory being P_t^{Ti}.

The individual finds that each theory usually makes a mistake P_t^{*i} in its predictions.

$$P_t^{*i} = P_t - P_t^{Ti}. \tag{6}$$

P_t^{*i} is not a constant over time, except in the stationary state. Considering two theories, T^i and T^j, P^{*i} may be less than P^{*j} in some periods and more in others. If the individual has a theory with smaller choice-theoretic errors than all other theories, the theories with the larger errors will be inefficient and will not be used. The theory with the smaller errors is a 'best' or 'dominant' theory. However, it is likely that there will not be any best or dominant theory in this sense: one theory may do better in some periods for some values of the exogenous variables and do worse than other theories in other periods. There may not thus be a best theory, as postulated by Walters (1971).

The variation over time in P_t^{*i} can be described by a frequency distribution. Defining a composite theoretical prediction of P_t as P_t^{Tc}, based on the predictions of P_t^{Ti}, $i = 1, \ldots, n$, we have

$$P_t^{*c} = P_t - P_t^{Tc}. \tag{7}$$

P_t^{*c} also has a frequency distribution, which is a function of the frequency distributions of P_t^{*i}, $i = 1, \ldots, n$ and the weight assigned to each such prediction. To illustrate, in the simple linear case and considering only two theories, $T1$ and $T2$,

$$P_t^{Tc} = a_1 P_t^{T1} + a_2 P_t^{T2} \tag{8}$$

for given weights a_1 and a_2. Let $a_1 + a_2 = 1$.

$$P_t^{*Tc} = P_t - a_1 P_t^{T1} - a_2 P_t^{T2}. \tag{9}$$

Hence, looking at the first two moments of the distribution of P^{*Tc},

$$E(P_t^{*Tc}) = E(P_t) - a_1 E(P_t^{T1}) - a_2 E(P_t^{T2})$$

$$\sigma_{cc}^* = \sigma_{pp} + \sum_i \sum_j a_i a_j \sigma_{ij} + \sum_i a_i \sigma_{pi} \tag{10}$$

$$i, j = 1, 2$$

where E is the expected value operator, $\sigma_{c^*c}^*$ is the variance of P^{*Tc}, σ_{pp} is the variance of P_t, σ_{ij} is the covariance of P_t^{Ti} and P_t^{Tj} and σ_{pi} is the covariance of P_t and P_t^{Ti}.

Looking at the predictions of the individual's theories, the individual can be expected to choose a composite theory that maximizes his utility. Assume that the individual has a von Neumann–Morgenstern utility function over $(P_t^e - P_t^T)$ since $(P_t^e - P_t^T)$ represents the extent to which his decisions would be based on the incorrect information. Incorrect information involves a loss. Assuming, for illustration, a quadratic utility function, the cardinal utility function is,

$$U(P_t^e - P_t^T) = -a\,(|P_t^e - P_t^T|) - b\,(P_t^e - P_t^T)^2. \tag{11}$$

That is,

$$U(P_t^{e^*}) = -a|P_t^{e^*}| - b(P_t^{e^*})^2. \tag{11'}$$

Assume that $\mathrm{d}U/\mathrm{d}|P_t^{e^*}|<0$ and $\mathrm{d}^2U/\mathrm{d}(P_t^{e^*})^2 < 0$. The individual would maximize the expected value of his utility function, subject to a constraint on $P_t^{e^*}$. Assuming that the individual has a certain amount C_0 that he wishes to spend on collecting information on $P_t^{e^*}$ and that his cost function[4] for acquiring such information is $C(P_t^{e^*})$, the cost constraint is:

$$C(P_t^{e^*}) = C_0, \tag{12}$$

where it seems reasonable to assume that $\partial C/\partial|P_t^{e^*}| < 0$. (12) is unlikely to be linear.

The individual can vary $P_t^{e^*}$ by choosing among theories. Since $P_t^{e^*i}$ is likely to depend, for a given theory T^i, on P_t^{*Ti} and P_t^{*Ti} has a frequency distribution specific to that theory, each $P_t^{e^*i}$ is likely to have a subjective probability distribution. Combinations of different theories, along with their cost functions, will yield the efficient cost function $C(P_t^{e^*})$ in (12).

The problem here has certain similarities with the standard portfolio selection analysis (Tobin, 1958, 1965). Confining our analysis to the mean-variance space, (11) implies that indifference curves have a negative slope in the $\mathrm{E}|P_t^{e^*}|$, $\sigma_t^{e^*}$ space where $\sigma_t^{e^*}$ is the standard deviation of $P_t^{e^*}$ and where the individual prefers less of $\mathrm{E}\,P_t^{e^*}$ and $\sigma_t^{e^*}$ to more of them. These indifference curves are shown in Figure 4.4 as I_1, I_2 and I_3. Note that since both $\mathrm{E}(|P_t^{e^*}|)$ and $\sigma_t^{e^*}$ are 'bads', the individual will prefer to be on the lowest possible indifference curve. The concavity of the indifference curves follows from our

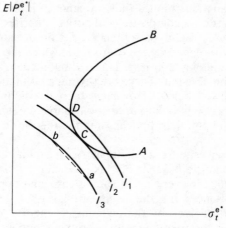

Figure 4.4

assumption that, given points *a* and *b* on an indifference curve, the individual will prefer a linear combination of *a* and *b* to *a* (and to *b*).

(12), given that P_t^{e*1} is unlikely to be perfectly positively correlated with P_t^{e*2}, according to the individual's subjective evaluation, implies a non-linear constraint.[5] We have assumed this to be given by the curve AB, where the point A is given by one theory and the point B by another one, and where the individual has only two theories available to him. The efficient opportunity locus will be the segment AD.

The optimal combination of $E|P_t^{e*}|$ and σ_t^{e*} in Figure 4.4 is given by the point C. In general, an optimal point will require the use of more than one theory, since only at the end-points A and B of the opportunity locus will only one theory be used.

We have so far examined the role of various theories as determinants of P_t^{e*}. But the individual need not rely only upon theories. He can also use, and probably does use, hunches, other persons' predictions, etc., in forming his subjective probability distribution of P_t^{e*}. Each of them can be considered to be a prediction in the same sense as the predictions of theories. Such a prediction would also have a subjective probability distribution. Therefore, the qualitative nature of the above analysis does not change in the presence of such non-theory predictions. This analysis implies that the individual will use a diversified set of information consisting of theories, hunches and other persons' predictions, etc., in making his decisions. Among these, or perhaps the fundamental part of each of these, will be the individual's experience on how well or badly each of these elements has done in the past.

The above analysis implies that, in general, individuals will base their predictions on a composite of theories, hunches, etc. But individual economists usually base their predictions on only one theory. This may be a purely academic exercise, in which the question of an optimal choice among theories is ignored, but it could also be a result of an optimizing decision. There are several possibilities here. Three of these are listed below. However, their decisions on their own investments may be based on predictions derived not only from their theory but also upon their hunches and the theories that they do not espouse.

First, the given economist might have such a faith in the predictions of his theory that he *believes* P_t^{e*}, as predicted by *his* theory, to be identically zero, for every t.[6] In such a case, the opportunity locus degenerates to one point, the origin, in Figure 4.4, and the optimal prediction is that given by the economist's theory. This prediction dominates over the predictions of all other theories, assuming that the economist in question considers them to yield predictions with non-zero choice-theoretic errors.

A second possibility is that while the given economist's own theory is expected to make choice-theoretic errors, he expects these errors to have a smaller mean and variance than the errors of other theories, and the opportunity locus and the indifference curves are such that the optimal prediction is given only by his own theory. This is shown in Figure 4.5, with the point A representing the predictions of the economist's own theory.

A yet third possibility, with the opportunity locus of any type, is if the given economist's theory is represented by the point A in Figures

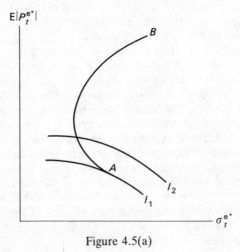

Figure 4.5(a)

4.4, 4.5 and 4.6 but the individual is indifferent to $\sigma_t^{e^*}$, the dispersion of his predicted errors. The indifference curves are horizontal in this case, as shown in Figure 4.6, and the optimal point is point A.

Economists are usually aware that no one theory is a true theory such that its expected choice-theoretic errors would be always zero. Such knowledge would make it difficult to believe in the first possibility above as an explanation of their faith in their own theory. The second is always a possibility for a given individual economist but is a variation of the general case in Figure 4.4, so that, in general, we would still expect most economists to use composite predictions rather than those of only one theory. The third is a strong possibility. Economists *qua* economists, and not as individuals staking their wealth on their predictions, could quite plausibly have a utility function that is linear in the choice-theoretic error: they want to choose the theory that has on average the minimum such error. Note that there is an *obiter dictum* to this: the self-same economist who espouses only one theory as an economist may use a composite one in making his own investments, where he does have something to lose.

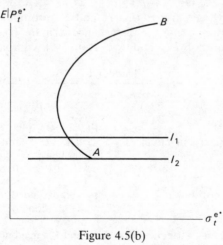

Figure 4.5(b)

(d) Choice-Theoretic Errors and Stochastic Errors

The framework of section (a) extended to include stochastic errors implies that, *ex post*,

$$P_t = P_t^T + P_t^* + u_t \tag{13}$$

where u_t is the stochastic error.[7] We assume it to have a zero mean and finite variance. Other assumptions usually made in simple least squares regression analysis can be added. Hence,

$$E(P_t) = P_t^T + E(P_t^*). \tag{13'}$$

In terms of expectations,

$$P_t^c = P_t^{cT} + P_t^{c*} + u_t, \tag{14}$$

where P_t^{c*} is the anticipated value of the choice–theoretic error. P_t^{c*} is not a random variable. (14) implies that

$$E(P_t^c) = E(P_t^{cT}) + E(P_t^{c*}). \tag{14'}$$

It is usual to assume that P_t^T is a single number. However, from the *ex ante* viewpoint, it seems more realistic to assume that at least some of the exogenous variables that determine P_t^T are unknown prior to period t and that the individual has a subjective probability distribution of each one. P_t^T then would also have a probability distribution. This is reflected in our rewriting P^T as P^{cT} in equation (14) and in our not assuming that $E(P_t^{cT}) = P_tT$.

It has already been argued that P_t^* and P_t^{c*} are not stochastic variables in the same sense as the disturbance term u_t. To emphasize the distinctive nature of P_t^{c*} and P_t^*, Table 4.1 compares the usual

Table 4.1

	Assumptions on	
	u_t	P_t^* *and/or* P_t^{c*}
1	$E(u_t) = 0$	$E(P_t^*) \neq 0$, $E(P_t^{c*}) \neq 0$
2	var $(u_t) = \sigma_u^2$ (constant variance)	variances of P_t^* and P_t^{c*} need not be constant.
3	cov $(u_t, P_t^T) = 0$	cov $(P_t^T, P_t^*) \neq 0$, cov $(P_t^{cT}, P_t^{c*}) \neq 0$
4	u_t is normally distributed.	P_t^* and P_t^{c*} need not have normal distributions or even symmetric ones.
5	u_t has a constant distribution over time.	P_t^* and P_t^{c*} need not have constant distributions over time.
6	u_t is the result of a large number of independently distributed disturbances or determinants.	P_t^* and P_t^{c*} are due to systematic and possibly important factors whose value and impact are not precisely known. The number of such determinants could be small.
7	A precise theory exists or is postulated for dealing with u_t.	A precise theory cannot exist for dealing with P_t^* due to inherent deficiences in knowledge.

assumptions of least squares analysis on u_t with what would be reasonable to assume for P_t^* and $P_t^{e^*}$.

Suppose that (13) is estimated as,

$$P_t = P_t^T + e_t \tag{15}$$

where $e_t = P_t^* + u_t$. e_t clearly does not satisfy the assumptions of least squares regression analysis, whether one-stage, two-stage and its other modifications. Assuming that the relevant theory specifies P_t^T as,

$$P_t^T = b_0 + \Sigma_{i=1}^n b_i X_{it} \tag{16}$$

$$P_t = b_0 + \Sigma_{i=1} b_i X_{it} + e_t \tag{17}$$

where X_{it} is the value of the i'th variable in period t. If the researcher estimates (17), the estimates of b_i, $i = 0,1, \ldots ,n$, would not be unbiased and consistent.

The proper equation for estimation is (13). Substituting (16) in (13),

$$P_t = b_0 + \Sigma_i b_i X_{it} + P_t^* + u_t \tag{18}$$

where u_t satisfies the least squares assumptions. But we do not have observations on P_t^* that are independent of P_t and of $(b_0 + \Sigma_{b^i} X_{it})$. (18) cannot, therefore, be estimated directly.

(e) The Revised Rational Expectations Hypothesis

From (13') and (14'), we get

$$\mathrm{E}(P_t^e) = \mathrm{E}(P_t) + \mathrm{E}(P_t^{eT}) - P_t^T + \mathrm{E}(P_t^{e^*}) - \mathrm{E}(P_t^*). \tag{19}$$

This equation follows from our assumption that the individual uses all the knowledge – imperfect and inadequate – at his disposal. It thus embodies rational expectations. It differs from the cruder version $P_t^e = \mathrm{E}(P_t)$ in Muth's simpler framework. In Muth's framework, the individual has probability distributions of P_t^e and P_t^{eT} that are confined to their mean values – that is, $\mathrm{E}(P_t^e) = P_t^e$ and $\mathrm{E}(P_t^{eT}) = P_t^T$. Further, in this simpler framework, theories do not make choice-theoretic errors, implying that $P_t^* = 0$, nor does the individual expect them to make such errors. No stochastic errors occur in the predictions of the exogenous variables. That is, $P_t^{e^*} = 0$. (19) then becomes Muth's version of the REH:

$$P_t^e = \mathrm{E}(P_t).$$

(19) can be regarded as our bounded rationality version of the REH.

(f) The Choice-Theoretic Hypothesis and Distributed Lags

We have assumed that the individual does not have a theory for predicting P_t^{e*}. He is not irrational enough to ignore it or to assume that $P_t^{e*} = 0$. His guesses about it will most likely be based on his past experience with P_t^* as well as his knowledge of the extent to which the relevant state of the world seems to have changed. Write P_t^{e*} as

$$P_t^{e*} = P_t^{e*'} + P_t^{e*''}$$

where $P_t^{e*'}$ is the part of P_t^{e*} that is based on past experience with P_t^*. We cannot say much in formal analysis about $P_t^{e*''}$, the component of P_t^{e*} that is based on some idea of the emerging and unprecedented events. On P_t^{e*}, we have assumed that

$$P_t^{e*'} = f(P_{t-1}^*, P_{t-2}^*, \ldots). \tag{20}$$

Looking at P_t^{eT} in (2), P_t^{eT} can similarly be broken down into two components: $P_t^{eT'}$, which captures the effect of continuing trends in the exogenous variables, and $P_t^{eT''}$, which reflects the influence of deviations from past trends. Write

$$P_t^{eT'} = g\,(P_{t-1}^T, P_{t-2}^T, \ldots). \tag{21}$$

(20), (21) and (14) imply that,

$$P_t^e = g\,(P_{t-1}^T, P_{t-2}^T, \ldots) + f(P_{t-1}^*, P_{t-2}^*, \ldots) + P_t^{eT''} + P_t^{e*''} + u_t. \tag{22}$$

(22) may be approximated by

$$P_t^e = h\,(P_{t-1}, P_{t-2}, \ldots) + P_t^{eT''} + P_t^{e*''} + u_t. \tag{23}$$

Relatively stable conditions would have $(P_t^{eT''} + P_t^{e*''})$ close to zero, while turbulent economic conditions would have large values for this sum. Appropriate distributed lag models should, therefore, do better in relatively stable conditions.

(g) The Revision of Expectations

A change in the anticipations of the individual could come about in one of three ways:

1. A revision of his estimates of the expected values of the exogenous variables.
2. A revision of his theories.
3. A revision of the choice-theoretic errors.

Of these three models of revision of anticipations, (2) would probably take the longest time to complete. The costs, in terms of time and money, of revising one's theoretical knowledge are usually fairly high and the individual may choose to maintain the body of his theoretical knowledge even when it performs poorly. We could here apply the usual optimizing rule: the public would revise its theoretical knowledge only if the benefits from this revision exceed its costs. The costs to the layman of increasing his virtually non-existent, theoretical knowledge of economics by any significant extent by learning economics are phenomenally high. The costs of acquiring the relevant forecasts by employing an economist or subscribing to the reports of an economic consultancy agency specializing in what he needs are also quite high. The cost to a given economist of revising his theories is also extremely high. In fact, in general the individual economist hardly ever shifts from his attachment to theories that he learnt early in his professional career. He may instead choose to revise his estimate of the choice-theoretic error for the next period. Such revisions are low-cost ones and do not have to take time. We could assume that, if the individual finds *ex post* errors in his anticipations, he will revise his anticipations for the future by revising his estimate of the choice-theoretic error. This seems to be a sensible short-run assumption, with the revision of theories being left to the long run. This is analogous to the concepts of the short run and the long run in the theory of the firm: in the long run, the firm can revise its plant size and its theoretical knowledge; it cannot revise these in the short run.

NOTES

1 This usage of the notion of bounded rationality is consistent with that of Simon (1979), who defines it as intended rationality within the limits of man's abilities to comprehend and compute in the face of complexity and uncertainty, or as 'rationality is bounded when it falls short of omniscience. And the failures of omniscience are largely failures of knowing all the alternatives, uncertainty about relevant exogenous events, and inability to calculate consequences' (Simon, 1979, p. 502). This can be taken as one description of the world assumed in this paper.

2   This assumption is often made by those who believe in the REH.
3   Economists have probably studied the demand and supply of money (M_1) as much as any other topic. Yet their predictions of it have never satisfied a hypothesis that would assert that $M_{1t} = EM_{1t}$, where M_1^* is the anticipated money supply and EM_1 is its mathematical expectation.
4   The cost function does not take account of the losses arising from mis-estimating the price level. Such losses would be taken account of in the utility function. Alternatively, the optimizing problem can be changed to one of cost-minimization where the costs include both those of collecting information and the losses from misinformation.
5   $P_t^{e^{*i}}$ is the choice-theoretic error expected for the i'th theory's prediction.
6   Note that $P_t^{e^*}$ has a *subjective* probability distribution.
7   P_t^T is defined in the rest of this paper as the prediction of the individual's optimal composite theory.

REFERENCES

Feige, E. L. and Pearce, D. K. (1976) 'Economically rational expectations: are innovations in the rate of inflation independent of innovations in measures of monetary and fiscal policies', *Journal of Political Economy*, Vol. 24, pp. 499–522.

Muth, J. F. (1961) 'Rational expectations and the theory of price movements', *Econometrica*, Vol. 29, no. 3, 315–35.

Popper, K. (1963) *Conjectures and Refutations*, New York: Basic Books.

Simon, H. A. (1979) 'Rational decision making in business organizations', *American Economic Review*, Vol. 69, 493–513.

Tobin, J. (1958) 'Liquidity preference as behaviour towards risk', *Review of Economic Studies*, Vol. 25, no. 67 (February), 65–86.

Tobin, J. (1965) 'The theory of portfolio selection', in F. H. Hahn and F. B. R. Brechling (eds), *The Theory of Interest Rates*, London: Macmillan, pp. 3–51.

Walters, A. A. (1971) 'Consistent expectations, distributed lags and the quantity theory', *Economic Journal*, Vol. 81, 273–81.

Each of the three branches of conservative economic theory has now been shown to be deeply flawed. Replies and rebuttals will, of course, be forthcoming, but the difficulties we have examined are so fundamental that to rectify them will virtually require reconstructing the theory. If the theory has be be rebuilt altogether, then it is certainly not valid to assume that it will reach the same conclusions about equilibrium, the role of government and so on.

Let us review the main points. Supply-siders oversimplify their theory of incentives, even in neoclassical terms, on top of which we all know that people respond to many other kinds of incentives besides the purely economic ones. Essentially, supply-side theory is modern-day 'vulgar economics', apologetics for the crudest doctrines of capitalism; it is unsophisticated in form, content and method. Not so the other two. Monetarism has generated a serious body of work, both theoretical and empirical. But it has never faced up to, much less resolved, the problem of the connection between monetary changes and real variables. This problem, called the 'dichotomy' by neoclassical writers and the 'transmission' problem by monetarists, continues to plague the theoretical literature, as we showed in our examination of Friedman's work. The result is that the models are either under- or overdetermined, that is, either inadequate or inconsistent. Finally, the rational expectations school differs from Keynesians less in its treatment of expectations than in its reliance on simple neoclassical models, which are supplemented by *ad hoc* and often unjustified assumptions about knowledge or learning. In any case there is no reason to assume that market agents believe neoclassical theory, since even many economists do not. If we allow *varied* beliefs, the results would be more plausible but they would no longer support the conservative cause. In short, conservative economic programs cannot be supported on theoretical grounds.

5 Social Policy: Private Reactions to Public Decisions

Gary Becker's influential *A Treatise on the Family* (1981) applies conservative economic theory to marriage and the family, and shows in the process that attempts to regulate or influence these practices through laws or redistributive measures will be undercut by the private market responses of rational individuals. The book is typical of the conservative approach to policy issues.

ECONOMIZING LOVE

Gary Becker is a renowned economist whose claim to fame rests largely on the ingenuity with which he argues that there is a calculating little capitalist concealed in all of us. In *A Treatise on the Family* he applies his technique and point of view to what most people would regard as a highly unlikely area – the field of marriage, where one would expect the heart to dominate the purse. Not so, according to Becker. His conclusions are startling, to say the least, and not all of us will recognize ourselves.

Here is why rational people – and Becker sees us all as more rational than not – marry:

> . . . persons marry each other if and only if they expect to be better off compared to their best alternatives . . .
> . . . rational persons marry even when certain of eventually finding better prospects with additional search, for the cost of additional search exceeds the expected benefits from better prospects. (Becker, 1981, p. 39)

As for whom we marry: '[In] efficient marriage markets, . . . high-quality men are matched with high-quality women and low-quality men with low-quality women.' Prospective marriage partners estimate one another's 'quality', in Becker's world, primarily by earning power, although they also calculate the value of intangibles, like satisfaction. Nevertheless, 'Men with higher earnings or other income . . . can attract several wives or higher quality wives. This explains why they marry at younger ages and remarry faster when widowed or divorced'. (p. 25).

As for the place of women:

> . . . comparative advantage [implies] that married men will specialize in the market sector and married women in the household sector. Therefore the market wage rates of married men will exceed those of married women . . . (p. 25)

As for love, Becker says it comes from the interaction between an altruist, who takes other people's happiness into account in making his choices, and the altruists' selfish beneficiary, who characteristically thinks only of the pleasures she will get. (Becker's choice of pronouns is always consistent.) In a family or relationship the recipient concludes that someone else's altruism is good for her, and so in turn behaves altruistically enough to make sure the altruist is well enough off to continue to perform kindnesses for her. In short, love is disguised efficiency.

Of course, 'love [altruism] and other personal characteristics are less readily ascertainable prior to marriage than are family reputation and position'.

> . . . The average divorced person can be presumed to be more quarrelsome and in other ways less pleasant than the average person remaining married because an unpleasant temperament is one cause of divorce . . . (p. 234)

If such traits emerge after marriage, they are 'unexpected information', which leads to divorce when it reduces the couple's wealth from remaining married 'below their wealth from a divorce'. Thus, since there will be mistakes in an uncertain world, 'modern societies have what may appear to be a paradoxical combination of many love marriages and high rates of divorce'.

Let us now go through the entire argument and see what it really says, for it will emerge that there is a very strong underlying political message – Reaganomics, in fact.

Becker begins with the gains from specialization and division of labor in the household. These explain why marriage is instituted in the first place: the wealth of the parties after marriage will be greater than before. To the altar men bring 'human capital' that is oriented to the market, such as job skills, plumbing or accounting. Women bring 'human capital' that is oriented to the household, such as cleaning or child-caring. Hence, men take jobs outside the home, while women do the housework. This is efficient, i.e. specialized according to comparative advantage. When the distribution of potential 'quality' – productivity or earning power in their separate worlds – is about the same for both the men and women in the pool of suitable marriage partners, monogamy will prevail; but if, say, there is one group of high-quality men with the rest clearly made of inferior stuff and the women are all more or less equal, then an efficient marriage market will theoretically require more than one woman to balance one man's productivity, and hence will promote or at least condone polygamy. Even when pools of partners are about even in 'quality', high-quality men will usually be matched with top-drawer women and low-quality men with the leftovers, as dictated by the canons of efficiency. Children result from a complex decision involving a tradeoff between their quantity and their 'quality', which depends both on their cost and the earning potential of both parents but particularly of the mother, since child-bearing will fall on her. This explains both the low birth rates in modern societies, and the recent decline, as women's earnings outside the home have risen. Divorce results from a recalculation of advantages in the light of new information; so that, when it is clear that the wealth from parting exceeds that from remaining married, a couple will divorce. Combined with an analysis of 'optimal bequests', and mixed with some assumptions about 'luck', the foregoing can be pulled together into a theory of income distribution, showing this to be a function of 'investment in human capital', modified by various circumstances.

Without exception, Becker applies to each of the topics he discusses a bald idea of motivation derived from economics: people try to satisfy their preferences (which may include preferences for being altruistic) as far as possible subject to the constraints of scarcity. Exchange takes place because it permits higher levels of satisfaction, e.g. because of 'comparative advantage', that is, each party specializes in what he or she can do *relatively* best, even if one party can do everything better. Investment in physical or human capital takes place because the sacrifice made now (by not consuming the goods or income) will be more than compensated by the increased income later. Investment in physical capital – building a factory, buying a machine – is no different in principle from investment in human capital – getting a degree, taking a course – except that machines can be scrapped or sold off but degrees cannot.

A delectable morsel, but not cooked up for science alone; there are implications for social policy. There are two important messages. The first is that the marriage market cannot work efficiently if it is meddled with. Welfare programs, like Aid to Dependent Children, will raise the rate of illegitimacy and increase the divorce rate essentially because they reduce the penalties associated with each. Welfare undermines the family. The second is that the government can have no significant long-run effect on income distribution. Government supplementary programs, like Head Start or school lunches, lead to offsetting reductions in parents' investment spending on their children. Less spending means less attention. The government causes child neglect. Hence these programs are wasteful failures. Similarly, the equalizing effects of government 'transfer programs' from rich to poor and inheritance taxes will be offset, eventually, by changes in private behavior, e.g. by reductions of earning efforts by the poor. Nothing can be done to change the income distribution, except temporarily, because it reflects the rational behavior of private households investing in education, given their tastes, their market information – and their luck.

In fact, government transfer programs are worse than wasteful; they undermine the incentive to private charity which *can* make a difference, precisely because it is voluntary and therefore does not provoke offsetting reactions. But the existence of government programs (even though they will ultimately fail) reduces private charity. There is, however, one way the government could help: by underwriting private bank loans to the poor, making greater investment by them possible. The poor should go into debt, and the government should be the debt-collector.

In short, Becker sees all decisions (including those of many non-human species) as explainable by means of the model of maximizing 'utility' subject to the constraints imposed by scarce resources. The same calculus that explains the market for goods and services can be adopted to explain the market for husbands and wives. The marriage market, an 'implicit' market, nevertheless works according to the same principles that govern explicit ones and, indeed, simply reflect the making of rational choices subject to the constraints imposed by natural scarcity.

A common reaction to this book will be that best expressed by Wordsworth:

Count not the cost: High Heaven rejects the lore of nicely calculated less or more.

The cold-blooded and cold-hearted calculation of gain has no place in the analysis of marriage, the having and caring for children, or in the tragedy of divorce. These are affairs of the heart; the proper function of the head is in the world of business and politics or in matters intellectual. If allowed a place here it will only create confusion; analysis is inappropriate since the decisions are properly made on the basis of emotion rather than reason.

To reject Becker on these grounds is too easy – and concedes him far too much. No doubt his calculations often oscillate between the ridiculous and the disgusting; some nevertheless have a point. There *is* a marriage market, and has always been, as bride prices in primitive communities and the novels of Jane Austen testify. For, after all, the family does perform economic functions and, moreover, within the family there is an often controversial division of labor. Children are both costly and capable of earning income and, as they get older, helping to support their parents. Divorces are often economic as well as emotional disasters or liberations. To reject Becker on the grounds that family life is an area in which economic calculation has no place is absurd; but, worse, it implicitly concedes the field of economics to him.

For Becker's book is not merely an application of economic analysis to the family; it draws on a very special and strongly ideological version of modern economic theory that is highly suspect in the profession today. Economists respect much of the work done at Chicago, but by and large they do not believe it. And Becker's work, in particular, stands out in its uncompromising purity. His version of economic theory is uncontaminated either by reality or by the arguments of critics outside his own narrow tradition. Both are ignored.

Enough of this. Now let us examine his terms.

Becker's analysis of income distribution and the prospects for redistribution is actually flawed even on his own terms. For example, he suggests that the progressive tax system redistributes incentives in such a way as to increase long-term inequality. Yet, even using Becker's own assumptions and methodology, the opposite conclusion is more plausible. For individuals are supposed to choose their lifestyles, then adapt rationally to relevant variables, including government policies. To demonstrate the ineffectiveness of government intervention, Becker focuses on government income redistribution programs – the progressive income tax and transfer payments. He postulates that families, including the poor, the unemployed and the illiterate, make life-cycle human capital investment plans that span two generations. These investment plans weight the expected rate of return on investment, and consider the families' preferences for leisure and for present and future consumption. Progressive income taxation aimed at redistribution will lower the expected rate of return to investment in human capital, causing families to cut back their investments. Becker feels that the lack of significant change in the percentage distribution of income in the USA during this century, despite the progressive income tax, is explained by this incentive effect (Becker, 1981).

The reduced incentive to invest in human capital, where income is taxed progressively, will not be equally distributed, however, for clearly the well-off are more severely affected than the poor (assuming no tax loopholes, of course). Thus the wealthy would cut back investment in human capital more than would the poor, resulting in *less* second-generation inequality (assuming differential earnings actually do reflect human capital investments, of course).

Other government programs designed to redistribute income – welfare and other outright transfer payments to the poor – are also counterproductive, in Becker's view. They weaken family ties, discourage labor force participation, and encourage illegitimacy, high fertility and divorce in poor families. Becker presents no empirical evidence to back up these propositions, but from his point of view he need not – rational agents will maximize their net family income, and if they can do so by having more babies or abandoning the family, so be it. Becker *must* take this view, since the decision to marry and to stay married and the demand for children are, in his view, simply governed by the desire to maximize household income. But in fact, of course, poor women had lots of babies and poor men abandoned their wives and families long before there was Aid to Families with Dependent Children (AFDC); and illegitimate birth rates are highest in American states such as Alabama and Mississippi where AFDC payments are lowest.

Even if Becker's methodology did not preclude his recognizing other human emotions besides the lure of the dollar, he could still take a different view of transfer payments. Transfer payment programs change initial endowments. So, even according to neoclassical theory, these could affect the final equilibrium. Indeed, the possibility of government action to change initial endowments has been a standard consideration of neoclassical 'welfare economics'. Usually, of course, this is presented as 'lump-sum' taxation, transferring wealth from one set of endowments to another. But entitlement programs, financed by taxes, can be treated as lump-sum transfers of 'human capital', simply by capitalizing the taxes and the payments stream. Moreover, if the taxes fall on income that would have been spent on luxuries or socially damaging consumption (e.g. cigarettes) and the payments support better health or education, the consequence should be judged a *net* increase in 'human capital', and not merely a transfer.

Becker, however, feels that income supplement programs do not improve the lot of the poor because, he contends, they reduce their efforts to earn in proportion to the grants they receive. Food stamps do not raise the nutritional standards of the poor; they simply make it easier for them to eat and allow them, for example, to avoid taking the low-paying jobs, which are supposedly commensurate with their skills, in order to survive. But as a practical matter (Becker is seldom practical) the vast proportion of poor in the USA are frail old ladies and small children and their mothers. The reasons these people fail to take paying jobs have nothing to do with inflated wage expectations. They do not work because, given their circumstances, they cannot.

For these people, redistributive government programs make the difference between having an income and not having one, between eating well and eating poorly. Even in the strict terms of rational expectations and human capital theory, such programs make a difference. If individuals maximize utility subject to constraints and the constraints are changed, the consumption patterns clearly shift. Welfare payments permit the poor to increase their 'human capital investments', so that when they do enter the labor or the marriage markets they do so as well-fed rather than sickly individuals, promising greater contributions to prospective employers or spouses, thus landing better jobs or catching more eligible mates.

Becker, on the other hand, feels that income-providing government programs actually feed people who would otherwise be cared for by 'private charity' – family, friends, neighbors or even errant husbands. This is hard to understand. The inadequacy – and arbitrariness – of private charity was one of the reasons for starting the government programs. In any case, in order for the distributional effect of government programs to be zero, the private charity discouraged must be equal and similarly distributed to the government largess handed out. No one could seriously argue this. For example, the family and neighbors of the poor are generally also poor. So government programs, by redistributing income from the well-off to the poor, may offset private charity that would have redistributed from poor to poor. Thus, in contrast to private charity, the government program would change the income distribution to improve the ability of the poor to invest in human capital, and thus enhance their position in labor and marriage markets – to put it in Becker's terms.

Following the well-trodden path of Jeremy Bentham, Becker assumes that we choose courses of action because they satisfy our preferences as much as possible given the costs and the alternatives, where the costs arise ultimately from scarcity. Both sides of this paradigm – the benefits, ranked by preferences, and the costs, imposed by scarcity – are faulty.

Take the costs first. Many costs, of course, do arise from scarcity, that is, from production, from our ways of transforming what Nature provides into what is useful for human society. But many do not, as people living in Chicago should know. Many costs are *imposed* by one party on others, as parts of strategies to improve income or social position. Thus Al Capone imposed costs on others as part of his strategy to sell liquor. Businesses regularly impose costs on other businesses, on their employees and on their customers. And, just as regularly, the other parties undertake expenditures for defense and/ or for retaliation. Becker would no doubt argue that such activities have no place in perfect competition, but surely that is simply another reason why the model of perfect competition should be ignored. When it comes to family life, to the division of labor in the household, and to the distribution of income either within the family or within society as a whole, surely the process of economic warfare – imposing costs and defending against them – must be considered central. Yet for all Becker's apparent hard-nosed rational calculation, he never considers what 'costs', for example, a husband could impose on a wife, at minimal inconvenience to himself, to compel her to do his bidding, or what her optimal defense would be. For Becker, marriage is an exchange relationship and exchange, in his economics, always leaves both parties better off. So much for realism.

Now let us look at the other side – choice based on preferences. According to Becker, *all* of our actions can be explained as choices based on our preferences and constrained by the costs arising from scarcity. But we know this is nonsense. Many of our actions have nothing to do with our preferences in the ordinary sense of the term, particularly when we come to the economic behavior of the family. They are *imposed* on us, often against our real wishes, by our jobs, family responsibilities or social positions. They are obligations resulting from prior commitments. Our present choices and actions reflect the past. Of course, Becker would argue that institutions are simply contractual relationships between individuals, chosen on the basis of their preferences. Most philosophers and social theorists would disagree, but Becker has never confronted the issues in any of his writings. Yet the point is utterly basic: if jobs or social positions or institutions are *not* 'reducible' to the voluntary decisions of individuals, then their independent influence must be taken into account. Becker's framework is not sufficient.

Think of the effects of the development of the modern corporation out of the family business, and along with it, the development of modern agriculture. Together these largely determined the shape of the modern city, and there can be no doubt that the urbanization – and suburbanization – of the working class has brought immense changes in the family.

Over the last century a large number of functions formerly performed by the family have been taken from it. Education (more generally, socialization) may be the chief example, but pensions, insurance, welfare and much medical care are now provided by the state, where in the past they were the responsibility of the family.

Moreover, private capital now performs for profit many tasks formerly handled in the home. Food processing and preserving, the handling of births and deaths, the making and mending of clothes, and the care of the aged, among many others, are all now major businesses, although they once figured among the provinces ruled by our great-grandmothers.

Becker would explain these developments by reference, on the one hand, to the greater 'efficiency' of the market system and, on the other, to the rise in the market earning power of women, who, as a result, choose to work less in the home. This rise in the relative earning power of women is itself unexplained, however. An institutional economic approach, by contrast, would explain the changed position of the family by reference to the shift away from family farming, the resulting urbanization and changes in occupational structure, particularly the rise of large hierarchical bureaucracies. Furthermore, the pace of change also matters, since each generation must be prepared for an occupational structure that is not only new but will change during its working life. Becker's commitment to individualism requires him to try to explain the changes in the family in terms of changes in the characteristics of its members – in this case the earning power of women. Both as description and as explanation this account of the new position of the family is inadequate.

So both sides of Becker's paradigm are flawed. On the cost side he overlooks imposed costs (coercion and economic warfare) and on the preference side he ignores institutional factors. Yet these intellectual defects do not explain the real aversion – even disgust – that reading this book provokes. This deeper problem lies in the paradigm itself, in the idea that human behavior can – or perhaps should – be represented by a model of rational, mathematical choice – 'internalizing the external mechanization of life', in Wilhelm Reich's memorable phrase. Rational choice is *reactive;* facing given conditions people calculate and make the best of what is presented to them. They change their calculated optimum packages reactively, as the conditions they face, and accept, change. In such a model nothing is created, nothing happens; people choose commodities, not their destiny. They do not weave the fabric of life.

> Let me not to the marriage of true minds
> Admit impediments; love is not love
> Which alters when it alteration finds
> Or bends with the remover to remove.

Two of the most powerful motivating forces in mankind's nature are love and fear. Becker understands neither; all he can analyze is a form of greed – the individual pursuit of pleasure or gain. But he cannot do even that adequately, because he cannot situate his analysis institutionally, or combine it with accounts of the other forces that motivate people. He sees 'free choices' where there are in reality, and necessarily, social constraints, obligations, pressures and coercion; and he fails altogether to see the truly creative freedom of the human spirit, which refuses to accept the given, and brings forth inventions, imagination and poetry – the freedom inherent in love.

REFERENCE

Becker, G. S. (1981) *A Treatise on the Family*, Cambridge, Mass.: Harvard University Press.

PART II: Practice

By now the catalogue of conservative economic disasters has become rich and varied. To be sure, there are some successes: Reagan and Thatcher, for instance, have brought down their country's respective inflation rates – but only by generating the highest unemployment in forty years. In every country where conservative economic programs have been tried, they have led to increased unemployment, more bankruptcies and widespread economic disaster. Why then are their policies popular? We have seen that their theoretical underpinnings are almost wholly without merit. When the evident, frequently observed and wholly predictable result of adopting their policies is a downturn in the economy, why do so many people support the conservative position? Indeed, many fervent supporters of Thatcher and Reagan are now out of jobs or in bankruptcy court, yet they often still remain loyal. What is is that has so attracted them, even against their own interests? What is the program actually accomplishing that keeps them loyal, in spite of hardship?

One answer, of course, is that the program, working more slowly than is desirable, but just as steadily as ever, is going to bring about Economic Recovery, meaning full employment without inflation and with a strong currency and high productivity growth. Eventually. We must be patient.

Well, perhaps. True believers are after all entitled to their fantasies. But there isn't a shred of evidence and the theoretical case is full of holes. So let us rule this answer out of court. Then the problem becomes interesting: what *are* the conservatives doing? How can they mobilize the backing of most of the business community for a program that throws an unprecedented number of businesses into bankruptcy court? How can they mobilize widespread – even if clearly a minority – labor support for a program that generates unprecedented unemployment?

In what follows we look at three case studies (Reagan, Thatcher and the milatary regime of Pinochet in Chile), run by 'Chicago boys'. In each case a different answer is suggested. First we have Amott on Reagan. Her contention is that conservative economic policies have chiefly served as a platform on which to bring together and reconcile the diverse elements of a new political coalition. This, she holds, is more significant than the actual content of the conservative program, which in fact is incoherent. Hodgson, by contrast, holds that the policy program is essential; it is what the Thatcher government is all about. The program is a set of mistakes and outmoded ideas that do not work, but in not working undermine the welfare state. The real meaning of Thatcherism is class revenge; it is a reactionary movement in the most basic sense of that term. Schneider, on the other hand, argues that, in Chile, the purpose of the policy program was not, as some have suggested, to destroy the labor movement, but to dismantle the quite effective and non-corrupt government bureaucracy (which was capable of managing the economy, but was also responsive to popular, democratic pressure), and replace it with a set of financial institutions organized around the capital market, which will perform essential but limited coordinating functions and cannot be affected by democratic pressures.

These three positions are different, but not necessarily in conflict. Perhaps we've said enough, and it is now time for readers to decide for themselves.

6 The Politics of Reaganomics

The ideas of economists and political philosophers, both when they are right and when they are wrong, are more powerful than is commonly understood. Indeed, the world is ruled by little else. Practical men, who believe themselves to be quite exempt from any intellectual influence, are usually the slaves of some defunct economist. Madmen in authority, who hear voices in the air, are distilling their frenzy from some academic scribbler of a few years back. I am sure that the power of vested interests is vastly exaggerated compared with the gradual encroachment of ideas. (Keynes, 1964, p. 383)

Forty-five years after Keynes wrote these words, it is common to find them quoted in discussions of the relationship between economic theory and policy; if anything, the passage has lost its power to provoke us into speculation on the ways in which policy-makers merge academic recommendations with political realities to produce economic policies. What ought to be startling is how different a picture Keynes painted from the one we observe today: more than twenty years passed before a durable consensus emerged on Keynesian policies of demand management, but the notions of 'supply-side' economics had barely begun to work their way into academic economic discourse before they were revealed as the pillars of the Reagan administration's macro policy. The radically different policies adopted by these 'madmen in authority' have not been distilled from the writings of some 'defunct economist'; rather, the Reagan campaign and administration played a decisive role in elevating a set of journalistic analyses and speculative propositions to the status of economic theory – and, indeed, nearly to the status of religion, so fervent are supply-siders in praise of their theories. What is the source of this conviction? How did supply-side economics gain its ascendancy, and why were traditional economic remedies abandoned by the US administration, in rhetoric, if not in practice? Can supply-side economics succeed in conquering the stagflation that has characterized capitalist economies since the 1970s? In what follows, the interaction between politics and economics is explored in order to shed light on the fall from grace of the neoclassical synthesis in economic theory and the demand management policies that grew out of that synthesis.

In the space of a very short time, the United States saw two clear changes in the direction and content of political and economic discourse. At the political level, the 1980 election brought to office a President who had previously been considered far too extreme ever to hold national office. At the economic level, policy-makers rejected Keynesian demand management and embraced a theory of economics that moved unusually quickly into the policy arena. We shall argue that these two changes are related, and that the ascendant political coalition and economic theory are mutually determining. We begin with a brief discussion of supply-side economics and its differences from the neoclassical synthesis it displaced from administration policy discussions. Next, we discuss the politics of supply-side economics, and its origins in the construction of a new Republican coalition. In that section, we pay particularly close atttention to the administration's relationship to organized labor and we describe the wide latitude enjoyed by the administration. Next, we point to some contradictions inherent in this political and economic coalition, concentrating on the problems of combining a fiscal expansion through supply-side measures with monetary restraint. These contradictions suggest that the new coalition may be less durable than its initial strength would imply. Finally, in the last section, we examine the outcome of these contradictions, documenting the economy's downward slide from 1980 through 1982.

SUPPLY-SIDE ECONOMICS

The goal of supply-side economic policy is surprisingly simple: inflation and unemployment are to be eased by increasing aggregate supply, thus avoiding the painful choices imposed by policies that operate on the aggregate demand curve. Demand management forces us to choose lower inflation or higher employment, whereas supply-side policies allow us to have our cake and eat it too. Supply will be expanded by tax cuts for business and wealthy individuals, as well as by a weakening of government regulations that have altered the pattern of business investment in the past. Tight money, kept rigorously in check by the Federal Reserve, serves two purposes: first, it holds down the otherwise inflationary effects of the tax cuts, and second, but more problematic, it dampens inflationary expectations so that interest rates fall. While the administration's supply-siders cheered the Fed as it held the money supply in check through the first two years of the administration, we shall see later how they were forced to call for easier money, and assigned the blame for the failure of their policies to the Federal Reserve.

The last piece of the policy that has now become known as 'Reaganomics' was a cut in non-defense federal spending, ostensibly to remove the work disincentive effects of social programs. Defense spending, however, was projected to rise dramatically. As Alfred Eichner (1981) has pointed out, the increase in defense spending has no direct supply-side benefits but does, nonetheless, have demand-side effects that are highly stimulative in the short run.

The supply-side solution departs from demand management policy in many ways, but they can be summarized neatly by recalling Keynes' emphasis on the distinction between saving and investment. Firms invest, primarily in response to anticipated sales, but both firms and individuals save. That planned investment thus need not equal saving creates the problem of effective demand and the call for government intervention to maintain effective demand at a level that will sustain full employment. Supply-side Reaganomics hopes to stimulate investment through accelerated depreciation and de-regulation; however, if firms do not anticipate increased sales, the new investment that is required to stimulate productivity and restore the American competitive position in world trade will not take place. The administration has concentrated its tax cuts at the upper-income levels, in the hopes of expanding the pool of savings tapped by credit markets. As much recent research has demonstrated, however, large corporations need not borrow to finance investment, drawing instead on retained earnings (Davidson, 1980). Thus, higher personal savings are neither necessary nor sufficient for more investment, as seen in the neoclassical synthesis that underlies demand management policies.

Supply-side economics burst on the scene as a media phenomenon at a time when the neoclassical synthesis was in serious trouble. Created by forcing Keynesian insights into an advanced capitalist, monetary economy to lie in a procrustean bed with classical monetary theory, the neoclassical synthesis admits the need for government intervention in the interests of macroeconomic stability, but attributes this need to the presence of sticky wages and prices. In the absence of such imperfections, the neoclassical synthesis maintains that the economy would be a homeostatic, self-regulating set of markets that would never depart from full employment for any length of time.

This view, held by many economists, is, unfortunately, difficult to maintain on logical grounds, depending, as it does, on the *ad hoc* assumption of a certain kind of market imperfection. If it is the rigidity of wages and prices that leads to a role for government stabilization, and if markets left to their own devices would produce desirable results, it would seem that an equally logical policy prescription would be to remove these rigidities rather than intervene in their aftermath. Supply-side economics presents an appealing approach along these lines. It blames government for wage and price rigidities, citing microeconomic policies such as unemployment compensation and marginal tax rates which disturb work incentives. As a result of these policies, wages have no tendency to fall when unemployment is higher than the 'natural' rate. Since government is the problem, the obvious solution is to remove the microeconomic policies that have led to wage and price rigidities (with an emphasis on wage rigidities, to be sure), thus obviating the need for macroeconomic stabilization policy and returning us to the pre-Keynesian world of smoothly functioning markets. In short, government intervention has created a need for further intervention, and has produced the economic crisis in which we now find ourselves.

Supply-side economics is less a fully articulated theory than it is a vision of rugged, individualistic entrepreneurs and hard-working families meeting in smoothly functioning markets, free from uncertainty and from the directive influence of government in their economic affairs. How could a theory so ideological in its origins, and so bereft of empirical support, have succeeded in transforming the range of policy alternatives that figure in public and academic debate? The answer, we believe, lies in an examination of the political coalition that brought Ronald Reagan to office. In the next section, we discuss the politics of supply-side economics to explain its meteoric rise to prominence.

SUPPLY-SIDE POLITICS

The process by which ideas gradually 'encroach' and find their way into policy-making, which seems to underlie Keynes' words, is one of thorough-going competition in the marketplace of ideas. Some theories are demonstrated to be wrong, presumably through the appearance of empirical observations that do not fit the theories, and others theories, which do explain the facts, come into discussion. Their adoption by policy-makers rests on a learning process by which policy-makers are slowly convinced to abandon their entrenched notions in favor of new theories. The rise of supply-side economics came about as a result of a very different process from the gradual learning Keynes spoke about.

The vicissitudes of electoral politics in the late 1970s created an opening for a shift to the right, and the administration brought to power as a result of that shift actively sought a theory with which to legitimize the policies that it believed were needed. In our view, the eclipse of both the traditional monetarist view and the Keynesian/neoclassical synthesis by a supply-side theory that both incorporates and rejects portions of the earlier views is as much, if not more, a response to a political constituency as it is a result of academic research and subsequent persuasion of policy-makers.

The dismal record of the American economy throughout the crisis period of the 1970s certainly cast demand management policies into disrepute. Their validity would have been challenged under any political circumstances. However, the same events that threatened the existing mainstream economic consensus also threatened the political viability of its partisans, bringing into office an administration with a new coalition of supporters, quite distinct from the Democratic coalition which now seems so much in disarray.

The new conservative coalition was forged with the aid of supply-side economics, which became an ideological tool with which the disparate new constituencies of the Old Right and the New Right could be reconciled. The combination of tax relief for business and upper-income individuals with a drastic pruning of government expenditures on the welfare state appeals to the Old Right (the traditional Republican constituency) as well as to the New Right, a social movement concerned much more with a broad range of social issues surrounding the family and religion than with the conduct of macro policy. A decline in the role of the public sector is an important plank in the platform of the Old Right, but allegiance of the New Right had to be purchased. Linking supply-side economics with the tax revolt at the local level was an important part of the price, as was the promise of a cure to inflation that did not involve the painful recessionary policies that were being offered by the austerity program of the Democratic Party. If Catholics, Southerners and labor union members were to join the Republican coalition, supply-side economics offered a comfortable meeting-ground.

The neo-*laissez-faire* ideology with which supply-side economics is imbued now serves as the foundation on which the government's legitimacy rests. At some point in the postwar period, working-class support for Democratic governments was secured by the promise of sustained economic growth. This meant, of course, that Democrats had to be extremely careful to maintain 'business confidence', that elusive factor termed 'animal spirits' by Keynes. Ironically, this also meant that Democratic governments were placed in the peculiar position of needing the cooperation of capital in order to maintain the support of labor. Republican administrations, on the other hand, enjoyed this confidence almost as a matter of right. (From this perspective, it is not so surprising that it was the Republican administration of Richard Nixon that broke the free market faith by imposing the only mandatory peacetime wage and price controls ever seen in the United States, and did so without losing the support of large segments of the business community.)

Today, the Republican party has adopted the Democratic growth platform, promising that the economic pie will expand if its supply-side measures are adopted. The mechanism is, of course, very different: rather than relying on government management of demand, the essence of the supply-side economics is its faith in private sector supply. If liberalized depreciation allowances and personal income tax cuts are handed out today, productivity and investment will rise tomorrow, and the benefits of economic growth will trickle down to everyone the day after. Business confidence need not be won; it simply can be assumed. Working-class support thus becomes largely irrelevant to the success of the policies. As long as working-class supporters of the administration can be convinced that the redistribution of income that accompanies supply-side measures will be in their long-term economic interest, they will willingly surrender whatever voice they had in policy-making during the period of Democratic party control – however feeble that voice might have been in light of the government's basic dependency on business support. Thus, redistribution is erased from the political agenda and disguised as a purely economic issue. George Gilder's *Wealth and Poverty*, favorite bedside reading of many administration officials, unashamedly states this appeal:

> To get a grip on the problems of poverty, one should also forget the idea of overcoming inequality by redistribution.. . . To lift the incomes of the poor, it will be necessary to increase the rates of investment, which in turn will tend to enlarge the wealth, if not the consumption, of the rich. (Gilder, 1981, p. 67)

Supply-Side Politics and Labor Constituencies

This singular disregard for labor constituencies is an important difference from previous administrations, and will be explored in more detail, since it illustrates the extent to which the administration has rejected one possible alternative to demand management in inflationary periods.

If we view inflation as arising from the competing claims of different groups for the national product, one mechanism for reconciling these claims is, of course, an incomes policy such as that advocated by Edward Kennedy during his abortive campaign for the Presidency. Western European countries have taken the lead in these policies, and strategies that integrate labor and business into negotiations over wages and prices are certainly more common in Europe than in the United States. Political scientists call these integrative arrangements 'corporatist', referring to a 'hierarchical non-conflictual integration of the state and organised groups representative of both capital and labour' (Crouch, 1981, p.197).

Corporatist arrangements are not unknown in the United States, although comparisons with Europe naturally must be undertaken with caution. The Reagan administration thus stands out for its refusal to engage in even token corporatist negotiations. During the New Deal, in particular with the early National Industrial Recovery Act of 1933, which was intended to bring business and government together with the guarantee of independent representation for labor, some integrative strategies were attempted (Skocpol, 1980). As mentioned earlier, Nixon presided over an incomes policy initially administered by a tripartite Pay Board and Price Commission. More recently, even the Carter administration made feeble gestures toward corporatist integration. Carter appointed a tripartite Pay Board to implement his call for voluntary wage restraint and flirted briefly with an Economic Revitalization Board, to be co-chaired by the chairman of Dupont and the president of the AFL-CIO. The Board was to make a recommendation on an 'investment development authority', which, in turn, could allocate credit and other special treatment to particular industries (Miller, 1980).

In the past few years, enthusiasm for corporatism has made unlikely bedfellows of liberal policy analyst Gar Alperovitz, investment banker Felix Rohatyn, and the editors of the 30 June 1981 issue of *Business Week* who outlined strategies for 'The Reindustrialization of America' in a special issue calling for a 'new social contract between business, labor, government and minorities'.

The Reagan administration has not even dignified proposals for corporatist integration with a public response, instead turning to a set of highly coercive social and economic policies that are intended to discipline and demoralize the working class and the unemployed. These policies not only repudiate integration; they represent a departure from New Deal promises and from mainstream Republican platforms. Lacking effective resistance, the administration rolls back the welfare state, assists capital in its efforts to reduce labor costs, attacks various legislative components of the big capital–big labor accord of the postwar era, and reduces worker control over conditions in the workplace.

The administration's relationship with organized labor has gone from bad to worse as Reaganomics takes its toll of labor's programs and constituencies. The first type of attack on labor might be characterized as direct, consisting of dismantling many federal programs with strong labor support. Programs under siege range from the minimum wage, threatened for the first time in its forty–three year history, to the newer social regulations such as those administered by the Occupational Safety and Health Administration and the Equal Employment Opportunity Commission. The second type of attack works by swelling the ranks of the unemployed, thus weakening labor's bargaining power and encouraging workers to lower their wage and benefit demands. (There can be no doubt, for instance, that the United Steelworkers of America local presidents were influenced in their ratification of a concessionary contract by the fact that over half their membership had been lost to the unemployment rolls.) Bolstering this strategy are cutbacks in programs that mitigate the burden of unemployment, such as unemployment compensation, elimination of many public employment programs and mandatory work requirements for those receiving welfare assistance.

The severity of the recession in the early years of the administration forced it to abandon some of these cuts in what is sometimes termed the 'social wage' – the additional income that individuals receive from the state in the form of cash benefits. Nonetheless, substantial budget savings have been achieved through tightening eligibility requirements for unemployment compensation, denying strikers Aid to Families with Dependent Children, and cutting the Trade Adjustment Assistance Act.

The political implications of the administration's repudiation of corporatism are clear: the 'Program for an Economic Recovery' is also a 'Program for the Demise of the Democratic Coalition'. Reagan is not attempting to snatch the entire coalition from the hands of the Democratic party, but he is taking advantage of the selective inroads made upon the coalition by Republican candidates in the 1980 election. Defections by blue-collar whites, Catholics, Jews and Southerners split the coalition in 1980 – as in the 1972 McGovern débâcle – and opened up the way for a program of redistribution aimed squarely at labor and welfare constituencies (Orren and Dionne, 1981).

Supply-Side Politics and the Limits of Policy

Freed from the indebtedness to organized labor that constrained Democratic policy-making on the one hand, and confident that it enjoys the automatic support of capital, on the other, this administration seems to have unusual freedom in the policy arena. The speedy passage of the Reaganomics program stunned even its supporters in the first years of the administration. Later on in the life of the Reagan administration, it took unemployment at rates unseen since the Great Depression and budget deficits at historic highs to narrow the policy latitude enjoyed by the administration (see Table 6.1).

Reagan has indicated that he will be not be distracted from his

Table 6.1   *Federal Budget Deficits, 1973–86 (US $ bn)*

Fiscal Year	Deficit
1973	−14.8
1974	−4.7
1975	−45.2
1976	−66.4
1977	−44.9
1978	−48.8
1979	−27.7
1980	−59.6
1981	−57.9
1982	−110.6
1983	−207.0[a]
1984	−196.0[a]
1985	−205.0[a]
1986	−214.0[a]

[a] US Congressional Budget Office base line projections, based on current policy and Congressional Budget Office economic assumptions.

Source: US Congressional Budget Office, *The Economic and Budget Outlook: An Update*, Washington, DC: US Government Printing Office, August 1983, Table II, p. 59.

vision of a renewed US economy: not by unemployment, not by large Federal deficits, and not even by mass opposition. Nixon, Ford and Carter all engaged in 'stop–go' economic policies, but the signal from Reagan is that he will not be moved off course. Unlike centrist governments, which are more sensitive to pressures from diverse constituencies of the working class and the unemployed, we suspect that the Reagan regime will not be deterred by anything short of mass insurrection. Should the cities explode tomorrow in opposition to the Reagan program, his response would not be a renewed War on Poverty. For instance, Reagan's summary dismissal of strikers and his incarceration of some union leaders in the PATCO strike gives us an indication of his feelings toward organized labor responses. His law and order stance bodes ill for groups that attempt civil disobedience. Finally, an attack on the Voting Rights Act, aimed at disenfranchising many minorities, was not considered unthinkable by the administration, although the Act was defended successfully in the Congress.

CONTRADICTIONS IN SUPPLY-SIDE ECONOMICS AND POLITICS

We have shown how the Reagan administration was able to move forward on its broad agenda of restructuring the economy, and have suggested that the role of supply-side economics is largely a political role of legitimation. Nonetheless, the happy marriage of a new Republican coalition with supply-side theory is unlikely to last. There are many contradictions between the self-representation of this administration and its actual practices, as well as contradictions within the practices themselves. For instance, Reagan promises to 'get government off the backs of the people', but at the same time supports – however weakly – pro-family and pro-religion social policies that are clearly coercive and invasive to many people. (See Petchesky, 1981, on the rise of the New Right and social policies.) The contradiction between ideology and practice reflects the division described earlier between the New Right and the Old Right. These two groups may be united in their support of free enterprise and a strong nation, but only so long as those doctrines operate at a sufficiently high level of generality. The two groups diverge on many questions such as the all-volunteer army, free trade (particularly with the Soviet Union), and social security.

By invoking generalities and refusing to acknowledge, much less choose, sides, the Reagan administration has gained a certain freedom from the dictates of either conservative faction. Reagan nominated Sandra O'Connor for the Supreme Court over howls of protest from the Moral Majority and its New Right allies. The Old Right, many of them followers of Milton Friedman, are similarly outraged by policies such as import restrictions on Japanese automobiles, tariffs on Japanese motorcycles, and a follow-through of the Chrysler bail-out. Reagan wins this independence (even from his own ideological allies) through complex lobbying, deals and tradeoffs. While there are certainly indications of cracks in the New Right–Old Right alliance, the administration preserves a wide discretion in pursuit of its policies both because the alliance persists and because it is unstable.

Some administration policies seem designed to create a durable coalition despite their potential danger for the economy. The expansion of military spending in the hope of re-establishing US world hegemony and avenging 'humiliation' in the foreign-policy arena caters to an extremely wide audience. However, the rapid militarization of the economy threatens economic disaster, through bottlenecks and high Federal deficits (Thurow, 1981). Another example lies in the dismantling of the welfare state, which has been accomplished in many instances by changing eligibility requirements and introducing work disincentives. Thus, while there is considerable popular support for a cut in welfare programs, that cut is being achieved in a manner that may drive many of the working poor into unemployment and a reliance on the 'safety net', ultimately driving up expenditures on those programs (Danziger and Plotnick, 1981).

The various components of Reaganomics all reveal a new anti-welfarist, free market strategy for securing popular belief in the regime. A narrowly doctrinal celebration of the free market, rather than concern for the needs of particular factions of capital, seems to orient the Reagan macroeconomic policy. Nonetheless, the *laissez-faire* ideology remains dangerously divided against itself when it comes to policy initiatives. Under the auspices of Reaganomics, the administration is harboring two quite distinct constituencies and policies: groups favoring monetarism and groups favoring supply-side economics. The differences between these two groups mirror the ideological schism that lurks in the Reagan coalition, and the contra-dictory effects of their policies spell disaster for Reaganomics. We shall next describe the problems of uniting a monetarist reign over the money supply with a supply-side stimulus to the economy.

Monetarism vs. Supply-Side Economics

The Reagan administration inherited a Federal Reserve determined to tame inflation through tight monetary policies, and Paul Volcker enjoyed substantial support for that endeavor from monetarist economists and from the Old Right, which advocates a market-based and non-interventionist response to inflation and unemployment. According to the doctrine of strict monetarism, discretionary fiscal and monetary policies are to be eschewed in favor of a constant growth rate in the money supply. Monetarists claim that rules, rather than discretionary policy changes, allow the natural self-regulatory tendencies of the economy to work unimpeded. Supply-side econ-omics, on the other hand, involves a dramatic alteration of federal tax policies with the aim of unleashing a torrent of private sector produc-tive activity. As documented in Table 6.2, the share of federal revenues contributed by the corporate income tax nearly halved dur-ing the early years of the Reagan administration. Paradoxically, supply-side economics calls for drastic intervention on *behalf* of *laissez-faire*, and vividly exemplifies one of the central contradictions in the Reagan government's strategy.

Gilder (1981) even links supply-side economics with a traditionalist plea for pro-family intervention by the state, arguing that the (evidently male) entrepreneurial instinct must be spurred on by the dependency of wife and children. Thus, an interesting analogy to the Old Right–monetarist clash with the New Right–supply-sider can be found in attitudes toward social legislation on the family. Despite the strong backing Reagan received from advocates of new, conservative social legislation, the administration waited two years before

Table 6.2   *Tax Sources of Federal Revenues (Percentage of Total)*

			Fiscal year			
Tax Source	1960	1970	1980	1981	1982	1983
Individual income	44.0	46.9	47.2	47.7	48.3	47.2
Corporate income	23.2	17.0	12.5	10.2	8.0	6.6
Social insurance*a*	15.9	23.0	30.5	30.5	32.6	35.5
Excise	12.6	8.1	4.7	6.8	5.9	6.4
Estate and gift	1.7	1.9	1.2	1.1	1.3	0.9

a Includes Social Security, Medicare, Unemployment, Railroad Retirement and Federal Employment taxes.

Note: Totals may not add to 100% as a result of rounding.

Source: US Office of Management and Budget; quoted in Leslie Wayne, 'The Corporate Tax: Uneven, Unfair?' *New York Times*, 20 March 1983, p. F26.

throwing its active support behind programs such as the reinstatement of school prayer, the 'squeal rule' requiring parental notification of teenage birth control use, and removal of 'anti-family' literature from federally-funded curriculum programs. The Old Right's libertarian stance is much less compatible with many of these initiatives. Gary Becker's world, described in Chapter 5 by Edward Nell, is one in which the state does not intervene, but families and individuals pursue maximization strategies in the sphere of free market relations. The social agenda of the New Right is quite far from this Chicago School approach of freely contracting (and re-contracting) individuals.

During the Presidential campaign, then-candidate George Bush, a conservative of the Old Right school, denounced supply-side economics as 'voodoo economics', but, as Vice President, he apparently has found the faith and papers over ideological divisions that he might have with some of the President's economic advisers. It was not long, however, before these ideological divisions, apparent early on, were translated into economic problems, and these problems began to dissolve political consensus. The Kemp-Roth tax cut, cornerstone of the supply-side program, has encountered increasingly stiff opposition each year when the Congress has passed its budget resolution. Nonetheless, the administration has stood by the program in the face of this opposition and in the face of embarrassingly high budget deficit projections.

Monetarism and supply-side economics are not necessarily incompatible at all levels. Both place the allocation of credit and other resources among sectors in the invisible hands of the market, rejecting direct sectoral intervention (such as that proposed by adherents of an industrial policy) and enhancing the autonomy of capital. Under conditions when monetary growth can be pursued without fear of inflation, the expansion of tax cuts can be accommodated. However, with a tight money policy and a fiscal expansion resulting from tax cuts and high military spending, conflict will definitely result. This conflict tends to promote fragmentation between industrial and financial capital, and sets the stage for the strange drama of a Republican President at odds with Wall Street, and with part of the business community.

Reaganomics Meets Business

Wall Street has not given supply-side economics the hero's welcome the administration feels it deserves, mainly because forecasters such as Henry Kaufman of Salomon Brothers and Henry Wojnilower of the First Boston Corporation feared high deficits and crowding out from the beginning. If both the private sector and the federal government compete for a *fixed* pool of savings by issuing new stocks and bonds, an increase in the money supply will be required to keep interest rates from rising. On the other hand, if the stimulative effects of government spending expand income and saving sufficiently, 'crowding in' will take place, generating new savings for both private and public borrowers. Wall Street's fears of crowding out thus spring from two sources. First, to the extent that the Reagan program was seen as a conventional fiscal policy, Wall Street monetarists would predict a low probability of real expansion. Second, to the extent that the program was seen as a new type of policy, a supply-side policy, Wall Street was also predicting failure.

The debate between Reagan and Wall Street has been acrimonious, with Reagan noting that he 'never found Wall Street a source of good economic advice', and with Murray Weidenbaum, first head of the Council of Economic Advisers under Reagan, suggesting that Wall Street simply had not understood the nature of the supply-side experiment. The 15 June 1981 issue of *Newsweek* quoted Weidenbaum calling Wall Street 'a class of slow learners'. (Weidenbaum was later replaced by Martin Feldstein, a conservative economist of the old school, when it became apparent that supply-side policies had failed.)

Further conflict with the financial community emerged later, when the administration, hoping to lower deficit projections, sought to secure revenues already due to the government through compulsory withholding on interest and dividend payments by banks. Reagan went so far as to blame banks for keeping interest rates high, even though banks were quick to respond that rates remained high because of anticipated federal deficits.

Uncertainty about supply-side economics was slower to emerge in the industrial sector of capital. Earlier on, the Reagan administration had bought off individual industries that received no particular benefits from the Kemp-Roth plan with special policies such as the leaseback provision, which enabled even industries with low income to benefit from a tax break. However, by the second year of the administration, business began to indicate that tax breaks were not enough. On 30 January 1983, for instance, the *New York Times* ran an article entitled 'Business Talks Back to Reagan' (Wayne, 1983). The article quoted critical remarks by many chief executive officers and associations of manufacturers. The common theme of their remarks was concern over what the administration is calling 'outyear deficits', (one wonders if they mean out of office) and a recommendation of increased taxes and of cuts in both defense and non-defense spending.

One curious outcome of the hybrid monetarist–supply-side program is a blurring of the distinction between financial and industrial capital. The high interest rates feared by financial capital in the long run, none the less produced high bank earnings in the short run. Industrial capital, unwilling to borrow at high interest rates, and unable to secure lower interest rates, developed financial activities in response. If industrial capital could not beat financial capital, it would join it. Merger and acquisition activity reached a fever pitch in 1981 as idle cash balances accumulated by industrial firms were used to acquire the assets of other firms rather than finance new productive investment (see Lekachman, 1982, p. 143.) In addition, companies such as General Motors reported earnings from their financial activities (such as the lending arm General Motors Acceptance Corporation) that matched, or in some quarters even exceeded, their earnings on industrial production. As cash balances accumulated, financial instruments proliferated and retail companies such as Sears expanded their financial services.

That the Reagan administration refuses to surrender its commitment to supply-side economics, in rhetoric if not in reality, demonstrates its operational independence from particular factions of capital. At the same time, its ideology and its indifference to labor opposition demonstrate its unalloyed commitment to capital in general. Elsewhere, we have called the administration a 'hypercapitalist' regime, dictating to capital the specific content of its pro-capital macroeconomic program (Amott and Krieger, 1982). Within the administration's pro-capital strategy are New Right social programs and supply-side experiments that the Old Right, left to its own devices, would never have placed on the agenda. Thus, significant portions of the business and financial community remain extremely reluctant to endorse all the components of Reagan's economic policy, but are hampered in their opposition by the administration's rigidity and political resolve.

THE REAGAN ECONOMY

Table 6.3 documents the course of the economy during the supply-side experiment. By December 1982, the unemployment rate had risen to 10.8 per cent, and industrial production was at its lowest level since early 1977. In most respects, the recession followed the classic pattern of a tight money downturn: housing starts and automobile and other durable goods sales fell first, followed quickly by a

Table 6.3   *The Reagan Economy*

	1979	1980	1981	1982	1983:II
Growth in real gross national product (annual average to annual average)	2.8	−0.4	1.9	−1.7	9.2
Percentage change in implicit price deflator (annual average to annual average)	8.6	9.3	9.4	5.9	3.5
Index of industrial production (1967 = 100, annual average)	152.5	147.0	151.0	138.6	144.3
Unemployment rate (annual average	5.9	7.2	7.6	9.7	10.1
Manufacturing capacity utilization rate (Federal Reserve Board, annual average)	85.6	79.1	78.4	69.8	73.7
Corporate profits with IVA and CCAdj, after-tax[a] (billions of 1972 dollars, annual average)	64.4	50.0	55.5	51.1	66.6
Business failure rate (rate per 10,000 businesses)	27.8	42.1	61.3	90 (estimate)	n.a
Gross private domestic fixed investment (billions of 1972 dollars, annual average)	229.1	213.3	216.9	206.1	214.6

[a] Inventory valuation and capital consumption allowance adjustments.

Source: US Department of Commerce, Bureau of Economic Analysis, *Survey of Current Business*, Washington, DC: US Government Printing Office, selected issues 1980–3.

weakening of demand in other sectors of the economy. What distinguished this recession was its depth and length, as well as the administration's obstinate determination to 'stay the course'.

Not all sectors of the economy or groups of workers suffer equally. Unemployment hits minorities and youth the hardest; however, as politically disadvantaged groups, they can exercise no real muscle in favor of stimulative policies. The Congress was finally able to pass an emergency jobs bill providing funds for public service employment in early 1983, but the Reagan administration did not lend its support to the bill until the final hours when passage appeared certain. By industrial group, steel and auto workers face extremely high rates of unemployment, a fact that contributed to major wage concessions in these industries as contracts came due for negotiation. Federal, state and local government employees face widespread layoffs for the first time since the rapid expansion of these sectors in the 1970s.

With demand and production at recession levels, it is not surprising that Keynesian 'animal spirits' were low. Gross private domestic fixed investment in real terms fell from a 1979 high of $229 billion (annual average in 1972 dollars) to $206 billion in 1982, the lowest level since 1976. Other indicators of investment, such as planned capital expenditures and new orders for producers' durable goods, all painted the same picture.

Despite the generally bleak outlook, some individuals and industries have actually prospered during the Reagan years. While manufacturing earnings plummeted and business failures soared, banks continued to exhibit strong earnings. Wealthy individuals also did well as a result of all the components of the Reagan program. As shown in Table 6.4, tax and benefit changes alone produced a massive redistribution of income from those with incomes under $10,000 to those with incomes over $80,000. In addition, rising interest rates boosted the incomes of creditors throughout the economy (see Table 6.5). In fact, net interest as a share of personal income rose from 8.4 per cent in the first quarter of 1980 to 10.7 per cent by the fourth quarter of 1982.

Inflation did decline, as promised by supply-siders. A large part of this slowdown in prices came about because OPEC was unable to sustain oil prices in the face of a worldwide recession. Wage concessions also slowed the workings of the wage–price spiral. While there were many such factors contributing to the slowing of inflation, one thing that can be said with certainty is that inflation did not abate as a result of the promised increase in supply: industrial production, to name only one index of the decline, fell continuously throughout 1981 and 1982 after remaining essentially flat throughout 1980.

The decline in inflation was, however, sufficient for the Federal

Table 6.4   *Changes in Household Income as a Result of Budget Cuts and Tax Provisions Enacted in Fiscal Years 1981 and 1982*[a]

| | Households with incomes: | |
	under $10,000	over $80,000
1983	−$5.8 billion	+$14.4 billion
1984	−$6.1 billion	+$19.0 billion
1985	−$4.9 billion	+$22.2 billion

[a] These figures reflect only budget cuts in benefit programs, and do not include losses in service programs such as health services, legal services and other social services. Thus, they represent a minimum estimate of changes in household incomes.

Sources: US Congressional Budget Office, *Effects of Tax and Benefit Reductions Enacted in 1981 for Households in Different Income Categories*, Washington, DC: US Government Printing Office, February 1982, pp. 4, 25; US Congressional Budget Office, *Effects of Changes in Taxes and Benefit Payments Enacted in Fiscal Year 1982 for Households in Different Income Categories*, Washington, DC: US Government Printing Office, November 1982, p. 10.

Reserve to ease its tight control over the money supply, and a recovery (which began slowly and weakly, at first) was underway by the beginning of 1983. While monetarists can take some credit for the recovery, it is interesting to note that it was not accompanied by the inflation rates that a quantity equation perspective would have predicted as a result of easier money growth. Thus, while the course of the Reagan recession and recovery has demonstrated the essentially political character of the supply-side program, it has not vindicated the monetarist perspective. Both aspects of Reaganomics discussed earlier in this chapter – monetarist adherence to tight money and supply-side investment and savings incentives – are responsible for the current economic quagmire, but adherents of each program have the comfort of blaming the other for their failure.

CONCLUSION

The Reagan administration, like the supply-side economic theory it invented, is highly unusual. By no means typical of Republican administrations, it is more ideologically driven and far more radical in its policy initiatives. It differs in its determination not to play stop–go economic games, even when unemployment climbs to politically dangerous levels. Its public commitment to *laissez-faire* conceals an important set of contradictions between political practice and political self-representation. Like the Thatcher government described in the next chapter by Geoffrey Hodgson, this administration intervenes

Table 6.5   *Interest Rates, Money and Credit*

(a) *Percent changes in money and credit (December to December)*

	M1	*M2*	*M3*	*Bank credit*
1978	8.3	8.2	11.2	12.5
1979	7.1	8.2	9.2	11.1
1980	6.4	8.9	10.1	9.9
1981	6.4	10.1	11.9	11.9
1982	8.5	9.2	9.7	10.5
1983[a]	8.0	9.0	6.3	4.7

[a] December 1982 to August 1983.

Source: Board of Governors of the Federal Reserve System, *Federal Reserve Bulletin*, Washington, DC: US Government Printing Office, August 1983, Table 1.10; *Economic Report of the President*, Washington, DC: US Government Printing Office, February 1983, Table B-61.

(b) *Selected interest rates*

		Treasury bills[a]	*Mortgages[b]*	*Short-term business loans[c]*
1979:	I			
	II	9.38	10.35	12.34
	III	9.67	11.13	12.31
	IV	11.84	12.38	15.81
1980:	I	13.35	14.32	15.67
	II	9.62	12.70	17.75
	III	9.15	13.12	11.56
	IV	13.61	14.62	15.71
1981:	I	14.39	15.10	19.91
	II	14.91	16.15	19.99
	III	15.05	17.50	21.11
	IV	11.75	17.33	17.23
1982:	I	12.81	17.10	17.13
	II	12.42	16.63	17.11
	III	9.32	15.65	13.27
	IV	7.90	13.79	11.26
1983:	I	8.11	13.26	10.20
	II	8.40	13.16	10.30

[a] 3-month market yield.
[b] Average rates on new commitments for conventional first mortgages on new homes in primary markets.
[c] Bank rates.

Sources: For Treasury bills and mortgages, Board of Governors of the Federal Reserve System, *Federal Reserve Bulletin*, Washington, DC: US Government Printing Office, selected issues 1980–3, Table 1.10, 'Monetary Aggregates and Interest Rates'; for bank rates on short-term business loans, US Department of Commerce, Bureau of Economic Analysis, *Business Conditions Digest*, Washington, DC: US Government Printing Office, selected issues 1981–3, Series No. 67.

powerfully to restructure capital, alter the balance of labor–capital relationships and actively promote particular outcomes in the economy (and in the family), while simultaneously posing as the champion of state withdrawal from the economy. Similarly, it dogmatically asserts the necessity of private sector management and planning, while its macroeconomic policies limit the range of options available to business in important ways. In the strength of its pro-capitalist ideology, Reaganomics has exacerbated the crisis of advanced capitalism.

POSTSCRIPT

The 1983 recovery began weakly but picked up strength from consumer and defense spending. Although Reagan may benefit from the timing of the upturn, a closer look at the data indicates that Reaganomics can take no credit for the recovery. As this volume goes to press, the savings rate remains low, growth in capital spending is concentrated in equipment (particularly in cost-cutting machinery) rather than in new plants, and interest rates are stubbornly high. Despite predicted federal deficits in the vicinity of 200 billion dollars, and growing pressures for tax increases from both sides of the political spectrum, Reagan remains staunchly committed to the political content of Reaganomics regardless of its economic coherence.

The author is deeply indebted to Joel Krieger, whose political insights formed the basis of this paper, and to Michael Hillard, Arjo Klamer, and Edward Nell for comments and assistance.

REFERENCES

Amott, T. and Krieger J. (1982) 'Thatcher and Reagan: state theory and the "hyper-capitalist" regime', *New Political Science*, no. 8.

Becker, G. (1981) *A Treatise on the Family*, Cambridge, Mass.: Harvard University Press.

Blinder, A. (1979) *Economic Policy and the Great Stagflation*, New York: Academic Press.

Crouch, C. (1981) 'The changing role of the state in industrial relations in Western Europe', in E. Crouch and A. Pizzorno, eds, *The Resurgence of Class Conflict in Western Europe Since 1968*, London: Macmillan, vol. 2.

Danziger, S. and Plotnick, R. (1981) 'Income maintenance programs and the pursuit of income security', *The Annals of the American Academy of Political and Social Science* (January).

Davidson, P. (1980) 'Is there a shortage of savings in the US?' in *Stagflation:*

The Causes, Effects and Solutions, Special Study on Economic Changes, Joint Economic Committee, 17 December, Washington, DC: US Government Printing Office.

Eichner, A. (1981) 'Reagan's doubtful game plan', *Challenge*, Vol. 24, no. 2.

Gilder, G. (1981) *Wealth and Poverty*, New York: Basic Books.

Held, D. and Krieger, J. (1982) 'Theories of the state: some competing claims', in S. Bornstein, D. Held and J. Krieger, *The State in Capitalist Europe*, London: Allen & Unwin.

Lekachman, R. (1982) *Greed Is Not Enough: Reaganomics*, New York: Pantheon Books.

Keynes, J. M. (1964) *The General Theory of Employment, Interest, and Money*, New York: Harcourt Brace Jovanovich.

Miller, J. (1980) 'The emperor's new policy', *Working Papers for a New Society*, Vol. 7, no. 6.

Orren, G. and Dionne, E. J. (1981) 'The next new deal', *Working Papers for a New Society*, Vol. 8, no. 3.

Petchesky, R. (1981) 'Antiabortion, antifeminism, and the rise of the new right', *Feminist Studies*, Vol. 7, no. 2.

Skocpol, T. (1980) 'Political response to capitalist crisis: neo-Marxist theories of the state and the case of the New Deal', *Politics and Society*, Vol. 10, no. 2.

Thurow, L. (1981) 'How Reagan can wreck the economy', *New York Review of Books*, Vol. 28, no. 2.

Wayne, L. (1983) 'Business talks back to Reagan', *The New York Times*, 30 January p. 1F.

7 Thatcherism: The Miracle That Never Happened[1]

The Government's programme is as foolish as it is wrong. Its direct effect on employment must be disastrous . . . purchasing power is to be curtailed . . . the end will be that no one can be employed, except those happy few who grow their own potatoes, as a result of each of us refusing, for reasons of economy, to buy the services of any one else . . . If we carry 'economy' of every kind to its logical conclusion we shall find that we have balanced the budget at nought on both sides with all of us flat on our backs starving to death. (John Maynard Keynes, writing in 1931; 1972, pp 147 and 239)

From 1945 to 1970 or thereabouts, there was a Keynesian 'interlude' in economic policy in Britain. Full employment was a primary objective. State intervention in a 'mixed' economy was accepted. The limitations of the market mechanism were recognized, to some degree, by both Labour and Conservative administrations.

The election of the Conservative government with Margaret Thatcher as Prime Minister in May 1979 radically changed all that. Keynesianism was dethroned. To some extent this had been heralded by the abandonment of the primary goal of full employment and repeated attempts to cut public expenditure by the preceding Labour government. With Thatcher's elevation to office in 1979, a marked swing to the right in economic policy had been accomplished. The Keynesian era had been left far behind.

In many respects this meant a return to *pre*-Keynesian policies. The antiquity of Thatcherism was masked, initially, by the apparent novelty of 'monetarism' as an alternative to the postwar Keynesian orthodoxy. But little, in fact, was really new. Like the economists of the 1920s and 1930s who were criticized by Keynes for putting too much faith in the market system, the 'new' priorities were for 'sound money', 'balanced budgets', 'more competition', 'private initiative' and an overall reduction in public ownership and expenditure. Like the 1920s and 1930s, the 'new' relationship of the Thatcher government to the trade unions was one of practised and explicit confrontations, rather than cooperation.

A comprehensive and objective assessment of the first four years of the Thatcher experiment is impossible. Complementary or contrasting evaluations have appeared elsewhere.[2] The aim of this assessment is to concentrate on, first, the money supply and inflation, second, industrial output and productivity, and third, trade unions and industrial relations. If ever there was clear evidence of the destructiveness and impotence of the economic policies of the 'New Right' it is provided by the first four years of Thatcher's Britain. Yet whilst we should all be reminded of the soaring unemployment and industrial decline, these issues will not dominate this account, for two reasons. First, the New Right is attached to the Victorian doctrine that all good medicine is painful medicine, and if it does not cause pain then it cannot be doing any good. In these circumstances the cries of pain from the patient do not alone lead to a change in diagnosis or remedy. Second, the concern here is to lay bare the rationale of Thatcherism and its extraordinary success in capturing the hearts and minds of economists, businessmen, civil servants and much of the population, despite its evident failure to bring about the promised economic recovery. It will be argued here that Thatcherism is much more a vision of an 'ideal' world than a remedy for economic decline that can be 'tested by reference to conventional economic indicators. That, in part, is its appeal.

THE MONETARIST SMOKESCREEN

Monetarist theories of inflation rapidly increased their influence in the early 1970s. By the mid-1970s this 'new' creed had won adherents amongst economists and politicians from the right, centre and left of British politics.

As Milton Friedman has willingly admitted, the idea that there is a close and causal relationship between the quantity of money and the overall price level is as old as economics itself. Friedman's contribution was to add some theoretical rigour and apparent empirical support to this hypothesis, partly by emphasizing a lag of about two years between increases in the money supply and the consequent effect on prices. After gaining some converts in the 1974–79 Labour government, monetarism became the battle hymn of Thatcher's general staff, at least in the beginning. Lord Cockfield, Minister of State in the Treasury, assured the House of Lords in 1980 that

there can be no doubt, based on theory and practical experience

that a growth in the money supply is followed after a period of time
by a rise in the rate of inflation, and equally, and more hopefully,
that a fall in the rate of growth of the money supply is also followed
in due time by a fall in the rate of inflation. (House of Lords, 1980,
col. 517)

As we shall see, this simple causal relationship is now open to considerable doubt. More of this later.

It is important to note an important adjoining element in the
'monetarism' of the Thatcher government. As Chancellor Sir Geoffrey Howe announced in his 1980 Budget: 'there is no doubt that public sector borrowing has made a major contribution to the excessive
growth of the money supply in recent years' (UK Treasury, 1980,
p. 16). The vast majority of 'monetarists' would accept that public
sector borrowing is the primary causal factor in bringing about an
increase in the money supply (which, in turn, brings about an
increase in prices). It is certainly an article of faith for the Thatcher
government.

If we are to accept the conventional view of the development of
economic theory and policy, economists first gather evidence; they
then test hypotheses and construct theories about the economy, from
which 'scientific' policy recommendations flow. In the late 1970s
there did *appear* to be strong evidence supporting the idea of a causal
relationship between the money supply and inflation. In 1973 the
money supply ($£M_3$) increased at a high and peak rate of 26.9 per
cent. Two years later the inflation rate peaked at 24.2 per cent. The
monetarists were triumphant. This dramatic correlation, with a two-
year lag, seemed to give strong support to monetarist theories.

What of the evidence supporting a relationship between public borrowing and the money supply? Here the monetarists were on shakier
ground. There was no clear evidence to support this hypothesis,
which was sustained for different reasons. One view, held apparently
by many leading members of the Conservative party, was that the
main component of the money supply was paper money and coin
printed and minted by the state. However, as every economist
knows, this is inaccurate. In all standard definitions of the money
supply, bank credit is another major component. Whilst Milton
Friedman did entertain analogies of governments dropping money
from helicopters to win popularity (and cause inflation), when
pressed he would admit that this ignored the phenomenon of credit
money created by private and other banks. Thus the expansion of the
money supply could not be blamed solely on the capacity of governments to create new banknotes and coin.

The aversion to public spending and public borrowing is a symptom of something much more fundamental than the monetarist theory of inflation. When the evidence began to contradict the monetarist theory of inflation, the aversion to public spending and borrowing remained. An understanding of what happened is important, particularly for those of us brought up on the doctrines of 'positive economics'.

What did happen? By the late 1970s, empirical work on the alleged time-lag between the growth of the money supply and price inflation had undermined the idea of a fixed lag of two years or thereabouts. As Tanner (1979) and others point out, if a time-lag exists it is of variable and indeterminate length. Events after 1979 did not dispel these doubts. A Treasury Committee on Monetary Policy met to gather evidence from the experts. Evidence was given, verbally and in writing, by a number of leading economists in the field, including Milton Friedman, David Laidler and Nicholas Kaldor.

Kaldor's evidence was crucial, and we shall dwell on it here (see Kaldor, 1980). He examined the relationship between the increase in the money supply and inflation for the period after 1973–5. For example, in 1975–8 the money value of GNP in the UK increased by 15.7 per cent. Yet the growth rate in the money supply ($£M_3$) was only 10.5 per cent in 1973–6 (corresponding to a two-year lag), and 9.5 per cent in 1974–7 (one-year lag). This evidence contradicts the monetarist theory. Further evidence from the UK in the 1960s tells a similar tale, and Kaldor was able to show that in less than six out of twenty-seven observations in nine other countries is there a semblance of a two-year lag in recent years.

What, then, of the remarkable correlation between the growth in the money supply in the UK in 1973 and the rate of inflation in 1975? Kaldor explains this as

> a pure fluke. They are the accidental result of the dominating influence of two events which were themselves wholly unrelated to each other; the adoption of the system called 'Competition and Credit Control' by the Bank of England in 1971 and the Arab–Israel War (the so-called Yom-Kippur War) on October 1973 which resulted first in an oil embargo on certain countries and then in a fourfold rise in the world oil price, which in turn induced the world-wide inflation in the years 1974–75. (Kaldor, 1980, p. 302).

The effect of the change in banking rules in 1971 was to increase interest-bearing time deposits by no less than 117 per cent in two years, largely accounting for the big increase in the money supply in 1972 and 1973:

This terrific 'bulge' in interest-bearing deposits was largely the consequence of banking policy changes – the clearing banks, freed from control, successfully diverted funds from normal channels and indulged in, or tolerated, a great deal of financial manipulation . . . There was no conceivable connection between these events and the large world-wide inflationary wave induced by the 'oil shock' of 1973, which had particularly grave consequences on the severity of inflation in the United Kingdom in 1974, on account of the 'threshold' arrangements (these were part of Phase 3 of the Heath Government's incomes policy but fixed before the big oil price rise) which, by the end of 1974, nearly doubled the inflation rate as compared with what would have happened otherwise. (Kaldor, 1980, p. 304)

Once the evidence of a time-lag had been put into doubt, the empirical foundation for the hypothesis of a causal relationship between the money supply and inflation was undermined. Kaldor's alternative, non-monetarist, explanation of the events of 1971–5 added further to the doubt.

In the same paper Kaldor goes on to present more damning evidence. Considering the alleged relationship between the public sector deficit and the money supply, Kaldor found that the unfunded element in the Public Sector Borrowing Requirement (PSBR) was quite insignificant as a statistical explanation of the change in the money supply for the 1966–79 period in the UK. A far better statistical explanation of the growth in the money supply is found by looking at lending by banks (which in the UK are almost wholly private institutions), to the UK private sector. This latter variable explained as much as 83 per cent of the variance, according to Kaldor's statistical analysis. The role of *public* borrowing is, on the face of it, much less important.

Kaldor's evidence had undermined two crucial postulates of Thatcher's monetarism. The causal relationships between the Public Sector Borrowing Requirement and the money supply and between the money supply and inflation were both put into doubt. As a result, even if the government were to be successful in reducing the PSBR, this would not necessarily lead to a reduction of the money supply; in turn, there was no guarantee that a reduction in the money supply would be followed by a fall in inflation.

In March 1981 the Treasury Committee on Monetary Policy published its report. The committee, of no left-wing bias, was composed of twelve MPs, with a seven to five Conservative majority. They produced a classic and damning indictment of monetarism, concluding that the changes in the level of the money supply did not provide a single and convincing explanation of changes in the price level. Furthermore, the Select Committee accepted that attempts to reduce the PSBR would not help an economic recovery. (Treasury Committee, 1981).

Yet the Conservative government did not change its course; it continued in its attempts to reduce public spending. The explanation for this apparent intransigence is not simply that leading members of the government had a limited understanding of economics. It had more to do with the fact that Thatcher's attack on the public sector was primarily based, not on a simple theory of inflation but on other, deeper, presuppositions. When asked in February 1981 whether unemployment in excess of 3 million might lead her to decide that the human cost of monetarist theory was too high, Thatcher replied: 'It is not a theory. It is borne out by everything that's happened in this country in the last 30 years' (*The Guardian*, 2 February 1981). This clumsy assertion points beyond the smokescreen that was generated by the 'purely economic' and apparently 'value free' arguments of the 1960s and 1970s about monetarism and the causes of inflation. The 'last 30 years' were the Keynesian era. It is not simply a question of 'abandoning' Keynesian *theories*. It is more a matter of rejecting Keynesian and social democratic *objectives*, namely the visible hand of government guidance and a publicly financed welfare state.

James Tobin had reached a similar conclusion as early as 1976:

> Distinctively monetarist policy recommendations stem less from theoretical or even empirical findings than from distinctive value judgements. The preferences revealed consistently in those recommendations are for minimising the public sector and for paying a high cost in unemployment to stabilise prices. (Tobin, 1976, p. 336)

There are those who are persuaded by theoretical discourse and empirical evidence and those who are not. The Thatcher government fell clearly into the latter category. Its economic experiment helped to undermine the classic 'positive economics' version of monetarism that had prevailed amongst economists in the 1970s. However, those economists who, unlike Keynes, believed in the overall efficiency of the market mechanism still had plenty of alternative theories to support their predilection. Thus, in the early 1980s, there was the vogue for 'Austrian' economics, 'rational expectations' theories, and the neoclassically minded 'economics of politics'. There were still many theoretical delicacies to tempt the connoisseurs of New Right ideology.

To add irony to irony, by 1983 the Thatcher government had achieved the singular economic success of bringing down the annual rate of price inflation from the level it inherited in the second quarter of 1979 of 10.6 per cent to a significantly lower figure of 6.2 per cent in the last quarter of 1982. (It should be noted, however, that inflation was accelerating in 1979. It reached a peak rate of 21.5 per cent in the second quarter of 1980.) Yet the cost of this success was not simply an unprecedented postwar recession and an increase in unemployment from 1.3 million in 1979 to nearly 3.1 million in the last quarter of 1982. It was also the refutation of the classic monetarist doctrine. The reduction of the rate of inflation over the period did not correspond to appropriate changes in the supply of money.

From the third quarter of 1979 to the third quarter of 1982, the money value of GDP rose by 36.3 per cent and the price level rose by 39.7 per cent overall (i.e. an average annual inflation rate of 11.8 per cent). According to the orthodox version of monetarist theory there should have been an increase of about 36 per cent, in the supply of money over a period of three years, about two years in advance (i.e. from 1977 (III) to 1980 (III)). In fact the money supply ($£M_3$) increased by a massive 51.2 per cent in that period. From 1978 (III) to 1981 (III) the increase in $£M_3$ was even greater – 53.6 per cent. Neither a two-year nor a one-year lag is confirmed.

The irony is that *if* the classic (two-year lag) version *were* correct then the rate of inflation would not have come down at all. A 51.2 per cent increase in the supply of money would 'predict' an overall increase in prices of 57.5 per cent in 1979–82. (Note that GDP volume declined by about 4 per cent in real terms in that period.) This amounts to a mean annual rate of inflation of no less than 16.3 per cent. If monetarist theory were valid we would have witnessed a rate of inflation of about 15 per cent in the second quarter of 1983, as the money supply was growing at the rate of 17.1 per cent two years earlier, and GDP volume was growing at about 2 per cent in late 1982. Paradoxically, monetarism has been discredited by the Thatcher government's real success in bringing inflation down and its failure to do the same for the rate of increase of the money supply. The government strikingly refuted one of the theories that helped it into office in the first place.

There are other aspects of Britain's monetarist experiment that should be noted in brief. First, not only did the first Thatcher government fail to control the money supply, in addition it presided over a big increase in public spending, in both real and monetary terms. Much of this increase went to finance unemployment. Second, and partly as a consequence, the Thatcher administration has failed to fulfil one of its major promises: to bring down the level of average personal taxation. In fact, the tax burden for the average family increased by about 7 per cent in the four years from 1979. This is despite the reduction of the standard marginal rate of income tax from 33 to 30 per cent in the June 1979 budget. This reduction, combined with a big increase in VAT, favoured a rich minority of the population only.

There are 'supply-side' aspects to monetarist ideology that are worthy of note. The aim is not simply to reduce inflation but to increase 'incentives' and improve the efficiency of the market mechanism. The Thatcher experiment shows that, to a large degree, deflationary policies aimed at combating inflation and tax-reducing schemes to increase 'incentives' are in conflict with each other. Attempts to reduce the public sector deficit (aimed, mistakenly, at bringing down the money supply and thereby inflation) are bound to put a squeeze on programs to reduce taxation. Under Thatcher, the 'supply-side' elements of the monetarist package have frequently been put in second place.

Both standard monetarism, based on the alleged link between public deficits and the money supply, and the money supply and inflation, and 'supply-side' monetarism, based on attempts to reduce taxation, have been discredited. A second term of office for the Thatcher government will, in all likelihood, put less emphasis on both parts of the monetarist package. Instead, the thrust of government policy will be concentrated in its program to extend the privatization of the British economy (by selling off public enterprises and franchises), and in its efforts to reduce the power of the trade unions through legislation and confrontation. The monetarist smokescreen will be removed. The true meaning of Thatcherism, which is summed up in the slogan 'free economy and strong state', will become clear.

INDUSTRIAL OUTPUT AND PRODUCTIVITY

Even to supporters of Thatcher's economic policies it was no great surprise when their immediate result was to bring about an economic recession. This was regarded as a necessary 'tradeoff': it was either unemployment now or even greater unemployment in the future. The 'resolute approach' meant 'accepting this reality'. We were warned of the 'short-term' costs, but repeatedly assured that the policies would bring about an economic recovery in the 'near future'. Naturally, this argument was not accepted universally, even within the Conservative party, and government policies found many critics.

The argument was not simply about the length of severity of the recession but about its costs and benefits. In some ways the latter is the more crucial issue. For if Thatcher and her supporters were to be wrong by underestimating the depth and duration of the recession to come, they could then claim that this even more painful medicine was doing all the more good. We should not confine our attention to the adequacy or validity of the simulation models of the economy that were employed in Liverpool or Cambridge, the Treasury or the London Business School. None of these models claims to be able to predict the different effects on productivity and entrepreneurial drive of boom or slump. Differences of attitude to a recession are much more fundamental. The crucial question is whether a recession is to be viewed as having either vitalizing or debilitating effects on the economy.

An axiom of Thatcherism and New Right thinking is that slumps and recessions purge the economy of its inefficiencies. The present leadership of the Conservative party is fond of phrases such as 'getting rid of the fat' and 'emerging fitter and leaner from the recession'. It should also be pointed out that the same underlying axiom is found elsewhere: amongst many thinkers on the Far Left. For example, John Harrison (1982) argues that the evidence indicates that Thatcher's policies could herald a 'dramatic' rise in productivity. Although Harrison and like-thinkers are socialist by political conviction, they still endorse the idea that economic recovery could result from a spell of right-wing government and recession.

First of all, however, let us examine the scale of the recession that has unfolded since 1979. Selected indicators for output and investment are presented in Table 7.1 . These show an unambiguous tale of woe: a slump in manufacturing investment, in manufacturing output, and in industrial production, and a declining level of GDP. Despite repeated assurances from the government, there is little sign of recovery. If we take the fall in manufacturing output from the last quarter of 1979 to the last quarter of 1980 it is no less than a staggering 13.4 per cent. This collapse is the second greatest in the history of British capitalism, rivalled only by 1920–1. Manufacturing output has

Table 7.1   *Selected Indicators of Output and Investment in the UK (Volume Terms, 1975 = 100)*

Year	Gross domestic product at constant factor cost	Industrial output at constant factor cost	Manufacturing output at constant factor cost	Manufacturing gross fixed investment
1979	110.4	113.2	104.6	112.7
1980	107.4	105.6	95.1	101.5
1981	104.8	100.1	89.0	83.4
1982	105.8	101.1	88.3	74.9

Source: Economic Trends, (London: HMSO), March 1983.

continued to fall, reaching an even lower level in the last quarter of 1982. The British economy has fallen into the abyss, and there is no sign of it bouncing back.

The consequences in terms of mass unemployment, social depriva-tion and industrial decline are plain for all to see, and we shall not dwell on them here (see Tomlinson, 1983). Perhaps shocked by the scale of the recession, the Thatcher government attempted to argue that it was simply a reflection of a slump in the world economy and Britain was doing no worse than its rivals. This is quite easily refuted. The decline in output in Britain has been much greater than in the 'major seven' OECD countries taken as a whole. (The 'major seven' are the USA, Japan, West Germany, France, UK, Italy and Canada.) From 1979 to 1981 aggregate GNP or GDP in these coun-tries increased by 2.2 per cent. In the UK it declined by 4.3 per cent in the same period. Employment actually increased from 1979 to 1981 in the 'major seven' – by 0.6 per cent. In the UK it declined by 6.9 per cent (OECD, 1982, Table 5). On the whole, the recession in the UK has been much more severe than in other advanced capitalist coun-tries.

Is the UK recession 'working' in the way that the Thatcher govern-ment argued? Is it weeding out the inefficient and spurring on the alert and self-reliant to greater competitiveness? The government never tires of reminding us that a 'miracle' in productivity growth is unfolding in the midst of gloom and despair. Is the miracle really hap-pening?

Table 7.2 shows that, in terms of productivity, the initial result of the slump was a marked decline. This ended, for both the whole economy and the manufacturing sector, in the last quarter of 1980. For the first eighteen months of the Thatcher government, output was contracting even more rapidly than employment, thus explaining the fall in productivity. For the next two years the decline in employ-ment was greater than the fall in output, hence productivity per worker (and per hour worked) began to rise.

Table 7.2   *Productivity in the UK since 1979 (1975 = 100)*

Year	Output per person employed in whole economy	Output per person employed in manufacturing	Output per person-hour in manufacturing
1979	109.1	109.5	108.7
1980	107.0	105.5	107.4
1981	108.3	109.4	112.7
1982	n.a.	115.3	117.5

Source: Economic Trends, (London: HMSO), March 1983.

The rise in productivity after late 1980 was initially quite rapid. Much of this, however, was a result of firms 'adjusting' to the recession by shedding labour that did not seem to be required with contracting demand. In addition, many firms – some of them weak and inefficient – were going bankrupt (at a record rate of 12,039 per year in 1982). If it were the case that the average productivity of the bankrupted firms was less than that of those that stayed in business, then overall productivity would have risen as a result of the recession. But it would not be a consequence of any general improvement in work practices, organization and efficiency in the surviving plants. It is like killing off those of poor intellectual capacities in order to raise the average level of intelligence of the population: it does not necessarily correspond to a real and enduring social and economic gain.

It is too early to disentangle all the factors that have been at work and reach firm conclusions, but some preliminary attempts have been made. One more obscure set of data casts some light on the processes involved. Since 1971, S. A. N. Smith-Gavine and A. J. Bennett have been gathering information on the intensity of work in a sample of manufacturing plants in order to compute an index of 'Percentage Utilisation of Labor'.[3] The PUL index is a composition of units of effort performed (according to the standard ratings of the work-measurement officers in the plants concerned), per unit of real time. If the work is performed at the rate that is deemed 'reasonable' or 'standard' by work-study experts, then the PUL index will be exactly 100. Thus the PUL index is an attempt to measure the level of activity of labor itself in the heartland of the economy. According to the data, the PUL index was actually at a historic maximum of about 102 at the time of the general election in May 1979. Subsequently, like the other main indicators, it fell with the recession and the general contraction in the economy. It reached the 'floor' in about January 1981 with a figure of 97. Since then the index has recovered and moved back towards its 1979 level.

The PUL index suggests that much of the growth in manufacturing productivity in 1981 and 1982 can be explained simply by the restoration of work intensity to Spring 1979 levels, and not by more efficient work practices or the introduction of new technology. Furthermore, as the 1979–80 fall in the PUL index is *greater* than the actual decline in manufacturing productivity this suggests that technological and other improvements *were* having an effect during 1980, *before* the full effects of the recession had worked through. It has been suggested that these 'improvements' resulted from (a) a dishoarding of 'excess' administrative and managerial labor, and (b) the technological results of the 1978–9 investment upturn (during the preceding, Labour government) becoming established in practice, (see Kellner,

1982; Jones, 1983). Thus it is difficult, on the basis of the evidence, to claim that Thatcherism is the root cause of the gains in productivity that have been observed since 1979.

In any case, the overall record does the government no great credit. There has been an overall decline in output per person employed in the whole economy from the second quarter of 1979 to the last quarter of 1981, with a slight increase during 1982. The *net* improvement in overall output per person employed from 1979 (II) to 1982 (III) is merely 1.4 per cent. This is equivalent to a mean annual improvement of little more than 0.4 per cent. The net figures for manufacturing are a little better, but a source of no great consolation. The improvement in productivity per person employed in that sector from 1979 (II) to 1982 (IV) amounts to 3.1 per cent overall, or a mean figure of 0.9 per cent per annum. The equivalent figure for productivity improvements on a per person-hour basis over the same period is 5.9 per cent overall, or a mean annual figure of 1.7 per cent. Thatcherism has brought no miracle in the productivity performance of British manufacturing industry.

Kilpatrick and Lawson (1980) have argued that Britain's poor industrial performance largely results from the defensive power of the trade union movement and its capacity to resist technological change and work reorganization. The Thatcher government has been at great pains to reduce the power of trade unions, and to a large extent this power has been checked by the big rise in unemployment since 1979. If the Kilpatrick–Lawson thesis is correct, then more recent improvements in productivity should be observed where the power of the trade union movement has been reduced.

There is some anecdotal evidence in support of this view. For example, within the British Leyland car company the power of the shop stewards has been confronted and successfully undermined by a new, aggressive management, and there has been a significant improvement in the productivity figures there. The MacGregor era at British Steel has also raised average productivity. However, a general pattern of productivity improvements resulting from weakened trade unions and authoritarian management has not been confirmed.

Some of the evidence on changes in work practices has been collected together in a recent study (Income Data Services, 1981). However, far from giving unambiguous evidence of the benefits of Thatcherism, it also shows that in many cases the introduction of automation and new technology has been delayed because of the continuing domestic and world recession. In fact, in the manufacturing sector as a whole, plant and machinery investment fell by 8 per cent in 1980, 17 per cent in 1981 and 13 per cent in 1982. This hardly heralds a technological revolution. It is unlikely that this will occur

without an expansion of effective demand for the products of manufacturing industry.

Clifford Pratten, an accepted British expert on industrial productivity, wrote in early 1982 with a degree of enthusiasm for the
Thatcher experiment:

> The positive aspect of the shake-out of labour is that efficiency has
> been increased . . . In spite of current problems the economic
> prospect for Britain in the 1980s could be exciting. There is now a
> realisation that a part of Britain's poor growth performance is attri-
> butable to kinds of inefficiency which many have never recognised.
> In the private sector a new generation of managers is being forced
> to tackle inefficiency in the face of international competition . . .
> (Pratten, 1982, p. 50)

Less than two years later Pratten had reached a much more critical
conclusion:

> Britain's economic decline has not been caused by worker indisci-
> pline alone. Industrial entrepreneurship, leadership and skills have
> been lacking. There are few signs that Mrs Thatcher's supporters
> are remedying these deficiencies on the scale required. Many
> companies are still seeking ways of reducing employment, not
> searching for new enterprise to increase employment. The Govern-
> ment places reliance on individuals to fill this gap. But it is naive to
> expect new small firms to compete with the giant international
> companies. (Pratten, 1983, p. 20)

TRADE UNIONS AND INDUSTRIAL RELATIONS

Thatcherism should not be characterized simply as an enthusiasm for
monetarism and market-based solutions to problems of low productivity. It also marks a break from the tripartite consensus – based on a
degree of cooperation between big business, trade unions and the
state – that has, to some degree, pervaded British politics since 1940.
Immediately upon attaining office, the Thatcher government
eschewed the institutional arrangements for negotiation and cooperation with the trade union movement that had been built up during the
1960s and 1970s.

The government's reasons for its hostile attitude to trade unionism
are various. The main thrust of its ideological attack is based on the
New Right doctrine that trade unions are an unwarranted and damaging interference with the workings of the 'free' market. In particular,

trade unions are said to create unemployment by 'pricing workers out of the labour market'. (See Minford, 1982).[4] They restrict the 'freedom' of individuals to negotiate the wage rate of their choice.

Consequently, the government brought in two rounds of restrictive legislation against trade unions, in 1980 and 1982. The 1980 Act restricted the right to picket and outlawed most sympathetic action in support of workers in dispute. The 1982 legislation went even further by making 'political' strikes illegal as well as 'blacking' and other forms of 'secondary' action, and by undermining the trade union closed shop.

There is no doubt, however, that one of the major corrosive influences on the power of the trade unions was the creation of mass unemployment. This above all was to bring down the number of strikes and to reduce the level of wage settlements. Thus Thatcher's anti-union policies did not meet the same resistance as those of Conservative Prime Minister Edward Heath in 1970–4, when the number of days lost through strikes reached a postwar record.

It is important to note that the organization, strength and militancy of the British trade union movement grew rapidly from 1968 to 1979. (see Hodgson, 1981, chs 5–7). In 1979, trade union membership as a percentage of the employed workforce reached an unprecedented 58.2 per cent. The 'success' of the Thatcher government in reversing this trend is portrayed in Table 7.3. It is clear from the table that there has been a significant reduction in the strength and militancy of

Table 7.3   *The Strength and Militancy of the Trade Unions in the UK*

Annual average for year(s)	Total trade union membership ('000s)	Percentage of employed workforce in trade unions	Number of working days lost through stoppages ('000s)
1960–9	10,148	44.7	3,555
1970–9	12,082	53.4	12,860
1979	13,447	58.2	29,474
1980	12,947	56.7	11,964
1981	12,182	56.2	4,266
1982	n.a.	n.a.	7,916

Source: Employment Gazette (London: HMSO), January 1983 and preceding issues.
Note: The Department of Employment definition of trade union membership is used; this includes trade unions not affiliated to the TUC. The workforce is defined as all persons in employment, excluding armed forces and the self-employed. Contrary to the DoE practice, and in line with a convention used in other countries, trade union density is here expressed as a percentage of the employed workforce only. This seems preferable to the practice of including the unemployed in the denominator of this calculation.

the trade union movement since 1979. However, this reduction is not as dramatic as popular belief would suggest. The membership of the trade union movement, in absolute terms, is still well above the average level of the 1960s, when there was much less unemployment. The annual reduction in trade union density has been only 0.5 per cent, and it is still well above the average for the 1970s. Indeed, trade union density has not yet been reduced to levels that preceded to 1974–9 Labour government. Whilst there has been a dramatic reduction in the number of working days lost through strikes since 1979, the 1981 strike level is still well above the average for the 1960s. And in 1982 the level of strikes began, once again, to rise, reaching a figure that was exceeded in only two years in the forty-two that followed the General Strike in 1926.

It would seem reasonable to suggest that if an economic upturn were to come the trade union movement would quickly regain the strength and potential militancy of the 1970s. The trade unions have been checked by Thatcherism and mass unemployment, but they have not yet suffered severe injury or major defeat. Consequently, a government that is bent on reducing the power and influence of the trade unions will have to mount a much more vigorous and authoritarian offensive against their legal rights and organization structures. Trade unions remain firmly implanted in the British politico-economic system, and they will not be removed without a major confrontation much in excess of 1926 proportions. The danger, of course, is that a New Right government will be tempted to use Draconian and authoritarian measures, thus building up the police state in its zeal to extend 'the freedom of the individual' and to undermine collective power. (see Gamble, 1979; Monffe, 1981).

Is there an alternative? A growing body of evidence exists to show that authoritarianism and confrontation are not only illiberal and anti-democratic, but also will fail to improve the performance of the British economy. Neither Thatcher's invisible hand nor her legislator's fist have brought about an improvement in industrial relations and structures. Trade union resistance to improved efficiency may have been a factor in the past, but there is still no evidence to suggest that a counter-strategy of confrontation from above will bring about a general increase in productivity. It is time to consider a different approach.

As I have argued elsewhere, there is plentiful evidence to indicate that democracy rather than despotism may be a more effective remedy in the industrial sphere. (Hodgson, 1982).[5] This evidence suggests that an increase in real worker participation in decision-making may have a significant positive effect on both productivity and worker morale. Whilst economists have been preoccupied with market-based solutions, involving 'incentives' and the price mechanism, they have largely ignored the effects of different organizational structures within the 'black box' of production itself. This amounts to a negligence of academic research effort, alongside which the 'shirking' behavior of the trade union movement is dwarfed by comparison. We have an extensive empirical and theoretical literature on the workings of the market, but very little in contrast on the sphere of production. Yet the evidence that does exist is almost unanimous in supporting the view that industrial democracy and worker participation have a great deal to recommend them in economic terms.[6]

HAS THATCHERISM A MEANING?

The long-term benefits of the Thatcher medicine have been lauded by the Right. Many on the Left have accepted that *in capitalist terms* it may indeed have restorative properties. Both these views share the assumption that there is a *rationale* for Thatcherism. It is said to represent the economic interests of big business; it is believed that the slump will purge, and from it the fitter capitalist firms will emerge.[7]

The contrary view has been expressed elsewhere. As Tomlinson has put it:

One may suggest that the whole rhetoric of 'shake out', 'slim down' and so on misunderstands the nature of the competitive process. In the short-run deflation is likely to 'weed out' those companies with cash flow problems, high current investment levels or other short-term problems rather than those inefficient in some long-term sense. Deflation may, therefore, generate a process of 'survival of the lucky' as much as 'survival of the fittest'. (Tomlinson, 1834, p. 44)

The evidence here presented supports that latter rather than the former view. It may well be that the ideology and economic policies of Thatcherism represent neither the short-run nor the long-run interests of the business community (and the majority of the population). Most of the evidence suggests that an informed businessman or economist should not support such monetarist and deflationary policies.

Yet if this conclusion is established a number of perplexing problems are raised. How are we to explain the enduring support for Thatcherism and the low ratings given to the Keynesian and radical alternatives, amongst 'experts' as well as over 40 per cent of the British electorate? How can we explain the phenomenon of an experienced and established 'ruling class' espousing a doctrine that seems contrary to its material interests?

As yet, we do not have satisfactory answers to these questions. Traditionally, Keynesians have tended to view Thatcherism (and Reaganomics) as products of misjudgment or blinkered vision, resulting from 'some academic scribbler of a few years back' (Keynes, 1936, p. 383). The appropriate response, in their view, is careful theoretical examination of the underlying assumptions involved, an appeal to the facts of the real world, and reasoned and educated persuasion with the persons concerned. As Donald Moggridge has written: 'Keynes always believed that "a little clear thinking" or "more lucidity" could solve almost any problem.... Reform was achieved by the discussion of intelligent people' (Moggridge, 1976, pp. 37–8). Yet there are many highly intelligent people in the Cabinet, at the Treasury, within the Confederation of British Industry, and even, perhaps in 10 Downing Street. If the Keynesian view of the workings of the advanced capitalist economy is valid, then there must be more to the erroneous policies of Thatcherism than a failure of the powers of reason. Something in addition must be preventing a change of mind. Otherwise people would have been persuaded, in all likelihood, by the waste and failure of 1979–83. Paradoxically, if Keynes was right in policy terms, then we are drawn to the conclusion that he must have been wrong in his view of the development and acceptance of those very same policies.

Orthodox Marxists take a different view. Ideology, including economic policies, is regarded as being an expression of class interests. Thus orthodox Marxists are inclined to regard the policies of any government within a capitalist system as having the function and design of furthering the interests of the capitalist class. Thus Thatcherism is a 'ruling class strategy', which is bound to have problems and drawbacks but also has an inner rationale in harmony with capitalist interests. However, all attempts to describe and analyze this rationale have been defied by the facts. Thatcherism has not increased productivity by a great amount, it has not created 'more favourable conditions for the accumulation of capital', it has not even substantially undermined the power of the trade unions. On the contrary, it has resulted in a record postwar recession and bankruptcies at an all-time record. In these circumstances the idea that somehow capitalist interests are being served is difficult to sustain, at least without considerable qualification.

A slightly more sophisticated orthodox Marxist argument is that Thatcherism represents the interests of financial as opposed to industrial capital. There may be a grain of truth in this, as a faction of the Conservative party has always put the interests of finance before industry, and the institutional division between finance and industry has been a feature of the British capitalist system since the Industrial Revolution. However, it is difficult to overcome the objection that the financial sector has a long-run interest in a healthy *industrial* base, and they would not support Thatcher-type policies if they thought that this base was being steadily undermined as a result.

What is assumed at the outset in the orthodox Marxian view is that capitalist ideology is always in close approximation to its real interests. In contrast to subordinate classes, such as the proletariat, it is assumed that under existing circumstances the capitalist class cannot have a 'false consciousness'. The rise of the New Right puts such a view in question. As Alan Wolfe has written in *New Left Review:*

> the traditional Marxist theory of the state was insufficient for understanding the right because it did not possess a sharp enough distinction between ideology and interest. Marxists understood that the quest of each particular capitalist for profit could not take place without some guiding mechanism that would represent the interests of capitalist society as a whole. From this perspective, laissez-faire beliefs were consigned to the realm of ideology; this is what the ruling class tells the people to preserve its rule, not what members of the ruling class actually believe themselves. It may well be the case, however, that right-wing businessmen actually believe in laissez-faire. In contrast to the essentially Marxist notion that ideology speaks for interest, the new right seems to assert its ideology even when it is not in its interest to do so.. . . a theory that conflates ideology and interest will miss much of its significance. (Wolfe, 1981, p. 15)

Not only must we abandon the optimistic rationalism of Keynes, but also the 'material interest' theory of capitalist ideology in the writings of Marx. What is the alternative explanation of the enduring support for Thatcherism?

As yet, no such systematic explanation exists. But in my opinion the following elements will have to be considered. First, it is no accident that the two countries that were first to elect New Right politicians to office were Britain and the United States, in 1979 and 1980 respectively. Whilst the New Right is making significant headway elsewhere, in West Germany for example, it is arguably more influential in the Anglo-American world. Unlike Continental European countries and Japan, Britain and America lack a sustained tradition of central state planning and regulation of the economy. The tradition of central planning on the Continent is a consequence of the social convulsions of the last 200 years which, at almost every stage, have resulted in increased centralization and state intervention. By contrast, the social systems in Britain and even America have been much more stable. An explanation of the differences in support for New Right ideas in different countries may have to proceed in such terms.

Second, it is necessary to explain the general growth in support for New Right ideas since the early 1970s. Here the major factor must be the end of the period of postwar economic growth and stability, marked by the breakup of the Bretton Woods agreement and the 1973 oil crisis. In these circumstances the prevailing 'Keynesian' ideas of the 1945–70 period were discredited by their apparent failure. Given the underlying strength of classical liberalism and *laissez-faire* ideology in Western society, a 'new' version of these same ideas was most likely to replace those associated with Keynes.

Third, it is important to note some features specifically associated with Britain. The adoption of Keynesianism in the 1940s in the UK was more thoroughgoing than in the United States, and greater force was required to dislodge it in the 1970s. The Conservative party was reluctant to accept Keynesianism in the 1940s, but Keynesianism became more acceptable when, after 1951, it ensured economic expansion, social stability and thirteen years of Conservative rule. Thus was established the 'Conservative Keynesianism' of Rab Butler and Harold Macmillan. The beginning of the end was Labour's victory in the 1964 election. The 1964–70 government simultaneously raised expectations, promoted a wave of trade union militancy after a restrictive incomes policy, and failed to deal with the underlying structural problems of the British economy. Britain entered the 1970s as a weak, class-divided country, with a standard of living much lower than that in other major capitalist countries. Thus began the dissolution of the Keynesian consensus. When the assurance of social stability and prosperity had gone, the postwar settlement broke down. The establishment reverted to its nineteenth-century liberalism.

Another factor should also be taken into account. From 1970 to 1974 the Labour party moved markedly to the left, and adopted a radical and interventionist economic program. It too abandoned the more cosmetic and superficial versions of Keynesian ideology and proposed extensive state intervention and economic planning. As Keith Joseph and others have pointed out, the conversion of several leading members of the Conservative party to the New Right ideology dates from the 1973–5 period when they perceived the 'threat' of a Labour government more radical than that which had gone before. The fear of the establishment of socialist policies, based as they may be on the strength and support of the trade union movement, remains as a sustaining influence on the ideas of the New Right.

Such an explanation of the rise of New Right ideas in Britain and elsewhere departs from the simple 'ruling class' explanation of the prevalence of a certain ideology that is found in orthodox Marxism.[8] Rather than viewing New Right ideas as an expression of the interests of a ruling class, it is preferable to see their origin in historical circumstances, class *relations* and prominent social *institutions*. If we are in search of a 'material basis' for New Right and *laissez-faire* ideology then it is nothing less than the reality and centrality of the *market* as an institution of capitalist society. The root of Thatcherism is not the alleged interests of a ruling class but the 'dull routine' of the market mechanism that permeates our everyday lives.

Unlike his earlier theory of ideology as an expression of 'ruling class' interests – the view that is found in *The German Ideology* and is prominent in orthodox Marxism today – Marx also expressed the 'institutional' view. In *Capital* he wrote of the market in the following terms: 'this sphere of simple circulation or the exchange of commodities, which provides the "free trader vulgaris" with his views, his concepts and the standard by which he judges the society of capital and wage-labour' (Marx, 1976, p. 280). The 'free trader *vulgaris*' is still alive and well, and his influence in the sphere of government, especially since 1979, should challenge the more prominent Marxist view that his ideas still represent the interests of a dominant capitalist class in a developed capitalist country.

It appears, therefore, that the primary influence in the formation of government policy is neither pure class interest nor the force of reason alone. It is more to do with the history of class relations and institutional arrangements, and their effect on prevailing conceptions of the world in which we live.

The first consequence of this argument is that we must re-examine the rise and establishment of Keynesian ideas in the 1940s. The victory of Keynesianism did not result simply from its cogency, empirical foundation and inner rationality. 'Persuasion' by gifted and intelligent people was not the only factor at work. More important was the establishment of a wartime and postwar consensus based on an accord between capital, labor and the state (Addison, 1977).

Second, in similar terms, a radical alternative to Thatcherism cannot rely on persuasion, or even the economic failures of the New Right, as sufficient to reverse the ideological tide. An alternative, radical consensus must be founded on real practices and institutions that exist, or can feasibly be created, within the advanced capitalism of the 1980s and 1990s. It must also relate to the tradition of limited democracy, the collectivist practices of trade unionism, the remaining elements of the welfare state, and the new worker cooperatives that, despite the economic recession, are expanding rapidly in number.[9]

SUMMARY AND CONCLUSIONS

The deflationary policies of the Thatcher government have been responsible for an unprecedented postwar recession, more intense than that currently experienced by other advanced capitalist countries. Most graphically, gross investment in manufacturing has fallen by about one-third since 1979, and Britain has entered a sustained recession from which there is no clear sign of recovery. Consequences include an increase of unemployment to 1930s' proportions and a significant erosion of the industrial base.

The very success of the Thatcher government in bringing inflation down to low levels in early 1983 undermines the monetarist theories that it has espoused. For, contrary to their efforts, the rate of increase in the money supply has been above target and generally well above the rate of increase of money GNP and prices. Thus the Thatcher government has demonstrated that there is not a close relationship between the level of inflation and the rate of increase in the money supply, contrary to monetarist theory.

Within the heartland of industry there has been no dramatic increase of productivity, despite the biggest shake-out of labor since the war. Despite the productivity 'successes' claimed by the new, aggressive and authoritarian managements in the motor car and steel industries, for example, a general improvement in performance has not come about. The severity of the recession seems to be constraining the investment in the new technology that has been heralded by the Thatcher administration.

In addition the Thatcher government attempted to shift the balance of power in favour of management and against the trade unions. Whilst trade union membership and militancy have fallen since 1979, they are still well above the levels of the 1960s. Consequently, if any economic recovery were to come about, it is likely that the balance of power would quickly shift back in favor of the trade unions. The clear danger is that a Thatcher government would attempt to prevent this by illiberal and highly restrictive legislation, unprecedented since the Combination Acts of the last century.

However, despite its record of failure on the economic front, the experience of four years of Thatcher government has raised many problems and issues. In particular it has been noted that the survival of Thatcherism challenges both Keynesian and orthodox Marxist notions of the relationship between economic policy, ideology and vested interests. An understanding of the influence of Thatcherism and New Right ideas should be related to the actual prevalence of the institution and associated practices of the market itself.

Thatcherism's immanent criterion of success is not in terms of the level of unemployment or output; it is in terms of its achievement in promoting private property and in particular market relations. Whilst Thatcherism may have failed in conventional economic terms, it may not have failed according to its primary criterion. The New Right has defined human freedom as 'that condition of men in which coercion of some by others is reduced as much as possible in society'. (Hayek, 1960, p. 11; see also Friedman and Friedman, 1962). They argue that coercion is absent in the voluntary contract between individuals, and the market, therefore, is the realm of freedom. Thatcherism has led to mass unemployment and industrial decline but this does not spell failure in its own language. It may have led, by its own definition, to an increase in 'freedom'.

Thatcherism not only presents a clear and, for some people, persuasive morality. It also contains a vision of a more self-reliant, individualistic and dynamic capitalist future. It offers a type of radical change and rejects the somewhat weary prescriptions of the past. It is not surprising that, by contrast, traditional postwar Keynesianism and social democracy look old-fashioned and outmoded. Fudge and compromise appear all the more ineffectual when the very severity of the crisis seems to call for more drastic solutions. Thatcherism has heralded the era of the radical, and those who desire humane and lasting policies in response to the crisis must learn its language and also think in bold and forthright terms.

POSTSCRIPT

A general election was called soon after the completion of this paper. In the poll of 9 June 1983 the Conservative party under Margaret Thatcher gained a crushing victory over the opposition by increasing its parliamentary representation to 397 seats.

NOTES

1 I am grateful to Nicholas Brealey, Stephen Johnson and Brian Roper for comments on an earlier draft of this paper.
2 See, for example, Best and Humphries (1981); Buiter and Miller (1981); Craven and Wright (1983); Coutts *et al.* (1981); Frazer (1982); Kaldor (1980, 1983); Keys *et al.* (1983); Lomax (1982); Pratten (1982); Reddaway (1982); Ward (1982).
3 Further information can be obtained from S. A. N. Smith-Gavine, Leicester Polytechnic, Leicester LE1 9BH, England.
4 For more serious studies of the relationship between trade unions, wages and unemployment see Thirlwall (1981), and the symposium in *The Economic Journal* (1982).

5. For up-to-date evidence see, in particular, Espinosa and Zimbalist (1978); Clayre (1980); and Stephen (1982).
6. There are hopeful signs that trade union leaders in Britain are beginning to accept and promote this argument. See, for example, the TUC–Labour Party Liaison Committee (1982); Murray (1983).
7. An example of this type of argument from the Left is found in Glyn and Harrison (1980), esp. pp. 138–43. Examples on the Right are numerous.
8. For a critical discussion of the orthodox Marxist theory of ideology see Abercrombie, Hill and Turner (1980).
9. 650 in number in January 1983, compared with less than 100 a decade earlier. According to the Cooperative Development Agency, the evidence suggests a superior survival ability of cooperatives, compared with conventional, private firms of similar size, despite the recession. See also D. C. Jones (1976). The rate of formation of cooperatives has greatly accelerated since 1979.

REFERENCES

Abercrombie, N., Hill, S. and Turner B. S. (1980) *The Dominant Ideology Thesis*, London: Allen & Unwin.

Addison, P. (1977) *The Road to 1947*, London: Quartet.

Best, M. and Humphries, J. (1981) 'Thatcherism', *Democracy*, Vol. 1 (July).

Buiter, W. and Miller, M. (1981) 'The Thatcher Experiment: The First Two Years', *Brookings Papers in Economic Activity*, Washington, DC.

Clayre, A., ed. (1980) *The Political Economy of Co-operation and Participation*, Oxford: Oxford University Press.

Coutts, K., Tarling, R., Ward, T., and Wilkinson, F. (1981) 'The Economic Consequences of Mrs Thatcher', *Cambridge Journal of Economics*, Vol. 5 (March).

Craven, B. M., Wright, G. A. (1983) 'The Thatcher Experiment', *Journal of Macroeconomics*, Vol. 5 (Winter).

Economic Journal, The (1982), Vol. 92 (March).

Espinosa, J. G., and Zimbalist, A. S., (1978) *Economic Democracy: Workers' Participation in Chilean Industry 1970–1973*, New York, NY: Academic Press.

Frazer, W. (1982) 'Milton Friedman and Thatcher's Monetarist Experience', *Journal of Economic Issues*, Vol. 16 (June).

Friedman, M., and Friedman, R. (1962) *Capitalism and Freedom*, Chicago: University of Chicago Press.

Gamble, A. (1979) 'The Free Economy and the Strong State', *Socialist Register 1979*, London: Merlin.

Glyn, A., and Harrison, J. (1980) *The British Economic Disaster*, London: Pluto Press.

Harrison, J. (1982) 'Thatcherism: is it Working?' *Marxism Today*, Vol. 26 (July).

Hayek, F. A. (1960) *The Constitution of Liberty*, London: Routledge & Kegan Paul.

Hodgson, G. (1981) *Labour at the Crossroads*, Oxford: Martin Robertson.

Hodgson, G. (1982) 'Theoretical and Policy Implications of Variable Productivity', *Cambridge Journal of Economics*, Vol. 6 (September).

Hodgson, G. (1984) *The Democratic Economy*, Harmondsworth, Middx: Penguin (forthcoming).

House of Lords (1980) *Official Report*, London: HMSO, 11 June.

Income Data Services Ltd (1981) 'Productivity Improvements', *Income Data Services Ltd*, Study No. 245.

Jones, D. C. (1976) 'British Producer Co-operatives', in K. Coates, ed., *The New Worker Co-operatives*, Nottingham: Spokesman.

Jones, D. I. H. (1983) 'Productivity and the Thatcher Experiment', *Socialist Economic Review 1983*, London: Merlin.

Kaldor, N. (1980) 'Monetarism and UK Monetary Policy' *Cambridge Journal of Economics*, Vol. 4 (December).

Kaldor, N. (1983) *Economic Consequences of Mrs Thatcher*, London: Duckworth.

Kellner, P. (1982) 'Exposed: The Great Productivity Myth', *New Statesman*, 30 July.

Keynes, J. M. (1936) *The General Theory of Employment, Interest and Money*, London: Macmillan.

Keynes, J. M. (1972), *The Collected Writing of John Maynard Keynes*, Vol. IX, 'Essays in Persuasion', London: Macmillan.

Keys, D. *et al.* (1983) *Thatcher's Britain: A Guide to the Ruins*, London: Pluto Press.

Kilpatrick, A., and Lawson, T. (1980) 'On the Nature of the Industrial Decline in the UK', *Cambridge Journal of Economics*, Vol. 4 (March).

Lomax, D. F. (1982) 'Supply-Side Economics: The British Experience', *National Westminster Bank Quarterly Review* (August).

Marx, K. (1976) *Capital*, Harmondsworth, Middx: Penguin, Vol. 1.

Minford, P. (1982) 'Trade Unions Destroy a Million Jobs', *Journal of Economic Affairs* (January).

Moggridge, D. E. (1976) *Keynes*, Glasgow: Fontana.

Mouffe, C. (1981) 'Democracy and the New Right', *Politics and Power 4*, London: Routledge and Kegan Paul.

Murray, L. (1983) 'How We Can Beat Unemployment', *New Socialist*, No. 11 (May–June).

Organisation for Economic Cooperation and Development (1982), *OECD Economic Outlook* (July).

Pratten, C. F. (1982) 'Mrs Thatcher's Economic Experiment', *Lloyds Bank Review*, No. 143 (January).

Pratten, C. F. (1983) 'Alternative Policies Neglected', *The Guardian*, 20 April.

Reddaway, W. B. (1982) 'The Government's Economic Policy – An Appraisal', *Three Banks Review*, No. 136 (December).

Stephen, F. H., ed. (1982) *The Performance of Labour-Managed Firms*, London: Macmillan.

Tanner, J. E. (1979) 'Are the Lags in the Effects of Monetary Policy Variable?' *Journal of Monetary Economics*, Vol. 5 (January).

Thirlwall, A. P. (1981) 'Keynesian Employment Theory is Not Defunct', *The Three Banks Review*, No. 131 (September).

Tobin, J. (1976) 'Is Friedman a Monetarist?', in J. L. Stein, ed., *Monetarism*, Amsterdam: North-Holland.

Tomlinson, J. (1983) 'Does Mass Unemployment Matter?' *National Westminster Bank Quarterly Review* (February).

Treasury (1980) *Financial Statement and Budget Report 1980–81*, London: HMSO.

Treasury Committee on Monetary Policy (1981) *Third Report from the Treasury and Civil Service Committee: Monetary Policy*, HoC Paper 163–1, London: HMSO.

TUC–Labour Party Liaison Committee (1982) *Economic Planning and Industrial Democracy: The Framework for Full Employment*, London: The Labour Party.

Ward, T. (1982) 'Mrs Thatcher's Economic Strategy in Practice', *Journal of Post Keynesian Economics*, Vol. 4 (Summer).

Wolfe, A. (1981) 'Sociology, Liberalism, and the Radical Right', *New Left Review*, No. 128 (July–August).

8 Supply-Side Economics in a Small Economy: The Chilean Case

During recent years, the economic thinking that shaped policy-making in Chile has rightly been identified with 'supply-side' economics and with monetarist doctrines. The faith in free markets, and in their ability to guide an economy towards higher growth and stability, has been predominant. Although similar policies have been applied in other countries, the radicalism in this case is unusual; of course, we cannot simply draw conclusions from this one case, but I think that the analysis will nevertheless suggest a number of common problems that are likely to emerge from the actual implementation of conservative economics, especially in the context of small economies in a semi-industrial stage of development.

Before attempting to interpret the case, the main elements in the blueprint of official Chilean economics are examined, in an analytical rather than a descriptive way. Conservative economic theory provides the notion that markets are the appropriate framework for economic performance and this overtly implies the withdrawal of the state to a secondary position. Monetarism enhances the importance of fiscal balance, stressing that a deterministic monetary policy has no effect on the economy's output and, therefore, governments should not attempt to tamper with this by creating more money than is necessary to maintain fiscal balance. From a standard Keynesian perspective, the role of the capital market as an effective coordinating sector for the development of the economy was combined in Chile with ideas on monetary restraint and on a restricted role for the state. Somewhat paradoxically, the expansion of finance and of financial intermediation was expected to boost development under monetary restraint.

Both of these perspectives entailed a radical transformation of the state. On the one hand, the rise of free markets implied extensive de-regulation of the economy and the privatization of state firms and property; on the other, the rise of finance extended the reach of legal and institutional arrangements that were required to promote the emergence of private firms and resources. From the outset, this shift from a state-regulated economy to a 'market'-regulated one seemed intrinsically contradictory: laws, institutional arrangements, regulations and supervising agencies, etc. all presupposed a considerable degree of intervention by the state. What apparently changed was the direction of state intervention, not its existence.

The actual success or failure of these general economic policies must be evaluated in terms of their efficiency and efficacy, for which a framework of assessment must be chosen. This may be the framework of orthodoxy, or it may be a different critical one. The results will vary. Within a conventional framework, what matters are the chosen objectives and the rationality of the means. Thus, assessing the results of conservative policy may produce a thoroughly positive judgement (lower inflation rates, a stable balance of payments, and sound financial positions of the main agents), or a thoroughly negative one (high unemployment, low levels of living standards, negative prospects of future requirements for balance of payments, concentration, centralization, etc.). It all seems to hinge on whose ox is being gored.

However, this is too simple. In order to develop an adequate critical insight, consideration of overt policy is not sufficient. Although it contains a number of important features, changes and adjustments also occurred at a covert level of policy. This is partly the result of the intricate fabric of finance, which, as it was extended and deepened throughout the economy, brought about subtle but significant changes. It transformed behavior and the structure of capital in the economy. Furthermore, the interplay of monetary restraint and policies of financial expansion within the framework of a free market system generated a number of much more significant transformations that effectively determined the character of overall policy-making. The covert level of policy involved, for instance, the provision of the necessary conditions for transforming the state, such as the creation of alternative agents to perform the functions formerly provided by the state. Also, financial expansion appeared to be systematically related to concentration, centralization and to specific trends in the restructuring of capital. Both levels of policy should be examined in greater detail.

OVERT POLICIES

The shift to a market economy in Chile required a major deregulation of the economy. For decades the state had been extending its sphere of influence through price controls, through the determination of interest rates, minimum wages, exchange rates and tariffs, and also through controls over quantities, such as production quotas and setting regional product allocation. The reach of state regulation was deepened during the Allende government – with the further extension of regulatory schemes into transportation and inter-factory trade – but its roots can be traced back many decades.

After 1973, de-regulation and privatization openly changed the characteristics of the state, of the private sector and of the relationships between them. An integral part of this program consisted in a package of monetary and fiscal policies designed to bring inflation under control. By imposing a strict monetarist course – reducing domestic credit and public expenditure – fiscal accounts were balanced by 1975; this was maintained thereafter. By eliminating special lines of credit financed by the state (introduced during earlier administrations in order to promote industrialization and production in lagging sectors – especially in agriculture), the level and the rate of growth of the money supply were controlled by 1974, which threw the economy into an expected recession. The annual rate of change in the gross domestic product in 1975 amounted to −15 per cent, while unemployment rose to unprecedented levels above 20 per cent and the share of wages and salaries in national income fell to an all-time minimum. Nevertheless, the rate of price increases, although accelerating at a decreasing pace, still produced record levels of over 30 per cent of domestic inflation in the following years, which caused doubts about the efficiency of monetarist policies.

Different factors may be singled out as the likely source of these inflationary tendencies. Let us examine them in more detail.

'Expectations' and 'exogenous' factors were pointed to as sources of continuing monetary instability. Because people were accustomed to highly inflationary and unstable conditions, they continued to act according to expectations determined by their 'rational behavior'; hence they anticipated increases in their costs and inputs, and moved 'ahead' of prices. Moreover, the opening of the economy, with an increasingly liberal foreign trade policy, introduced external pressures on domestic prices as the international economy experienced high inflation and instability during these years.

Yet a major cause of domestic inflation might well have been the impact of financial expansion and deepening. (Financial 'deepening' means building up a more and more complicated financial structure on a given basis of real assets – pyramiding, in short.) Government economists neglected this point, but I think that there are two good reasons for considering it. Consider first the effects of privatization and de-regulation, especially within the banking and financial system. After 1973, the role of this sector and its impact on the functioning of the economy changed radically. For many years the financial system had been totally subordinated to the state, through special re-financing and rediscount facilities, as well as direct control over financial firms. Then, during the expansionary phase, this changed to an open system ruled by private management within a liberal framework of operation and functioning – free interest rates, flexible instruments and issuing of debt instruments by the private sector, etc. A change in the hierarchy and the order of economic relations between the central monetary authority and the financial system was involved. Under the new system, the extension of debt covered a new and totally autonomous sector of agents and instruments. In fact, deepening implied the shifting of deficits from the public sphere to the private, so that the conditions for the stability of these relationships escaped more and more from the direct influence of the central bank. New mechanisms of regulation, such as reserve ratios and capital debt ratios, became the only possible methods of action. But obviously, the efficiency of these mechanisms depended more on the workings of markets than on the actual directives of the central bank. In the standard view, where markets are close to perfection, monetary effects on prices are supposed to be confined to high powered money (M_1). But the development of an open financial sector generates new kinds of money (M_i, $i=2, \ldots ,n$) whose effects on prices and monetary equilibrium are neglected by conservative economics. This is surely a mistake, since M_i has significant influence in the long and medium terms and may affect both prices and output not only in the short term, but especially under crisis conditions.

The second set of considerations relates to the use of financial resources. In principle, the extension of secondary debts and the deepening of finance in an economy should not impose additional costs on the users (causing further inflationary movements of domestic prices) because the new funds are supposedly efficiently allocated at equilibrium interest rates to finance new productive investments. Financial deepening should be offset by the increased productivity of financial intermediaries. But the case of the Chilean economy is quite different. Initially, there was a massive requirement for financial resources to establish and re-establish private control over economic activity. There were then further financial requirements for the deepening of concentration and centralization of the dominant forms of capital organization within the private sector itself. The first type of requirement is associated with the costs of state transferences, since privatization imposed financial 'costs' on the private sector and caused a drain of private resources into the consolidation of the firms that were taking over state enterprises. In this process, it was more than just the property transfers that required additional finance. The privatization of enterprises and activities meant that their working capital requirements increased along with their greater autonomy. None of these cost effects existed before; moveover the additional demand for finance brought higher levels of interest rates as well as new dimensions of credit.

Apart from the implications for inflation, the rise of the financial sector indicated a deeper transformation of the economy. Finance emerged, in fact, as an alternative coordinating sector capable of replacing state activity and regulation. During the expansionary stage, 1974–7, the financial system's assets doubled, and they more than doubled again by the end of 1980. Table 8.1 shows this kind of expansion in several different dimensions.

This extraordinary expansion of finance was not free from certain conflicting characteristics. First, the term structure and the level of domestic interest rates placed a burden on the users of credit, who were confronted with expensive short-term credit for medium- and long-term requirements. Second, the liberalization of financial markets, together with a restrictive monetary policy, generated extremely high levels of interest rates, which attracted an increasing volume of short-term speculative external capital into the country.

Table 8.1 *Finance and Investment, 1970–82*

Year	Banking placements[a] (US $ m.)	Total financial liabilities[b] (US $ m.)	Total money[c] (Ch$ m. Dec. 1974)	Total quasi-monies[d] (Ch$ m. Dec. 1974)	Domestic savings (US $ m.)	External savings (US $ m.)	Investments as percentage of Gross Dom. Product
1970	671.6	—	12.1	3.8	683.4	100.8	20.4
1971	917.8	—	25.8	7.2	403.5	186.0	18.3
1972	1,200.0	—	70.5	15.7	4.6	364.6	14.8
1973	277.9	630.7	361.8	74.2	290.9	89.4	14.7
1974	153.9	1,578.4	1,255.7	336.4	864.6	24.5	17.4
1975	193.2	1,533.1	473.6	163.9	543.5	216.5	15.4
1976	440.7	1,732.7	1,423.4	819.3	135.9	128.8	12.7
1977	1,069.0	2,490.3	1,559.3	1,130.5	147.9	384.6	13.3
1978	1,903.9	5,037.7	1,920.5	1,989.3	223.8	792.2	14.5
1979	2,142.8	9,420.9	2,204.5	3,450.3	538.0	1,059.7	15.6
1980	14,385.2	17,539.1	2,729.2	4,388.5	809.9	2,011.6	17.8
1981	22,634.2	18,217.6	2,548.1	5,597.1	615.0	4,775.4	19.5[e]
1982	15,981.9	11,231.4	1,922.1	7,009.7	—	—	14.0[e]

[a] Banking system's stock of credit, investments and other placements by the end of each year. Figures in US $ m. converted by the banking exchange rate on 31 December.

[b] Stock of liabilities at the end of each year.

[c] Includes private and public sector money.

[d] Private quasi-money.

Source: A. Schneider, 'Financial expansion and monetary restraint: the Chilean case', PhD thesis, New York: New School for Social Research.

Improvements in the balance of payments and a larger volume of foreign trade strengthened the appeals to increase capital inflows into Chile. Foreign financial capital came first as credit to the central bank (1976–8), which redistributed it to banks and to the private sector. Later credit came through operations involving only private banks and direct borrowing by domestic firms from foreign banks. After 1979, an increasing number of international banks opened branches and representative offices in Santiago; the prospects for the consolidation of an open financial system seemed bright as the authorities lifted limitations that forbade direct or indirect borrowing in dollar-denominated loans by domestic corporations and individuals. While financial activities soared, foreign direct investments remained sluggish and lagged behind, in spite of the adoption by Chile of one of the most liberal statutes on foreign direct investment in the world.

Measured in terms of fiscal balance, balance of payments accounts, reserves and financial variables, the results up to 1980 were unquestionably impressive. There were problems in the 'real' sector, but they were overshadowed, especially in the minds of journalists, by the success of financial and commercial activities. In order not only to explain the stage of contraction and collapse that followed, but also to account for the problems that were present throughout the period under consideration, the analysis must go beyond the monetary and financial spheres and consider the *covert* policies that were associated with the overt policies already described and that limited the economy's ability to adjust to external impacts.

COVERT POLICIES

Conservative economics has a characteristic simplicity that is one reason why many find it attractive. Under solid, simple principles of 'monetary constraint', de-regulation and privatization, the role of economic policy appears to be confined within neat limits. For their part, markets and their mechanism – prices – emerge in full force as operators of the economic system with the expected ability to correct all sorts of 'imperfections'.

Real economies, however, are in open contrast with this scheme. Although policy-making is usually confined to well-defined and determined limits, crucial transformations take place elsewhere, beyond the overt concerns of policy. Thus, while the entire policy apparatus for example was concerned with the fiscal budget or with interest rates, totally different economic problems – such as unemployment, recession, lack of new private investment, concentration and monopolies, dumping – emerged in unprecedented profile.

The Policy Package: Concentration and Centralization

De-regulation set the scene for a struggle to restructure capital. The state withdrew many forms of protection, and intervention shifted to 'market' conditions. Privatization intensified the competition, although at a cost, since it drew resources from the private sector, although it improved for a time the current and future flow of capital funds. The 'private' economy started to work. Initially, there was relatively little competition, since for most entrepreneurs old habits remained intact and they behaved according to their previous ways. Local entrepreneurs were few and consisted largely of family firms. This meant that the traditional form of organization was that of 'family capital', through which one firm was the origin and set the limits for investment ventures. Diversification under this form of organization is slow and difficult, requiring a break with established patterns based on social, economic and family traditions. Privatization and de-regulation precipitated the change in this pattern.

A few groups did anticipate these changes and faced diversification with greater flexibility. These groups were naturally related to old 'family' capital, but they transcended this form as they went into several different businesses at once, training managers and organizing their activities. Buying up state assets mainly required a decision to run a firm with no prior knowledge or specific experience. It implied a different approach to economic enterprise. Risks were involved, but so were compensations. There was a unique opportunity to control newly privatized markets for firms that had been oligopolies in the past or were large enough to have experienced state control. Naturally, many insignificant firms were also involved, but they were not really important in comparison with the larger ones. Furthermore, as a general rule, there was little interest at first on the part of foreign firms in entering this market, for two different kinds of reasons: (1) political uncertainties about the stability of the military regime, and (2) lack of management and local networks of support, which were dismantled after most foreign capital abandoned this market during the Allende regime.

The case of banks is relevant. By 1973, all but one bank were under state control. When they were sold (between 1976 and 1980), they were acquired by those domestic groups which had adopted wide-ranging strategies of diversification and expansion. Foreign banks entered the financial sector only in the later phase of this period, by establishing their own operations. Thus, the degree of control in banking by entrepreneurial groups was significant.

The same groups controlled export firms, such as wood, mines, fishing and agro-industrial firms. By 1980, five private exporters accounted for about 60 per cent of the total private export bill; all five of them were diversified groups, almost the same as those in banking.

The term 'entrepreneurial' group was coined to point to the clear connection between *persons* and *control*; that is, although there is individual ownership, there is no attachment to a specific area of activity. It is thus different from family capital or from corporate capital as a form of organization. The difference from the latter may be arguable since corporate capital may be highly diversified and may include venture capital, but the clue lies in the distinct and clear structure of ownership. In fact, in the case of an entrepreneurial group, property may be, as a norm, traced to individuals, whereas modern corporations have a tendency to show more interconnected ownership structures ('banks which own industries, which own banks', or corporations owned through trusts and endowments).

This transformation of the structure of the economy had extensive implications. It created a local managerial sector and changed the nature of the representative form of capital in the economy. Moreover, it may be argued that the kind of transformation involved in the shift of the state to a subordinate role makes this change in the organization of capital a necessity because, under a system of family capital, no one would undertake the risks, or deal with the complexities involved in diversified growth shaped by free market policies.

Another force that influenced and shaped these transformations was monetary restraint. When it was applied on top of the situation already described, an even *greater* concentration and centralization was generated. This is explained by two sets of factors. The first had to do with the contraction in aggregate demand that resulted from state contraction and general recession. The second was that, when the money supply contracted, the rates of decrease in the demand for credit associated with a decrease in economic activity were relatively small, since privatization implied an even greater burden on the private sector – a larger credit demand – and all these pressures coalesced to create a higher level of interest rates. Tight credit – the elimination of special lines of credit and poor initial financial resources – together with the establishment of new firms and management, placed pressures on the weaker firms and so bankruptcies intensified. Larger firms also became larger by default of the weaker or through mergers and acquisitions. Put simply, oligopolies *consolidated*. Trade liberalization could also be shown to have generated the same kind of effect. The markets, then, were increasingly characterized by large conglomerates and firms with strong oligopolistic powers, while a whole new set of institutional features became predominant. Markets in the real world had fewer and fewer of the abstract characteristics supposed by the theories that supported policy-making.

Changes in the Hierarchy of Capital

Transformations in the productive organization of capital were not the only consequences of shifts in the role of the state. The *role of finance* became fundamental in two dimensions: (1) in the order of magnitude of sectors, and (2) in the order of hierarchy between sectors.

Physical expansion of the financial sector changed the relative proportions of capital within the economy, although this also reflected the shift of finance capital into a position of control over other forms of capital, productive and commercial. This happened because, as the coordinating function was transferred to the financial sector, its technical and economic supervision of the allocation of resources favored those sectors that could best face the conditions of the policy package with regard to operations and expansion. There is a *real* 'intermediation' process. 'Lending' implies a more powerful position than 'borrowing', just as, under some conditions, 'supply' is stronger than 'demand'. When the supply side is oligopolistic, for example, the lender may select the sector, the recipient and the final use of its resources, in a succession of strategic and technical decisions. It will impose conditions up to the point where the borrower declares insolvency, which is when finance usually and ultimately *takes over the entire control of an operation.*

The establishment of a financial sector is conventionally taken to represent the 'modernization' of a capitalist economy. Moreover, in advanced economies the strength of financial capital is indisputable. These concepts may seem well-established facts, in both theory and practice. The reason for their analysis here is that they were new to the Chilean economy. The establishment of a large capital market came about as the result of a development policy applied by neo-liberal 'supply–siders' in a semi-industrial, peripheral economy. The oligopolistic features created in such an economy in fact impose a heirarchical rule that is both elitist among capitals and elitist with respect to the economy as a whole. The policy is not one for *managing* the economy, in the conventional sense. The point is to restructure the economy, and to replace the state by the private capital market.

Internationalization of Finance

Finally, the internationalization of financial capital implied a significant transformation: as the hierarchical ruling force of the system was itself increasingly internationalized (i.e. the interlocking of flows and stocks of resources between the domestic financial system and the international system was extended), the whole economy became more and more vulnerable to external dynamics.

In the end, the monetary system was to become uncontrollable in such a context. The system reflected and adapted instead to both domestic and international market activity: domestic, because the extension of private intermediation reduced the scope and the effectiveness of domestic policy by the central monetary authority; external, because no open system can resist pressures generated by the swings and cycles of international markets. A functional vulnerability exposed the system to monetary determinations of output and employment.

The evolution of monetary policy and the increasing influence of foreign exchange is illustrated by Table 8.2, which shows that exchange operations became for a while the main component of changes in monetary issues. The central bank moved to a secondary position, maintaining some influence over short-term interest rates and a very weak indirect ability to regulate some areas of the term structure. The issuing of private domestic credit was left to private banks through reductions in the level of legal reserves and their ability to channel resources from external financial markets. Monetary growth became less and less important to the central bank, creating a situation that may be taken as an illustration of the monetary approach to the balance of payments *in action*. After 1978, with an open financial sector and a fixed exchange rate, monetary primary issuing – high powered money – was determined basically by variations in international reserves.

This approach to issuing appeared to be efficient for the purpose of monetary restraint: real variations of the stock of issue were kept at relatively stable levels, as shown in Table 8.2. But this happened only while international reserves were growing: they expanded rapidly for some time until 1981, when they began to fall. Monetary and financial mànagement then turned into a real nightmare. A fixed exchange rate and an open system had been central for policy implementation. The apparently consistent monetary and financial system that they generated in fact eroded the economy in at least two respects. First, in real terms, the economy was weakened as a result of monetary restraint: with higher unemployment and slower expansion of productive capacity, especially in industry and manufacturing, and also because of dear money policies, the economy became less and less competitive in an increasingly open environment. Secondly, as money became more and more expensive, the monetary system opened in order to attract external funds, which led to a large

Table 8.2 *Prices and the Money Supply, 1974–82*

Year	Annual change in Price Index	Change in M_1+M_2	Changes in monetary issuing	Exchange operations	Operations with Treasury and notes	Changes in inside money	Total reserves	Net capital inflows	Deficit on Current Account
	(Percentages with respect to previous December)						(US $ m. at end of each year)		
1974	369.2	259.2	213.3	–12.8	229.9	–4.5	94.0	273	211
1975	343.3	294.7	269.1	210.1	–16.7	85.6	–129.2	584	491
1976	197.9	264.3	239.6	207.2	–39.1	71.4	107.9	–215	–148
1977	84.2	146.2	94.4	52.1	–4.7	52.6	273.3	459	551
1978	30.2	98.6	56.2	101.0	–1.6	3.6	1,058.0	1,234	1,088
1979	38.9	72.2	44.9	135.4	–0.0	–34.8	2,513.8	1,200	1,189
1980	31.2	70.6	36.8	109.5	–0.4	9.1	4,073.7	1,921	1,971
1981	9.5	20.0	–8.9	654.4	101.8	–356.6	3,775.3	4,699	4,814
1982	20.7	30.4	–26.2	—	—	—	2,577.5	2,500[a]	2,406

Sources

[a] More than half of this amount is explained by the fall of international reserves.
Source: A. Schneider, 'Financial expansion and monetary restraint: the Chilean case', PhD thesis. New York: New School for Social Research.

increase in short-term – vulnerable – foreign indebtedness. (Credit extension recorded a more than tenfold increase in less than three years, as shown in Table 8.1.) But the combination of a fixed exchange rate with monetary restraint accounted in turn for extremely high interest rates and real rate differentials, and this was precisely the bait for international banks. Policy guidelines attempted to maintain the inflow of funds and encouraged facilities for the direct operation of international banks in the domestic market; by the end of 1980 there were over twenty foreign banks with fully operational outfits in Santiago.

CONTRACTION AND COLLAPSE

By 1980 then, the model of financial expansion and monetary restraint appeared to work well in terms of its stated objectives, but looked terribly wrong from a critical perspective.

In terms of stated objectives the record in some respects was appealing: fiscal and financial consolidation, a growing equilibrium in the balance of payments surplus, which explained a rising volume of international reserves. Even monetary stability looked possible after more than six years of consistent monetarist anti-inflation policies had begun to create doubts about the ability of monetarism to control prices and construct a stable monetary society. Although the labor market continued to be extensively regulated and the exchange rate was not free, market de-regulation and liberalization in general appeared to work. Aggregate annual growth rates for the economy during 1977–80 were, at 7–8 per cent, above historical levels.

The analysis and exposure of apparent shortcomings and potential deficiencies was not an easy job in the social and political environment of a highly authoritarian regime. Criticism concentrated on two aspects of the economy, the real and the monetary.

As far as the real economy is concerned, the main criticisms stressed that the growth performance was illusory. The high growth rates of 1977–81 reflected rather a recovery of historical output levels after the 1974–7 recession had brought about a substantial drop in output (e.g. −15 per cent GNP for 1975). A higher output level was the result of accommodating to normal levels of capacity utilization and to the resources' endowment of the economy.[1] Investment figures support the view that little new plant and equipment was created: most investment was concentrated in house building and transportation equipment, while the aggregate investment to GNP ratio of about 14–18 per cent lags far behind comparable figures for rapidly expanding economies such as Mexico or Brazil (24–28 per cent) with similar growth rates during the period. Moreover, the expansion of exports in Chile seems to be explained by earlier development in the fishing, forestry and fruit plantation sectors, which was carried out with extensive government financing. Hence, the higher growth rates may be accounted for by output normalization, although the influence of reorganizing management and productivity may have been extensive.

From a macroeconomic standpoint, higher output and growth rates were to be expected as financial resources were increased and systems of intermediation were de-regulated. The standard view of 'the transmission mechanism', after all, connects increases in funds with new investments. However, a more than tenfold increase in credit placements between 1974 and 1979 failed to generate a compensating increase in investment activity. The standard view was obviously flawed. Saving schemes also failed: domestic savings ratios fell to historical lows, while the economy entered a frenzy of consumption; aggregate savings were made to look good by including 'external savings' – the net transfer of funds recorded in balance of payments – in the data.

The restructuring of capital experienced after 1973 by the Chilean economy involved a certain amount of adaptive reorganization, existing operations being trimmed up to meet international competitive standards. Labor discipline and the establishment of managerial systems by the emerging entrepreneurial conglomerates seemed to imply some degree of 'modernization'. But this involved trimming down rather than up if one considers the large number of bankruptcies, takeovers and mergers that occurred during the recessionary and post-recessionary stages. The industrial resources of the Chilean economy, however small and nascent, had not been directed by any consistent, programmatic development effort; in any case, the market was supposed to shape the economy. This led to rapid deindustrialization in the Chilean case, as shown in the changes in the composition of GNP, where manufacturing and real productive sectors lost ground to service, trade and finance.

Enthusiastic economic authorities were able to ignore deindustrialization, dis-investment and other negative trends affecting the real economy as long as bankers were willing to provide funds. Financial expansion was promoted by high domestic interest rates, but funds remained in the financial sector since the price of money was artificially supported by strict money policies, not by the development of the new sectors or technologies that could generate the profits required to sustain and pay for such financing. This was to be a source of a major imbalance, as financial deepening was based not upon new, more productive capabilities but rather on self-contained monetary and financial spheres. The capitalization process had little to do with real accumulation, and more with financial inflows from abroad, which in turn supported credit and monetary structures. The interlocking of this capitalization pattern with the domestic credit system remained confined to the financial sphere and, therefore, eventually could be affected by a sudden speculative wave, totally unrelated to real developments.

On the monetary side, criticisms focused on the monetary approach to the balance of payments, which determined domestic money issuing – and this liquidity – in accordance with the variation in international reserves. Government economists argued fervently for this, expecting that it would imply an autonomous mechanism for money creation, entirely beyond the control of the issuing agency. The dangers lay in the link with the international economy, a sector well known to developing economies for its wild fluctuations and abrupt swings.

A by-product of the issuing pattern was the fixed exchange rate system adopted in 1979. This was supposed to help control inflation by eliminating inflationary expectations associated with exchange rate variations and to support financial expansion by increasing the rate differentials implicit in credit allocation. The parity eroded steadily after 1979. This affected exports as usual but also caused problems for other domestic sectors as imports became more and more price competitive. A vigorous 'push' on imports was exerted by countries extending financial advantages or simply dumping their exports in other's markets. The effects became more obvious as Chile's market for imports was developed.

The course of events in the world economy during 1980–1 posed difficult problems. On the one hand, prices and markets for Chilean exports fell under the pressure of recessionary conditions in the US and Europe. On the other, although larger financial resources were made available as banks had their last free-wheeling fling with OPEC monies, semi-industrial economies found themselves faced with substantially higher interest rates. Risk assessment in Chile was very good, but loans were still heavily concentrated in financial, short-term lending. Further erosion of the real economy went hand in hand with stepped up financing, which appeared to improve the balance of payments, but implied a much more expensive burden in carrying costs for the future. External debt jumped from around $10 billion to almost $18 billion and the new loans were obtained at substantially higher rates than normal.

Such a framework spelt trouble. By mid 1981, international banks had begun to curtail lending to Chile, as well as to other countries where they suspected problems. Chile felt the impact immediately. A fall in foreign loans implied less income – less money according to the monetarist view – and therefore prices had to be reduced. There were two ways to achieve this: generalized price deflation, or currency devaluation aiming at a 'one shot' effect on prices. Other alternatives were not even considered.

Government economists firmly believed in the effectiveness of the monetarist route of price deflation. However, after some months with usually negative variations in the consumer price index, it became apparent that these were not sufficiently large to generate an adjustment that would restore equilibrium. Meanwhile, monetary restraint had raised interest rates to extremely high levels, thus reducing the operational ability of firms to stay in the markets. Unemployment jumped more than 10 full percentage points to over 28 per cent of the labor force; yet wages and salaries did not respond as orthodox theory expected. Confronted with such widespread inflexibility, the government considered passing a state law to force a general cut in labor payments. A 10–15 per cent cut was discussed, but the idea was dropped as politically impractical. It would have been too difficult to justify in the name of the free market mechanism.

The option of currency devaluation was then adopted. The price in pesos of the US dollar was increased from $39 to $47 in June 1982. The economic authorities expected a 'one shot' effect on the price level to restore the competitiveness of domestic production as it was absorbed over the next two or three months. A 20 per cent devaluation was expected to generate an inflation rate of 15 per cent, and to encourage activity led by export sectors and domestic manufacture. Greater liquidity and a higher inflation rate were expected to ease real interest rates and relieve monetary pressures. Instead, the economy went straight into a spin of instability. On the one hand, the financial impact of the devaluation went far beyond what was expected. On the other hand, the monetary accommodation to devaluation proved quite insufficient and un-coordinated.

Domestic firms and households had been contracting dollar-denominated loans thoughout the earlier period of fixed exchange rates and easy credit extension. Policy-makers encouraged such credit practices because they represented a direct demand for dollar loans and, at the same time, a lower interest charge. Hence, the proliferation of dollar-denominated liabilities among domestic currency earners was very wide. When the burden of devaluation was added to the already weakening cash flows typical of the recession, the pressure reached a climax and the economy tumbled into collapse.

For banks, good loans were transformed into bad loans so rapidly that by the end of the year the piling up of uncollectable debt comprised over three times the volume of capital and reserves. As firms and borrowers stalled on their payments, liquidity problems within the banking system became so serious that the entire monetary expansion created by devaluation was absorbed without spreading outside the banking system itself. More and more funds were utilized in roll-overs or re-financing extended by financial intermediaries to related firms within their entrepreneurial groups; the degree of manipulation of funds was large and illustrated the consequences of the great concentration and ownership patterns that had evolved under the earlier phase of policy. This method of credit allocation increased interest rates, arbitrary selectiveness, etc., but it had escaped every attempt by the monetary authority to restrict it. For a while, the attempts to control liquidity showed the complete lack of effectiveness of central banking or Treasury instruments. Financial legislation seemed totally inadequate; amendments just too late. The monetary authority appeared to have no control over the supply of money. Demand forces dominated the money markets, changing contractual terms in the financial system and rapidly transforming long assets into short, money terms.

Monetarist policies continued to feed the process of financial erosion and therefore to deepen the recession. Asset values continued to fall, amplifying even further the spread between credit and the collateral for it, and so accelerating the pace of transformation of good loans into bad loans. Policy management became highly erratic. Once the initial devaluation had been absorbed, inflation rates recorded positive increases but this had no effect on activity targets, while a run-down on reserves was actually accelerated.

A system of market-determined exchange rates was then introduced, which caused a further devaluation of the peso. This only increased the pressure on monetary and financial structures and the possibility of total collapse became apparent. The 'markets' were composed primarily of foreign banks and domestic firms wishing to cash out of an unstable, erratically managed economy. They attempted to withdraw dollar placements and to convert pesos into dollars. Thus, expectations stimulated dollar payments and a further drain on international reserves. Domestic investors and speculators also helped to throw the exchange market into a spin. A sliding scheduled exchange system was adopted, but it was already too late.

The effects were immediate, although they were manifested in a somewhat unexpected turn of events. The government decided to intervene in five large financial firms, including the two largest private banks, which were related in turn to the main entrepreneurial groups. This initiated a number of significant developments.

In the first place, it was the opening move in a wide process of monetary and financial sanctions. Extending credit to related firms was halted and roll-overs were prohibited by state-appointed managers; this forced a number of interrelated firms into filing for pre-bankruptcy status. Liquidation became very likely for many firms. For some of the entrepreneurial groups, sanctions would even imply partial or complete dismantling and divestiture. The scope of sanctions, and thus the extent of liquidation, will depend on the ability of the government to engage in bargaining and compromise according to legal procedures. However, the privatization laws made this difficult.

In the second place, the intervention measures panicked the capital market so that the stock market and many investment funds collapsed. These funds had channelled resources into the schemes of the entrepreneurial groups, supporting stock prices and encouraging the new entrepreneurial structures. When many related firms faced bankruptcy and liquidation, the whole sector collapsed, causing extensive losses for private domestic investors.

For the banking system, the sanctions were disastrous, since they meant that groups had to account for all bad or uncollectable loans, and then face their own creditors – with predictable consequences. There were two kinds of creditors: external and domestic. Domestic depositors were protected by state guarantees. External banking debt, which was added to the private corporate debts of firms involved in the intervention, was sufficiently large to provoke renegotiation. This was a traumatic outcome for a country that had applied the whole set of ideas favored by most international bankers. The process of debt renegotiations also had domestic implications, for the state had to cover and commit itself to pay for banking and corporate debt acquired by a few individuals or by leading entrepreneurial groups. Although this move was widely resisted, the regime has until now had the political ability to make all Chileans pay for debts the proceeds of which were enjoyed by only a few in developing their expansionary schemes.

The process of debt renegotiation has also taught Chile a lesson. When private debts were contracted in the earlier phase of expansion and liberalization of finance, the fees and charges were higher *because* there were no state guarantees. The state encouraged this situation by stating that it assumed a subsidiary role with respect to the economy. However, when the banks and private corporations defaulted and debt renegotiation became unavoidable, the banks demanded a recognition from the state of all obligations. The arguments for this were that the government had compelled defaults by intervening, or simply that if the government wanted banks to resume lending operations – which it did desperately – it had first to reschedule the whole amount of past, accrued debts. The state has granted significant concessions – as yet unknown, but certainly large. In the end, debts were 'private' only within a given framework, and became 'public' by a simple change of terms made possible by the pressures confronted in a crisis. But this change conceals the actual payment of much higher interest charges and commissions carried by 'private' contracts. The abstract, political denomination of debt as 'private' may have cost the country several billions of dollars.

Government sanction and intervention involve a radical change in economic management: they mean a *de facto* return to a state-managed economy. There is still a theoretical, abstract commitment to the free market in Chile, but the need to control financial convulsions, to prevent further collapse and eventually to protect the stability of the political regime, has compelled increasing state interference. By controlling the main firms – the large public enterprises that still remained in state ownership and now the largest private ones – the state has regained control over the economy. At the same time, the managerial systems have been paralyzed. They have been partially replaced in shuffles and reshuffles, and expect orders from some higher authority. These orders remain ambiguous, sometimes unknown, as the economic authorities reject programming and planned state coordination. The superimposition of conflicting layers of authority is apparent. The policy-makers are largely unaware of the full political consequences of their failure; they have succeeded only in opening the 'Chicago road to socialism', and have set the scene for an eventual twist in the regime's economic philosophy, if not a complete about-face. For political survival will not be easy after a disaster of this magnitude.

It is now very difficult to predict the final outcome of these events. The succession of four economics ministers in less than one year, as well as the successive shifts of policy in the face of changing realities, all make for a confusing picture. On the one hand, some degree of financial stability has been attained by extensive 'lending of last resort' accompanied by a firm check on monetary issuing of high power monies. Some degree of control has been regained through sweeping intervention in banks and entrepreneurial groups so that, to some extent, the state now commands key sectors: a large segment of the public sector and now a large segment of manufacturing, banks and commercial firms. For several years to come, the central bank will compel profit transfers from all banks to pay for the rescue of uncollectable portfolios. The unemployment situation has been dealt with by extensive subsidies and transfer programs. These expenditures – consisting not in unemployment compensation but in programs of 'minimum employment' managed by county authorities – cause largely unproductive transfer payments, which do not generate much demand stimulus but do lead to further erosion of fiscal and monetary policy effectiveness.

On the other hand, the renegotiation of external debt is inescapable. Whatever the terms or the framework, this restores a high risk rating for the Chilean loan market for at least a few years. The extension of state guarantees and government participation in clearing the formerly 'private' commitments are also unavoidable. The stability and prospects of the Chilean economy will thus depend – if they do not depend entirely already – on what the state does. An autonomous, fully operational private sector is now some kind of archaic illusion.

It is clear that the adoption of orthodox monetarist ideas proved to be totally inadequate to deal with the Chilean crisis: they allowed the full and amplified transmission to Chile of the recession in the advanced economies through open trade and monetary systems. This episode illustrates the distance between theory and reality, and the persuasive misunderstandings that result from perceiving a market not as it really is – with all its institutional aspects and inflexibilities – but as a simple textbook portrays it. Alternative policy options were discarded on purely ideological grounds and the policy actions that were adopted came up against the effects of the transformation of the economy realized under the combination of covert and overt policies during the phase of monetary restraint and financial expansion. A completely devastating collapse of industry and finance was prevented only by a major reversal of the role of the state in the economy, which returned to a position of central command. Monetarist policies have thus produced exactly what they intended to erase.

Yet the policy-makers continue to be committed to privatization and a dominant role for the private sector. As a result, large public firms do not invest because it is intended that they will be transferred to the private sector. Large private firms, in turn, do not invest because their current managers are transitory, because their horizon is limited by the prospect of liquidation, and because they expect at best only to consolidate the financial position of the firm prior to reassignment. The contrast between what the regime and its supporters in the private sector say and what they do is made even sharper by the difficulties inherent in circumventing laws designed to protect the private sector from government interference and by confused bargaining processes.

The fact that monetarist theories and policy-making in Chile remain the dominant paradigm in the government, press and academic life is clearly related to the association of the military regime with these views and its ability to remain in power, rather than to its ability to manage the economy or to predict its behavior. The source of conservative economic policies and ideas is clearly connected here to an undemocratic, unyielding authoritarian regime. The events in Chile give more and more support to those who believe that the development of a just and stable society is impossible under monetarist guidelines because of their impact on economic activity and distribution.

NOTE

1   A similar argument on the issue of the 'Brazilian miracle' is put forward by E. Bacha, L. Taylor, *et al.*, *Models of Growth and Distribution for Brazil*, Oxford: Oxford University Press, 1980.

9 Conclusions – Cowboy Capitalism: The Last Round-up

The consequences of the conservative revival are now in plain view. The rule of defective theories and misguided policies has steered the ship of state on the reefs of world-wide economic collapse. Yet in spite of these well-foreseen and well-explained disasters, conservatism remains widely popular and strongly supported, particularly by the business community. How are we to explain this? Let us review the position.

WHAT CONSERVATIVE ECONOMICS MISSES: THE WAY THE WORLD WORKS

Modern conservatism presents no less than three distinct theoretical approaches to economics, each of which purports to demonstrate the optimality of the working unfettered free markets and the undesirability and/or ineffectiveness of government intervention. Each fails to understand the theory of effective demand, leading to the absurd view that all unemployment must be, in some sense, 'voluntary'. Each fails to provide a coherent account of the problems of the modern economy.

Supply-side incentive theory

Basically, this fails to understand how business enterprises work. Business expansion depends on expected market growth, i.e. on (long-term) sales growth. Current production and employment depend on current or immediately anticipated sales. A slowdown of spending – it does not have to be actual increased saving, it can be merely a postponement – will lead to a production slowdown, with layoffs and short time, which *further* reduce spending – the multiplier effect. Supply-siders, rehabilitating Say's Law, fail to understand this, and hold that every act of supply is necessarily an equivalent demand, thereby missing the central point of a monetary economy. So, cutting back government budgets reduces sales, which sets off further multiplier reductions. Cutting taxes, on the other hand, might provide an offsetting stimulus, although for the most part the taxes being cut are those of the rich, who have a low propensity to consume. Moreover, supply-siders want to cut taxes for the effect on supply incentives, not to stimulate spending, as the Keynesians would. They claim that cuts for workers will increase the supply of effort: workers will work harder for bonuses, or longer hours for overtime. Tax cuts for executives and the rich will increase the supply of savings, and this will lower interest rates and stimulate investment. Yet many studies have shown that the supply of effort depends chiefly on job satisfaction, which in turn depends on workers having some control over the nature, pace and quality of their work and working environment. Increasing their take-home pay either by raising wages or by cutting taxes will have little effect. As for the effect of tax cuts on savings and investment, the supply-siders fail to notice that their proposal simply transfers withdrawals from government to the private sector. This has to be analyzed carefully. Suppose initially that the budget is in balance, and that private savings equal private investment. That is, using the diagram developed earlier, the LM locus cuts the JW locus where the latter cuts IS. Then let there be a tax cut, that is, a lowering of the tax rate from t_0 to t_1, with government spending, G, constant. From Figure 9.1 we see that this causes the JW locus to swing out from JW_0 to JW_1. With a given LM locus, we see that the result is a *rise in both interest and income*, with the emergence of a government deficit and a corresponding private sector surplus of savings over investment. (If G were also cut in the same proportion as

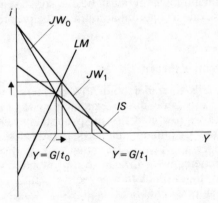

Figure 9.1

taxes, there would be *no effect* on either interest or income. JW_1 would simply rotate about the initial equilibrium point within the angle defined by IS and JW_0.) So the consequences of a tax cut are quite different from what supply-side doctrine asserts. In short, supply-siders ignore the evidence on the causes of labor effort, while their account of the effects on savings and investment overlooks most of the principal interactions studied in the theory of effective demand. Supply-side theory, as Rinder shows, relies on a literal-minded and simplistic version of conventional economics that is wholly inappropriate for modern, or perhaps any, social conditions.

Monetarist Macroeconomics

Again the central failure is to understand the theory of effective demand. Monetarism tries to link spending – effective demand – with money, and money with wealth, basing these links, respectively, on the traditional quantity theory, and on the fact that money is a store of value. But household spending depends primarily on earned incomes, which is to say, on real wages and employment, while business spending for investment purposes depends largely on the expected growth of sales, which in turn is considerably influenced by the present level of sales and recent changes in that level. As Friedman admits, the demand side of the monetarist approach is weak, but the treatment of money is no better, as we saw. Monetarism has no answer to the problem of the relation between real and monetary phenomena. It cannot accept the real balance effect without accepting most of the Keynesian approach along with it. Yet it has no answer to the challenge posed by the 'invalid dichotomy'. The Keynesians are no better off, for the real balance effect saddles them with as yet unsolved, if not insoluble, problems, not the least of which is that the concept of wealth involved is incoherent. The monetarist challenge has at least opened the Pandora's box of monetary vs. real concepts in economic theorizing.

Rational Expectations Theories

First, there is the question of the underlying model, in which the 'expectations' are embedded. If this is a model with uncertainty and a monetary organization of the sort Keynes studied, then 'rational expectations' will lead to Keynes' results: underemployment equilibrium will be a possibility, and policy can be effective. Second, there is a problem of internal consistency. The approach requires making quite asymmetrical assumptions about the behavior of different economic agents – chiefly, firms and workers, though sometimes businesses and households – and this asymmetry is inconsistent with the theory of markets underlying the models. Further, there is the problem that all agents – firms, households, workers – are supposed to believe the same economic theory. But the actual diversity of economic theories is very great, ranging from crank opinions all across the political spectrum, to serious academic theories all across the political spectrum. Moreover, because of identification and specification problems, it is inherently impossible econometrically to establish anything stronger than that the evidence at present is consistent with a particular theory – and an infinite number of variations on it! Hence, appeals to the facts will not – cannot – settle the issues dividing the proponents of various theories. But once 'imperfect knowledge' is permitted, the conservative conclusions of the rational expectations theorists no longer follow.

All three approaches thus fail to grasp the central idea of the theory of effective demand; all three assume that free markets in practice will approximate the idealized markets of the textbooks; none pays more than ritual attention to economic power, corporate oligopolistic practices, mark-up pricing, community pressures, indivisibilities and other market imperfections, or to the possibility that the textbooks might have failed to grasp something essential in the way prices are set and actually function. Textbook theory holds that prices reflect scarcity, that the price system allocates scarce resources efficiently. But it is possible that the textbooks are either wholly or partly wrong, that, in reality, the price system performs some quite different function or functions alongside, or in place of, the allocative function. For example, it has been suggested that, through changes in the mark-up over wage costs in response to variations in aggregate demand, prices adjust to provide the profits to finance the investment that business wishes to carry out. If this or something like it were the actual mission of 'the price mechanism', then very few of the conventional conclusions about market efficiency or optimality would hold. Yet conservative economists never seem even to consider the possibility. For them, the efficiency of the free market approaches the status of a revealed truth.

What all such theories have in common is a certain kind of *unreal* quality. It is not that their assumptions are abstract or 'unrealistic'; it is the *working* of the models that is unreal. It is like a theory of automobiles that explains their movement by the spirits that turn the wheels. Say's Law, the tax wedge and the work/leisure choice, the real balance effect, and rational expectations are all just such spirits. Of course, there is a place for spirits and, similarly, there may be a place for some of these ideas – but in works of fiction or quasi-religious ceremonies, not in what purport to be works of science, leading to practical policies that will affect the daily lives of millions of people. And this is really the clue. Conservative economics is not, in fact, science at all. It is ideology *masquerading* as science; romantic individualism in scientific drag.

If that is so, then what are we to say of the policies that follow from such theories?

POLICY ON THE ROCKS

It was billed as a 'Program for Economic Recovery' in the US, as 'shock treatment' to bring the nation to its senses in Chile, and as the strong medicine, bitter but necessary, that would restore economic health in Britain. In each case the conservative program was comprised of essentially the same elements, though mixed in somewhat different proportions. Basically, the elements have been tight money, budget cuts, tax cuts for the wealthy, and de-regulation together with dismantling of the regulatory agencies. In each case the program has had essentially the same results: recession deepening into depression, steadily growing unemployment and widespread bankruptcies, particularly in manufacturing, inflation first increasing then tapering off, declining investment and profits, which, combined with high interest rates and a strong exchange rate, lead to bankruptcies, takeovers, mergers and a general restructuring of capital. By and large, the concentration of ownership and control has increased and, broadly speaking, the giant multinationals and international banks have benefited. Yet this conclusion cannot be pressed too strongly; national capital probably got the lion's share in Chile, and both banks and multinational giants have suffered extensively in both Britain and the US.

In any case – some recovery! Unleashing the free market has led to unquestionable, and wholly predictable, disaster. No doubt, recovery will come eventually, as the normal business cycle reasserts itself, and when it comes it may be fairly strong. But the recovery will then be followed by another bust. The Keynesian object was to control or at least dampen this cycle of boom and bust. De-regulation and budget-slashing have led to the dismantling or weakening of many of the mechanisms that dampened and controlled the cycle. The result, of course, has been to remove the brakes that stopped us from lurching down the economic roller coaster. So, down we go.

Why this should appeal to the business community is, on the face of it, something of a mystery. Government spending and government regulations have both had as their chief object the maintenance of orderly markets, with high levels of demand requiring high levels of employment. To plunge the system into recession hardly seems to the benefit of either business or labor. Is it anything more than sheer obstinate thickheadedness?

This answer cannot be absolutely ruled out, but there are two others that ought to be considered. One we have already mentioned – the revival of the ideology of individualism, to which we shall turn in a moment. The other is closely related, but intensely practical. It is a kind of capitalist Luddite response – to destroy the machinery that is replacing them and controlling their lives. Just as the followers of Ned Ludd broke up the machinery that threw them out of work, or worsened their conditions, so capitalists are now hell bent on wrecking the institutional machinery that, in populist or revolutionary hands (sometimes even in liberal hands), could come to dominate or even replace them.

CAPITALISTS AS LUDDITES: DESTROYING THE MACHINERY OF DEMOCRATIC CONTROL

It is frequently argued, especially by Marxists, that the conservative economic policy is simply a disguised attack on labor. Capital is better placed to withstand a recession; hence generating one will put labor on the defensive and roll back real wages. Moreover, it will force weak firms to the wall, and they will be swallowed up by the strong. One trouble with this scenario lies in the fact that, in general, at least since World War I, both real wages and labor's share have *risen* in recessions and fallen in the upswing. Granted that capital is (usually) better placed to withstand hard times, it nevertheless also seems to be hit harder by them. If the capitalists' aim is to increase profits and the rate of profit, the should do their best to engender booms, not recessions.

A similar point applies to the related claim that recessions will improved labor discipline, thereby making possible higher productivity advances. Productivity in fact increases most rapidly in boom conditions, as shown by nearly all postwar statistics in all major capitalist economies. Again, on the face of it, business should support an expansionary policy package, not a contradictory one.

Yet these points do have more than a grain of truth in them. Business is concerned, intensely concerned, with labor costs and labor discipline, but this is simply because labor costs are usually the largest or one of the largest cost items, and labor discipline is the key to productivity. Business is concerned with all costs, and with more than labor discipline – it is concerned to keep open the *field of action* of capital. Any restraints or restrictions on the free movement of capital, on its prerogatives, its decision-making rights and powers, are necessarily anathema, since they reduce the range of possibilities for making money. Whether the restrictions come from labor, consumers, environmentalists, local communities or political parties does not matter. Whether they concern workplace safety, pollution, product safety, truth in packaging, truth in lending, price-gouging or anything else, is immaterial. Whatever they are, they are restrictions on the freedom of business to choose the best strategy to make money. Such restrictions must be resisted, for if they are allowed to stand, they will stand as a precedent. First an inch, then a mile. If labor gains the right to a say in workplace safety, why not a veto power over working conditions? Why not over the pace of work? Why not a share in the profits? Why shouldn't consumers have a say in price-setting? In plainly oligopolistic industries it is difficult to appeal to the virtues of perfect competition. Perhaps more to the point, since jobs depend on it, why shouldn't labor have a say in the location of industry, in particular a veto over runaway industries, those moving from Toledo to Mexico, New York City to Hong Kong?

It is important to see what is quite evident to many business leaders: once the legitimacy of these questions is granted, there then follows an interminable and essentially undecidable dispute over the exact division of powers and responsibilities between business, labor, consumers, local communities, environmentalists, etc., with the chief dispute, the core of the matter, being between business and labor. Once capital has conceded the right of labor and/or others to challenge its authority and prerogatives, there is no obvious stopping point. Each group will push for as much as it can get, and will mobilize all the political and other resources at its disposal. The election of Allende in Chile, and the legislation enacted subsequently, shows quite clearly how far this can go in a democratic system. A well-planned, capably organized political coalition, relying on an efficient and well-trained state bureaucracy, can take over and run virtually the entire economy, essentially *displacing the rule of capital*.

But this also provides capital with the essential key to preventing this. None of these groups – labor, consumers, environmentalists – is itself able to operate the economy or to police business to ensure compliance with legislation or agreements. All depend on the state bureaucracy for that. Thus, *dismantling the state deprives popular movements of any means to enforce their will*. Even if they succeed in putting legislation on the books, if budgets are cut and state agencies are gutted and demoralized, nothing will be done. Without an agency like OSHA, labor cannot enforce workplace safety standards, except by the expensive and imprecise weapon of the strike. Without the Environmental Protection Agency, environmental groups cannot enforce legislation, except by costly and time-consuming lawsuits. Without a consumer protection agency, consumer groups are likewise reduced to lawsuits to enforce consumer safety standards. And so on. Cutting state agencies, de-regulation and budget-cutting are all ways to prevent popular groups from effectively exercising their will. The cutbacks in welfare, unemployment compensation, food stamps and similar programs also weaken those dependent on them, and deprive many political organizers of essential or helpful means of support while doing political work.

However, it would hardly do to advertise this as the purpose of the program. Hence the need for an apparently well-grounded scientific-seeming theory to provide suitable sheeps' clothing for the lupine policy package. But there has to be more. Besides dismantling the state agencies capable of expressing and enforcing the popular will on the economy, there has to be some program for restoring profitability to capital. Where is accumulation to take place? How can transformational growth be restored? How can the centers of capitalism, especially the US, be kept prosperous and strong?

In fact the conservatives have extremely simple answers to these questions, though they do not discuss the matters in these terms. Accumulation will take place on the basis of consumer-driven transformational growth, based, as in the past, on the auto-industrial complex, abetted by modern microelectronics and computers. The difference, however, is that it will now take place in the Third World, or rather in 'newly developing countries' (NDCs) of the Third World – South Korea, Brazil, Mexico, Chile, and so on. Here, in these nations, a large and relatively prosperous middle class is ready for a consumer boom, specifically for an automobile boom. The market is there, and the labor force is large enough, skilled enough and cheap enough to carry it out. So, the pattern can be repeated, with the US and European companies licensing or producing through subsidiaries. This is the importance of free capital mobility and free trade. Nor do the companies want their new operation tied down in a maze of safety or anti-pollution regulations.

So, the answer to the question, how is capital to accumulate, is easy. Capital must migrate to where the automobile and consumer durable product cycle is about to begin again. But that leaves the difficult question of how a strong and prosperous economy is to be maintained at the center of the system, in the US. Here again, however, conservatives have an exceedingly simple answer: through a military build-up. By greatly increasing domestic military spending and at the same time promoting military sales abroad, they hope to bring the economy back to full employment, thus keeping the industrial system strong, even if growth is no longer chiefly centered at home.

Moreover, the military build-up will provide the center with the strength to defend its client governments and its investments in the newly developing countries of the Third World.

On the surface, the policy is coherent. But it has two flaws, each devastating. First, the growth patterns of the NDC's are anything but attractive, quite apart from the human rights records of their neo-fascist military dictators. In every case, growth has caused the emergence of a dualistic society: the accumulation of capital has not only brought high wages and modern technology, it has also destroyed traditional concepts, traditional agriculture and older balanced ways of life, creating a seething mass of displaced, jobless, largely homeless humanity swirling in barrios around the great cities. Make no mistake, the military dictators are *necessary* if private capital is to maintain its sway. Necessary, but – here is the catch – maybe not sufficient. The development process generates its own contradictions and may throw up its own forms of government, and of economic organization, based on the national or indigenous culture. That is what happened in Iran, and it may well happen again in other places. Even earlier, Salvador Allende, in Chile, showed that a progressive, anti-capitalist government not only could get elected, but could carry out its program and increase its popularity even in the face of a massive undercover American campaign to 'destabilize' it. So the proposal to shift the center of accumulation to the NCD's of the Third World carries more than a little risk.

The second flaw is, if anything, even more serious. Prosperity in the US cannot be based on military spending, since military spending does not *grow*, at least not in any natural and regular way. Once a level of military power is decided upon, a certain sum of spending will be required – and that is it. It has to be maintained, but that is all. Of course the military–industrial complex has an answer – a new generation of weapons is developed as soon as orders have been completed for the old. 'Technological progress' makes the earlier weapons obsolete, and if we don't order the new weapons, the Soviet Union will develop similar advances and take the lead in the arms race. However, the 'progress' has turned out to hamper rather than improve the performance of the weapons, for the requirement of selling the new weapons to procurement officers has created baroque monstrosities that require almost unbelievable maintenance and servicing and frequently do not work at all. Moreover, even if new weapons systems replace old ones regularly, there is still no guarantee that *military spending will grow*. For the new systems may simply replace the old at the same or even lower cost, with the result that military spending will *shrink* as a percentage of GNP. Of course, it will be 'better' than if it fell to zero, as it would if the old (and often more workable) weapons were kept on. But it is no way to sustain prosperity, for, as we saw, the *level* of prosperity in capitalism depends on the *rate of growth* of investment and government spending. So prosperity cannot be based on a component of the system that contains no inner growth dynamic, let alone one that is completely wasteful into the bargain.

There is one way to make military spending grow, however, and that is to whip up war fever. Scare talk about the Soviet Union, as viewed through the 'window of vulnerability', with emphasis on the 'present danger', will do a lot to boost the military budget. Even so, it tends to be a once-for-all hike. It may last a few years, but then a new scare will have to be invented. There is no getting around it, the best way to keep military spending growing is to have wars, continuous wars. Not one big one; that is too dangerous. Lots of little ones – 'police actions' – carried out in the context of a permanent confrontation with the Soviet Union. Some action in El Salvador and Central America, confrontation in Africa over Angola and Namibia, something to restore American prestige in the Persian Gulf, perhaps – any or all of these will help. For the point is not just to keep military sales up; it is also, and much more important, to preserve the Free World, the world, that is, where capital can move freely. That is the basic message of conservative economics: capital must be able to move to where the markets are developing, the military spending will both keep these markets open and prop up the advanced and mature economies as capital pulls out of them to invest in areas of future growth.

In short, the free market program has a multi-faceted appeal. To some, it offers a program and justification for restricting the power of organized labor or organized consumer groups. To others, it offers a program for restricting the powers of the state to control and regulate economic activities – power that might well be exercised in the interests of the people at the expense of private profit. Most of all it offers a program for ensuring the world-wide free mobility for capital. And, of course, there is the ideological appeal: unlike classical or Burkean conservatism – or Adam Smith for that matter – the modern version argues that the interests of business and the people can never 'really' or 'truly' conflict. The Invisible Hand is always a helping one. Yet, in fact, we know better; we have all felt it picking our pockets. It is precisely the mission of conservative ideology to convince us that this is not so – that what we can see with our own eyes is not really happening. If we can't see it, we won't try to stop it.

So there are good reasons for the free market program to appeal to the business community, even when, in the short or medium term, it hurts business (especially if it is not too dogmatic about the need to eliminate government subsidies to industry). But there are deeper and darker reasons for its appeal to wide sections of the populace. This appeal, unfortunately, reaches out well beyond the business community to all who feel threatened by the pace of change in modern life. The free market is the keystone in an arch of ideology that supports the vision of the frontiersman, the rugged individualist who conquered the West, exterminated the Indians and walked on the Moon. As is well known, behind every such great man there stands a Woman. Moreover, what makes these heroic feats possible, and sustains the individual in moments of weakness, is Simple Faith. (In fact, British capital, the US army and Eastern banking conquered the West, and the vast collective effort of modern science, incorporated in NASA, a government agency, put men on the moon.) Mythology, like the cowboy hero of the Old West, dies hard. Can the second assistant vice-president, the insurance salesman, the commuter on the 8:05 from Bethpage, dress in buckskin and ride into the sunset? Why is the Woman standing behind him now pushing herself forward? Even pushing in front of him. How can one have simple faith when theologians talk about the death of God and priests join the communist guerillas in the mountains? How is the world to be understood and why is everything so difficult?

The answer comes in the form of a Great Simplification: all at once everything is clear – it is the fault of government. Government has destroyed incentives and weakened the economy; it has corroded the family and undermined simple faith. The values of our forefathers can be re-established if we can just get the government off our backs and out of our lives. (This means, of course, getting the government actively to promote the values of rugged individualism.) The virtues of the frontier must be restored. Let us see what these are and what their appeal is. Here is a recent account.

THE LAST FRONTIER: THE ENTREPRENEUR AS COWBOY

Adventure, imagination and boldness in the taking of risks – these are the central elements in the make-up of the entrepreneur, the true creator of the world we live in. It is a mistake to think of our civilization as sustained by material things (factories, roads, bridges) or by natural resources (such as coal mines, oil wells or top soil). The things of the world are built by entrepreneurs essentially out of their own vision and energy; the natural resources are discovered and mobilized by them, and when they are used up new ones will be discovered. The resources of the world are limitless, if we have but the energy and vision to seek them out and learn how to put their properties to use.

Of course, not all entrepreneurs will succeed, not all innovations will work. In fact, most will fail and most would-be entrepreneurs will lose their shirts and very likely their family's shirts, too. Nevertheless, this is as it should be. Settling the West was not easy either. Frontier life is harsh, and only the lucky will strike gold. But that is the way it should be; that is what gives capitalism one of its most essential qualities: it provides space for chance and for luck, for the unexpected, the wholly unforeseen and unplanned. This element of chance and luck brings novelty, the unknown, into our everyday lives and so accords with one of human nature's deepest wishes. Far from being a defect of capitalism, the inherent dependence of market success on luck is one of its strengths. Not only does it provide a great spectacle for everyone; it brings out the creative and gambling instincts in the competing entrepreneurs.

A further point is essential. Luck and creativity, boldness and imagination are essentially *individual*. A corporation cannot be creative, cannot be lucky, in the relevant sense. Only an individual can be, it seems. For if a corporation could innovate, why not any bureaucracy? Is Lockheed more efficient than the Pentagon? Is General Motors more innovative than NASA? The doctrine is that individuals are the true and only source of creativity; committees and bureaucracies, including private corporations, tend to stifle initiative, smother competition and compromise away innovation.

Of course not everyone is imaginative, daring and able enough to be an entrepreneur, or even willing to risk trying. Only the elite, the natural aristocracy, are capable of entering the race. The rest of us will have to be content with a humbler position, essentially working in someone else's grand schemes. However, such people as we are prove to be absolutely necessary, for without us nothing would get done. Hence it is essential that we be motivated, for example by having to support a family and having no other income but what we obtain from working.

Although celebrated, and highly rewarded, for his hardy fortitude in bearing risks, the entrepreneur is, nevertheless, in certain respects quite sensitive and delicate. He is, it seems, easily discouraged, especially by taxes and government regulations. Filling in forms and responding to the questions of government inspectors can easily drive him to despair or to Mexico. Lack of a proper competitive environment can lull him into lethargy. Criticism by liberal moralists, fussing over oil spills and rare birds, can sap his creative vitality. A breakdown of family morals can leave him without the prospect of bequeathing his just rewards to happy heirs and descendants.

Is this a parody? I don't think so, in spite of the slightly tongue-in-cheek air. Readers of George Gilder's *Wealth and Poverty* (1981) or Jude Wanniski's *The Way the World Works* (1981) should recognize the basic picture. The essential point is quite simple and was made a long time ago by Schumpeter: the crucial dynamic, the driving force of capitalism, comes from the 'creative destruction' wrought by the individual innovating entrepreneur – the Edisons, the Fords, the Rockefellers, the Vanderbilts – who transformed the world through the intensity of their vision and the force of their personalities. The corollary, of course, is that any bureaucratic restrictions that hedge in the activities of such geniuses will weaken that driving force and slow down the pace of progress. Indeed, this is perhaps the basic message conveyed by the novels of Ayn Rand – romantic individualism, the world as created by will. What are we to say to this?

The answer can be given in one word: nonsense. The world is never built by a single individual. People are interdependent. Inventions are never the products of isolated geniuses, struggling alone in their basements. There is always a social context, just as crucial as the impetus of leadership. Leaders *are* important, and great leaders are highly important, but they are important because they bring people together and forge teams out of them. The largest and most success-ful American business of the nineteenth century, the Pennsylvania Railroad, was not the creation of any of the robber barons. It was put together by committees, and was run from the start as a bureaucracy. It became the prototype of the American corporation. Everyone knows of Henry Ford, but what of General Motors, for five decades a far larger and more successful company? No single 'individual genius' was ever responsible for it. And what of the Manhattan Project, or the landing on the moon? How to explain the curious fact that crucial inventions tend to occur *simultaneously*, but independently, to 'indi-vidual geniuses' all over the world? (There were four inventions of the airplane, five or six of the automobile, all independent, all at about the same time. Newton and Leibniz both invented the calculus independently in the same year. Examples could be multiplied end-lessly.) Those who built the world we live in today, and those who are today building tomorrow's world, are not rugged individualists shoot-ing it out in OK corral, but people who work well in committees and function smoothly in bureaucracies, walking the corridors of power. We may not like it, but that is how it is. The 'free market' is adminis-tered by a committee consisting of at least the Sales Manager, the Production Manager and the Vice-President in Charge of Finance.

THE FREE MARKET AS THE LAST FRONTIER

Yet simply saying this won't do. There he stands, tall and lean, silhouetted against the fading sunset, guns slung low, the woman slightly in the shadows to the rear, fighting back the tears as he saddles up ready to ride on, new lands to conquer. The image, burned into our consciousness, will not fade though skyscrapers grow on the ranches. But if we are ever to understand our own world, we have to free ourselves from this kind of simplistic nostalgia, for at bottom that is what has captivated the modern conservative – not the contented cattle grazing in tranquillity under stately English oaks on well-managed estates – the Burkean vision of an older generation of conservatives. The plutocracy builds railroads to reach the great plains where hired men herd Texas longhorns across sweeping lands, and hired guns fight rustlers. And the moguls of oil move in to drill, buying out the cattlemen . . .

The terms of the vision, the particular images, don't matter. The essential feature is that the free market is the frontier. The rules are few, but the code is clear, and the battle goes to the strong and quick, although the Invisible Hand tips the scales in favor of the white hat. Justice triumphs. In a literal sense, that is all there is to it. The free market gives scope to individual initiative, and this entrepreneurship is the generator of progress, because the market will accept and reward only what people want and will pay for.

Even supposing this were broadly true – and, as we have seen, recent history and theory both show that it is not – is this any way to organize a society? Is this fair, or just or even sensible? Before we succumb to a romanticized vision of the frontier, we should ask ourselves what it is really like? In actual fact, the frontier was often chaotic and lawless, ruled by power, rather than consent. It was dirty and often brutal. Sometimes it prospered and grew rapidly, yet it could also collapse suddenly. So, in all these respects, with the free market.

Let us consider a few very basic elements in the picture of the risk-taking entrepreneur in the free market. He innovates, without hindrance from regulations or licensing or permission. He takes his risks on the market, on the chance that his product will be wanted. But he is not, in fact, the only one at risk. His workers are equally at risk, for if he loses his capital, they will lose their jobs. Why is his risk more important than theirs? Why should he make all the decisions, and reap the reward for risk, when they risk what is just as important to them – their livelihood?

In the conservative picture, the entrepreneur is able to live out his creative thought in action, but the worker, on whom the entrepreneur depends completely, is compelled to follow a repetitive, uncreative and boring course, spending his hours on someone else's project, where his own beliefs and vision are most likely irrelevant to the work at hand. Why should this be? Why should the great majority have virtually to separate themselves from their own minds to give their labor to projects that have no connection with their lives, projects defined by the pursuit of money? Why should the great majority be forced by necessity to work in unpleasant, boring, soul-destroying jobs, in order to make enough money to get by? It is true that economic progress may provide a large number, perhaps a majority, with a good deal more than enough to get by. But economic progress has not made the work any more satisfying. It hasn't even made it all that much safer. This is not to deny that there has been improvement; only to note that it has not been on anything like the scale of the rise in consumption standards – and it started very low.

Of course, the conservative answer is that if the workers had had any initiative, they wouldn't be workers; they would be entrepreneurs. There are several real problems here. First, if the proof of lack of initiative is the fact of being a worker, the claim reduces to a tautology, and is meaningless. But, then, how are we to tell who has initiative? And is there room for more entrepreneurs? Gilder, in fact, admits that a crucial ingredient in success is luck, so initiative and hard work are not enough. Nor, perhaps, are they even necessary. Second, why should those who either lack initiative, or have met with bad luck, be forced to work at boring and repetitive jobs over which they have no influence? The entrepreneurial virtues are not the only ones that deserve to be rewarded – and, in fact, when we study the robber barons, or even the ordinary practice of business, we find ourselves in a morass of half-truths, dubious practices, hard sell and soft soap. Some people may very well find this repellent. Why should they be penalized?

Why shouldn't the people who work in an enterprise on a regular long-term basis, even the lowest, have some say, some kind of vote, in how it is run? People vote on, and have a say in, how the country is run. Why not the company, then? This is not to deny the difficulties in working out the exact forms and degrees of participation (or to deny that some schemes will be fraudulent). It is rather to assert that these questions are the important ones; that it is inherently undemocratic to restrict the right to run the company and determine its impact on the community to those who formed it and put up the money. Those who are affected must be notified and give their consent. Those who do the work must have a say in how it is done and what for. How this is to be done, what kind of say, what form of consent, or extent of veto – these are the questions. Not whether.

This leads very quickly to perhaps the hardest question of all: how to organize economic life around some other principle than – or at least mitigate the negative effects of – the pursuit of money. Again, any answers will be complex and detailed, and will cover a wide range of political positions, but the question itself collides head-on with the basic presupposition of the plutocratic conservative vision. For that vision is based on the premise that the achievement of monetary profit is a sufficient condition, in general, for judging a project or activity to have been socially useful. The idea that the pursuit of money is inherently corrupting or demeaning, or an inversion of means and ends, is wholly alien to modern plutocratic thinking, though, it was, in fact, a strand in an older conservatism.

Much more could and should be said about the weaknesses, implausibilities and oversights in the plutocratic vision of the innovating, risk-taking entrepreneur, generating progress in the free market. Not least, it can be profitability compared and contrasted with the vision of the fruits of stability, law and order at the heart of the older, traditionalist conservatism – although this must be left for another time; it has been enough here to try to challenge the justification and undermine the appeal of plutocratic conservatism.

A NEW APPROACH TO THEORY

Yet we cannot leave things here. We have argued that free market economics is inherently defective, indeed disastrous, but as a by-product our argument has also pointed up deficiencies in mainstream theory. Nor should this come as a great surprise, for conservative economics rests on the same theoretical bedrock that underlies conventional neoclassical thinking. Hence we should expect the mainstream explanations of our recent economic problems to be similar to those advanced by conservatives, and to exhibit many of the same shortcomings. That is precisely what we find.

For example, mainstream Keynesian thinking attributes the problems of the 1970s to a combination of 'supply shocks' and mistaken policies, exacerbated by the redistributional effects brought about by the higher prices resulting from the supply shocks (Blinder, 1981). The decade began badly with food shortages, the devaluation of the dollar and the breakup of the Bretton Woods system, and the first great oil price hike. It ended with the dollar crisis and the second oil price shock. In between there was the worst recession, up to then, of the postwar era, a weak recovery and a second slump, all three attributable, at least in part, to policy errors.

Mainstream economists identify – and disagree about – a large number of problematic policy moves during the decade. The way controls were imposed, administered and removed; the failure to cut taxes early enough in the recession; the management of interest rates and the money supply; the extent and timing of support for the dollar; the degree of protection for ailing US industries; all these and others have been cited as policy errors that intensified the effects of the supply shocks, creating the condition of rising prices and slumping output – stagflation – characteristic of most of the decade.

The chief analytical tools of mainstream thinking are the aggregate demand and supply curves connecting GNP and the price level. Higher price levels are associated with lower levels of GNP on the aggregate demand curve, and with higher levels on the aggregate supply curve. The shape of the aggregate demand curve is explained largely by wealth effects, such as those criticized earlier by Nell and Azarchs, while the aggregate supply curve rests on labor market analyses of the kind examined and rejected by Cherry, Clawson and Dean. The mainstream tools, in other words, are for the most part the same as those used by their opponents. They see the economy in the same way, they describe and analyze it in the same terms, and they largely agree that the problems of the 1970s were due in substantial measure to erroneous policy reactions to exceptional supply shocks. Where they disagree, of course, is in identifying which policies were the mistakes.

Besides mainstream thinking, two other approaches to the problems of the 1970s have emerged that show striking affinities to conservative analysis, at least in certain respects. Perhaps surprisingly, both are radical, politically speaking. One is a kind of Marxist fundametalism, which holds that the nature of capitalism has not really changed since Marx's time, so that his categories and explanations can be applied almost without modification to today's world (Mandel, 1978). The crisis, therefore, is to be explained by the tendency of the rate of profit to fall due to competitively induced excessive increases in the organic composition of capital, that is, to the tendency of modern industry to replace labor with expensive automated processes. The decline in the rate of profit in turn leads to a slump in investment and to attempts to improve profits by manipulating the money supply, which just results in inflation. The crisis is understood as the way the law of value asserts itself under modern conditions; rationalization and competition lead to excessive investment, bringing a fall in the rate of profit, which in turn, further intensifies capitalist competition, leading to overproduction and a slump. To cure the slump, capitalist governments expand the money supply, generating inflation but having little or no effect on the recession, whose fundamental cause is the fall in the rate of profit.

In the hands of an expert, such as Mandel, this can provide a sophisticated and powerful approach to contemporary economic questions, clearly based on quite different categories from those that provide the common ground on which both monetarists and mainstream Keynesians stand. Yet there are two important affinities with conservative thought that deserve to be brought out. First, effective demand plays almost no role in the Marxist analysis of the problems of the 1970s. The crisis originates, so to speak, on the 'supply side', in the tendency of the rate of profit to fall. This tendency, in turn, is inherent in the way technology develops under the stimulus of competition. Formally, the analysis is the same as that of aggregate marginal productivity theory: an increase in the capital-to-labor ratio must be associated with a lower rate of profit. Of course, the use to which the formal relationship is put is quite different, but the relationship itself is the same, and is precisely the connection that was criticized in the 're-switching' debates. In general, there is no reason to suppose that higher levels of capital per worker must be associated with lower rates of return on capital, whether this association is interpreted in a neoclassical or in a Marxist way. (Nell, 1980, Part II).

The second affinity to conservative thought concerns the role of money. Inflation is caused by the over-issue of money, in a vain attempt to avert or minimize the crisis. Inflation is at bottom a monetary phenomenon, and is the result of policy. There is a further point of agreement here – Keynesian policies are powerless to stem the tide of crisis; the economy cannot be 'managed'. The effectiveness of policy intervention is strictly limited. So, in spite of a basic orientation that could hardly be more radically opposed, Marxists and conservatives end up agreeing on some very fundamental issues.

A second recent approach to current economic problems, also radical, has shown a rather different set of affinities to conservatism. Bowles, Gordon and Weisskopf (1983) have argued that the source of the crisis of the 1970s is to be found in the breakdown of what they call the 'social structure of accumulation' – roughly, a set of usually implicit agreements between labor, capital, local and national governments and various special interest groups, specifying who is to do what in baking the pie and how, then, it is to be divided up. These agreements prevent outbreaks of social unrest, strikes and other industrial disputes, and ensure a more or less smooth process of capital accumulation. But new technologies develop, new conditions emerge, and the old agreements are no longer appropriate. For example, German and Japanese competition requires changes in the agreements concerning heavy industry. Developments in the newly industrializing countries require the possibility of relocating plants. New technologies require a complete overhaul of labor relations. Faced with a new worldwide competitive situation, capital in effect scrapped the old agreements, in the process launching an attack on labor (long before Reagan), but as yet offered nothing to put in their place. Workers, rightly enough, have become increasingly disgruntled, and as a consequence unwilling to put forth much effort. The result, they argue, is the famous falling-off of the rate of growth of productivity, which in turn leads to a squeeze on profits, and so to cutbacks in investment, resulting in a slump. The inflation then resulted from the combination of stagnation – too few goods – with political stalemate, which meant too many claims, as competing groups, no longer bound by an implicit agreement, pressed their demands in money terms.

Once again, this approach explains the crisis from the supply side. Effective demand plays no role in the analysis. Indeed, the account given of inflation is not altogether inconsistent with a Keynesian perspective, for inflation is explained by too much money (resulting from the funding of competing claims through political process) chasing too few goods (too few because of the slump). But why doesn't this just lead to an expansion of output? The neglect of effective demand is not explained. The crisis results from a breakdown of an essentially political agreement, leading to a refusal of labor to work effectively. Here again the agreement with the conservative prespective is striking: the unwillingness of labor to put forth effort – lazy bastards – is at the bottom of the whole mess. Of course, Bowles, Gordon and Weisskopf argue that workers are *justified* in no longer working hard: capital has abrogated the implicit agreement and has not negotiated a new one. But they agree with conservatives on the fundamental cause of the current difficulties.

So both mainstream and recent radical thinking show some kinship to conservative ideas. And, as we have seen, the problems inherent in free market theories have exposed related difficulties in conventional economics, particularly in regard to real/monetary relationships and to questions of effective demand generally. Indeed, the most striking common feature in the preceding discussion is the failure of all the theories to take adequate account of effective demand. One reason for this is that the critical implications of that theory have not been clearly seen, since effective demand is usually studied in a neoclassical context.

Standard neoclassical theory has always sought (as Keynes himself did) to integrate the theory of effective demand with the vision of the market system efficiently allocating scarce resources. Keynes effected this reconciliation by arguing that standard theory was a *particular* case, valid only at full employment, but unobjectionable then. This created the problem of reconciling marginal productivity theory, according to which employment can increase only if the real wage falls, with the theory of effective demand, according to which employment could increase without any change in real wages (if investment spending rose), and would normally rise or fall as real wages (and so consumer spending) rose or fell, when other things remained constant. No adequate resolution of this contradiction has ever been put forth; indeed, the 'grand neoclassical synthesis' abandons Keynes' contention that modern economies can reach equilibrium at less than full employment. The neoclassical elements in that synthesis dominate the Keynesian. But the difficulties in conservative economics arise precisely in the central vision of the marketplace efficiently allocating scarce resources. Markets so conceived cannot be adequately related to monetary institutions; expectations cannot be reliably formed in a world of uncertainty filled with competing theories and ideologies; the simple conclusions of competitive models are unacceptable. The emulsion of effective demand and efficient allocation tends to separate under strong light.

This leaves the way open for a revival of the theory of effective demand, basing it not, as Keynes tried to do, on neoclassical foundations, but rather on the modern reconstruction of classical and Marxian theory. The rebuilding has taken place within the framework provided by Piero Sraffa in his magnificent *Production of Commodities by Means of Commodities* (1960), a work that has provided an altogether new perspective on the economic theory that preceded the 'marginalist revolution'. The central idea is that prices, far from allocating scarce resources, are themselves determined by (and not determinants of) the distribution of income between social classes, essentially workers and owners or managers of capital. The distribution of income will depend upon the labor force and its rate of growth, saving propensities, the bargaining power of the classes, political institutions and the state of world trade. Clearly some of these factors are exogenous to economics, while others are traditionally part of the subject. Given the real wage, however, economic forces determine what methods of production will be used, and this in turn will give us prices and the rate of profit, which, together with savings propensities, will yield the full employment (potential) growth rate. The theory of effective demand then will tell us how much of this potential will be achieved at any given time.

In other words, the modern classical theory of growth and distribution will describe the evolving structure of the economy, and this provides the *setting* within which the drama of effective demand – unemployment and inflation – is played out. No compromise need be made with marginalist principles; no synthesis exists. By situating the theory of effective demand in a modern classical framework, we can make a clean break with the orthodox theory of the optimal and efficient working of free markets. On such a basis we may hope to build a new theory of economic policy.

WHAT CAN BE DONE?

But we need more than a new theory; we need new policies. For, as we have seen, the Keynesian policies have run their course; to judge from the record of the 1970s, they are not capable of coping with stagflation. The failures of monetarism *et al.* do not mean we can go back to business as usual. So what new policies will be suggested by such a new approach to theory?

This is not a question we can deal with here. Our purpose has been to provide a critical assessment of the theories of free market conservatism and the policies of radical plutocracy. But since this critique has also indicated flaws in the mainstream approach, we owe it to our readers at least to suggest some of the ways in which we might be able to define new policies, and how they would relate to other policy stances.

Mainstream thought sought to strike a balance between the interests of capital and those of the state, where the former are understood to concern the search for profits and new markets, together with the prerogatives of capital in controlling and directing production, while the latter concern the general welfare of the citizenry. Clearly the interests of capital and the citizenry can conflict; equally, they can be complementary. (When the interests of capital and of citizens conflict, it cannot be presumed that the state will always take the part of the citizens. But this is too large and complex an issue to deal with here.) Mainstream theory attempts to find compromises in the areas of conflict, and to strengthen the complementarities. But such attempts tended to come to grief in the 1970s. The tradeoff between inflation and unemployment worsened, the conflicts over environmental spoilage and pollution intensified, the fight over the flight of capital to 'export platforms' in the Third World grew more rancorous, while the competition between the leading firms of Japan, Germany, France, the UK and the US grew fiercer every year.

Monetarism quite unabashedly seeks the maximum freedom of action for capital in these circumstances. Completely eschewing compromise, it seeks the repeal of legislation and, where that is not possible, the circumscription of administration of any and all forms of regulation of capital. Repression by means of recession tends to put labor and consumer groups in their place, while tighter job markets and bleaker prospects generally dampen the militancy of the campuses. And so on; we need not repeat the full program.

Very broadly, there are two directions in which to look for a new set of policies. One is to seek a new form of compromise between capital, labor and the general populace. The 'social contract' and most proposals for incomes policies, along with most plans for reviving industry, fall under this heading. Labor must show restraint over wages and working conditions, the general populace must be less demanding and impatient of matters of safety and the environment, while business aided by subsidy must move energetically to invest and expand. Labor's restraint is rewarded by an expansion of job opportunities, as the economy grows, and eventually, as the new investments raise productivity, with higher wages. The general populace is rewarded with general prosperity, while the state (and local governments, too) will receive higher taxes as a result of greater economic activity. Business, of course, gains in the form of lower costs. So everyone is better off. How could such a compromise be resisted? If it is so attractive, why isn't everyone jumping on the bandwagon?

The reason is surely that in the 1970s and even more in the 1980s, no one can be sure that 'giveaways' to business – wage restraint, deregulation, subsidies – will actually encourage expansion. Profits will rise, it is true, but it doesn't follow that business will invest at home. In fact, it may take advantage of its greater freedom, and move its capital abroad, either by lending or in the form of direct investments. In the 1970s, favored places were Western Europe and the so-called newly industrializing countries – Brazil, Taiwan, South Korea, Singapore, Iran (under the Shah) – where markets for consumer goods were growing rapidly as a large and prosperous middle class emerged and consolidated its position. In the US, by contrast, market growth slowed markedly, especially for consumer durables, at the end of the 1960s. So, on the one hand market growth is slowing in the US while it is accelerating in other parts of the world. On the other hand, the pressures of population on space and resources, together with the accumulated effluents from a century of industrial production, have created an environmental crisis plus serious workplace and community safety problems. Regulatory 'giveaways' are more expensive than ever.

So that route to recovery is not promising, though, of course, since it involves making concessions to capital, it will be strongly promoted and is the most likely to be tried. But, to repeat, it is unlikely to succeed for the simple reason that investment cannot easily be encouraged when market growth is sluggish. It is impossible to go into the causes of the slowdown in market growth in the US and the UK at this point, but, for the record, consumer durable spending, the government deficit, net exports and private investment all grew more slowly in the 1970s than in the previous two decades.

Let us now consider the second possibility, which will certainly not be popular with the business community, and so will face serious political obstacles. Instead of seeking a new compromise with capital, a set of policies could be defined on the basis of *dominating* capital. (Note that this still falls short of abolishing or expropriating it; these policies remain within the framework of capitalism.) Such domination would only be possible if based on a powerful and popular political movement of course, and would last only as long as such a movement held together. No such movement can presently be discerned on the political horizon in either the US or the UK. Nevertheless, it is still worth sketching the outline of this form of economic policy.

To begin with, there will have to be two kinds of controls – controls over prices and controls over movements of capital. Taking the first, this is not as formidable a task as it is sometimes made to appear. As Galbraith has said, it is not so hard to control prices that are already administered, and the prices of products manufactured by the 2,000 or so largest US corporations, comprising over two-thirds of US GNP, are all administered. *Politically* there will be furious resistance to a national pricing scheme, but *technically* the job is not at all difficult; it simply amounts to coordinating the separate pricing policies of the giant corporations, while constraining overall price increases in the national interest, together with passing on the benefits of technological advances to consumers in the form of lower prices.

A price control policy will imply a complementary money wages policy. But here new considerations enter. For when growth has slowed down, maintaining full employment will require a rise in consumption, most easily achieved by bringing about a rise in wages. Moreover, such a rise in wages can itself encourage both increases in productivity, as firms innovate to maintain their traditional profits, and new investment to provide the capacity to service newly affluent households. Here caution must be exercised – too great an increase in real wages will impose unacceptable costs on business, leaving too little surplus for investment, but too small an increase will not provide sufficient stimulus either to productivity or to investment. A policy of encouraging high wages, perhaps by systematically and regularly raising the minimum wage and extending its coverage, will have to be supplemented by subsidies to innovation, e.g. through low-cost government loans, and by retraining programs for displaced laborers. A major consequence of such a policy will be a change in the composition of industry, for low-wage, inefficient firms – even entire industries – will have to modernize or go out of business. However, the 'weeding out' under this policy would be directed at technologically backward and genuinely inefficient firms, not at firms whose debt structure was lop-sided, or whose markets tended to dry up in recession.

The second set of controls needed would prevent the flight of capital overseas. Some capital mobility would be permitted; the point would be to regulate it in the national interest, rather than permitting capital flows to follow anticipated profits (profits that may never be realized, as in the loans to some 'developing' countries, which went into the pockets, and Swiss bank accounts, of corrupt officials). Along with these controls, a policy of managed trade will be needed; countries must not be required to generate recessions in order to bring imports down to the level of their exports. Selective import controls must be permitted and balance of payments deficits must be financed without requiring 'austerity'. Again, it is not technically impossible to see how to do this; instead of penalizing the weak – those who run deficits – penalties could be assessed against the strong – the surplus countries – who would be required to promote the loans to finance the deficits. Instead of cutting back imports through austerity, deficit-running countries could be encouraged to modernize their export industries.

Finally, as mentioned, such an approach would require a considerable retraining and relocation program for workers, since it would strongly stimulate modernization and technological development, which perhaps always, but certainly with today's 'high tech', tend to displace labor and change the skill mix demanded in the labor market.

The preceding is only a sketch; it is not complete and is intended only to be illustrative. Yet we have seen enough to ask, is it impossibly utopian? Surely the political force necessary could never be amassed? However, many features of the program are already in place in many capitalist countries. Industrial policies and job retraining are a crucial feature of the Japanese economy. High wages, with real wages *leading* productivity, have been policy in Singapore. Price controls have repeatedly been used, though on a temporary basis, in most major countries, and import controls have been and are ubiquitous. Easy money and fiscal stimulus are Keynesian commonplaces. And so on. The idea is to change from relying on these measures as part of *ad hoc* crisis management, to weaving them into the fabric of a comprehensive, integrated expansionist policy program.

This is not the place to put forth an alternative to austerity. The point is rather that such an alternative is conceivable, and the crucial point is that it requires political domination of capital by the community – rather than compromise with capital, let alone domination by capital, as in the strategy of radical plutocracy, whose incoherence and disasters we have catalogued in this book.

REFERENCES

Blinder, Alan S. (1981) *Economic Policy and the Great Stagflation*, New York: Academic Press.

Bowles, Samuel, Gordon, David M. and Weisskopf, Thomas (1983) *Beyond the Waste Land*, New York: Anchor Press/Doubleday.

Gilder, George (1981) *Wealth and Poverty*, New York: Basic Books.

Mandel, Ernest (1978) *The Second Slump*, London: New Left Books.

Nell, E. J. ed. (1980) *Growth Profits and Property, Essays in the Revival of Political Economy*, New York: Cambridge University Press.

Sraffa, Piero (1960) *Production of Commodities by Means of Commodities*, Cambridge: Cambridge University Press.

Wanniski, Jude (1978) *The Way the World Works*, New York: Basic Books.

Index